# The Philosophy of
# Franz Rosenzweig

(Courtesy of the Josef Prager Collection, The National
and University Library, Jerusalem, Israel)

# The Philosophy of
# Franz Rosenzweig

*Edited by*
Paul Mendes-Flohr

Published for Brandeis University Press by
University Press of New England
Hanover and London, 1988

© 1988 by Trustees of Brandeis University

Printed in the United States of America

LIBRARY OF CONGRESS CATALOGING-IN-PUBLICATION DATA

Jerusalem Philosophical Encounter (4th: 1980)
   The philosophy of Franz Rosenzweig.
   (The Tauber Institute for the Study of European
Jewry series; 8)
   Meeting held Apr. 20–May 2, 1980 in Jerusalem.
   Bibliography: p.
   1. Rosenzweig, Franz, 1886–1929—Congresses.
I. Mendes-Flohr, Paul.  II. Title.  III. Series.
B3327.R64J47   1980      181'.06      86-40552
ISBN 0-87451-398-7

5 4 3 2 1

The Tauber Institute for the Study of European Jewry, established by a gift to Brandeis University from Dr. Laszlo N. Tauber, is dedicated to the memory of the victims of Nazi persecutions between 1933 and 1945. The Institute seeks to study the history and culture of European Jewry in the modern period. The Institute has a special interest in studying the causes, nature, and consequences of the European Jewish catastrophe and seeks to explore them within the context of modern European diplomatic, intellectual, political, and social history. The Tauber Institute for the Study of European Jewry is organized on a multidisciplinary basis, with the participation of scholars in history, Judaic studies, political science, sociology, comparative literature, and other disciplines.

## THE TAUBER INSTITUTE FOR THE STUDY OF EUROPEAN JEWRY SERIES

### Jehuda Reinharz, General Editor

# Contents

# Acknowledgments

The symposium from which this volume emerged was organized by the Shmuel Hugo Bergman Centre for Philosophical Studies at the Hebrew University of Jerusalem. At the time of the symposium I had the honor to serve as the director of the Centre; and I accordingly wish to thank its staff, particularly Eva Shor. Unassumingly, she led me, then a neophyte in the arcane world of administration, through the often baffling byways of organizing a symposium and the subsequent publication. I am deeply grateful to her. The Fourth Jerusalem Philosophical Encounter was cosponsored by the Israel Academy of Sciences and Humanities, the Van Leer Jerusalem Institute, and the Embassy of the German Federal Republic in Israel. Their generous support is acknowledged with gratitude.

The symposium was hosted at the residence of the Van Leer Jerusalem Institute, whose staff attended to the administrative and logistic details of the symposium with care and impeccable competence. I am especially pleased to record my thanks to Rivka Ra'am. I wish to express my gratitude to a dear friend whom I met by the grace of the symposium. Werner Marx of the University of Freiburg took great interest in the symposium from its very inception. With boundless enthusiasm and energy he helped secure the participation of German scholars in the symposium and the support of German funding institutions. Further, and more significantly, he lent me his unfailing moral support throughout the symposium.

The preparation of this volume was financed by the generous support of the Israel Academy of the Sciences and Humanities and the Pepita Haezrahi Memorial Fund. I gratefully acknowledge the graciousness of these institutions as well as that of the Jerusalem Fellows Program, which underwrote the costs of translating Professor Ernst Simon's essay. I also had the good fortune of enjoying the assistance of devoted and skillful translators and stylistic editors to whom I should like to reiterate my appreciation: Esther Cameron, Gabrielle Schalit, Arnold Schwartz, and Michael Swirsky. As always, the assistance of my devoted friend Hayim Goldgraber has been inestimable. Sabine Gass conscientiously prepared the index with the generous support of the Van Leer Jerusalem Institute. Kathryn Gohl deserves special mention for her careful and caring copy editing. The fact that this volume appears under the imprint of the University Press of New England is to no small measure due to the much appreciated efforts of Alfred Ivry and Bernard Wasserstein of the Brandeis University Publications Committee.

I am particularly grateful to Jehuda Reinharz, director of the Tauber Institute for the Study of European Jewry, Brandeis University. When the specter of financial and administrative difficulties threatened the publication of the volume, he interceded and resolutely guided the volume over all of many obstacles. The fact that the volume was adopted as a Tauber Institute publication is only a small indication of his generosity and friendship.

Finally, I am profoundly indebted to Nathan Rotenstreich, who first broached the idea of the symposium and encouraged me to undertake its organization. At every stage of the preparation of this volume I enjoyed his sapient counsel and untiring support. I trust he knows how dearly I cherish his friendship.

*March 1987*                                    P.M.-F.

# The Philosophy of
# Franz Rosenzweig

# Introduction:

# Franz Rosenzweig and the German Philosophical Tradition

*For Arthur A. Cohen (1928–1986)*

This volume of essays pays tribute to the philosophical legacy of Franz Rosenzweig (1886–1929), a German Jew who is now celebrated as perhaps the most creative Jewish religious thinker of the twentieth century. Despite his brief life—he died two weeks shy of his forty-third birthday after a heroic struggle to overcome a terrible disease—Rosenzweig served to inspire a veritable spiritual and religious renaissance of German Jewry.[1] From the midst of assimilation and, indeed, from the threshhold of baptism, Rosenzweig affirmed Judaism as a living faith that he deemed to be of urgent relevance to the modern individual. Based on the centrality of divine revelation as a historical fact and an existential possibility, Rosenzweig's theology led him to abandon his erstwhile pursuit of an academic career—as he himself put it, "one perfectly 'eligible' for a university lectureship"—and devote himself exclusively to the community of his fellow Jews.[2] This decision, however, did not mark a break with the ideals of German philosophical culture to which he so passionately subscribed. Indeed, both ideationally and spiritually there is a continuity between his deep involvement in the philosophical tradition of German idealism and his later theocentric affirmation of Judaism. This volume seeks to illuminate this continuity. When Rosenzweig's thought is placed in its biographical context—tracing his path from German idealism, beholden to the putative omniscence of reason, to religious faith—this continuity is particularly manifest and, indeed, takes on the contours of a dramatic tale.

In March of 1914 while researching a book on Hegel at the Prussian State Library in Berlin, Rosenzweig came across a newly acquired manuscript.[3] It was undoubtedly a momentous occasion for the young scholar. Purchased the previous year at an auction, this hitherto unknown manuscript was a two-page fragment of an essay indubitably written in the hand of Hegel.[4] Evidently composed during the last years of the eighteenth century, the essay presents an outline of what its author regarded as the proper and most urgent agenda of philosophy. Apparently addressed to colleagues as a proposed basis of discussion, the essay speaks of developing a "complete system" of all ideas that would allow ethics and physics to conjoin their efforts to further the supreme task of philosophy, namely, to illuminate how the individual as a "free, self-conscious being" could conceive of the natural world as amenable to moral freedom. "To our sluggish physics, advancing laboriously with its experiments, I would like to lend wings once more." A genuine philosophical system, dedicated to furthering "absolute freedom," the author of the fragment declared, should include in its purview not only ethics and physics, but political science, mythology, and religion as well. At its pinnacle, philosophy must be an aesthetic act. "For I am convinced that the supreme act of reason, because it embraces all ideas, is an aesthetic act, and that only in beauty are truth and goodness of the same flesh." It is ultimately the aesthetic act that joins the rational realm of ideas and the sensuous domain of nature. Further, "until we make the great ideas aesthetic, that is, mythological, they will have no interest for the people; and, conversely, until the mythology is rational, the philosopher will perforce be ashamed of it." The masses, beholden to sensuous images, must become rational, and philosophers must become sensuous. The author of the fragment concludes with a vision of a covenant between mythology and philosophy, in which the unenlightened and enlightened will "at long last" embrace. "Then universal freedom and equality of spirits will prevail!" The establishment of "this new religion . . . will be the very last and the grandest of humanity's works."

The cadence and voice of the fragment bespeak a buoyant, triumphal mood—a mood that suggested to Rosenzweig that although clearly written in the script of Hegel, the fragment was alien to the spirit of the young Hegel. Rosenzweig's immediate intuition was that it was actually written by Hegel's then close friend, Friedrich von Schelling (1775–1850). Rosenzweig followed through with a careful philological and ideational analysis of the essay, which ultimately lent confirmation to his initial intimation that Schelling and not Hegel was indeed its author. In the spring of 1917 Rosenzweig published the fragment in the proceedings of the Heidelberg Academy of Sciences, entitling it "The Oldest Program of a System for German Idealism" ("Das älteste Systemprogramm des deutschen Idealismus").[5] In the detailed commentary accompanying this first publication of the fragment, Rosenzweig concluded:

> Only one man in the philosophical German of the year 1796 possessed this youthful, victorious tone; the very first fleeting glance which we cast at the thoughts contained in the program informed us that it was he. This man alone employed the bold phrase "I shall" with such insouciance, employed it without cease to the end of his life when, an old man, he departed from a world disheartened. So busy with programs he never got as far as a completed work; so busy with "ideas" and "projects," "presentations" and "reports," promises and half-fulfillments he never got as far as wholehearted deeds. "I shall" was to be his last word, as it was his first.[6]

The ever exuberant but erratic Schelling was the author of the document transmitted to later generations in Hegel's hand—a supposition that is more plausible should one recall that in an age when photostatic-copying machines were not even an idle fantasy, if one wanted to retain a document for later perusal one simply copied it by hand. Such, Rosenzweig surmised, was the case when the twenty-one-year-old Schelling—the *Wunderkind* of German philosophy—showed Hegel his essay. The latter copied it, and it is this copy that eventually found its way to the Prussian State Library.[7]

Researching this article, which served to establish his reputation as an up-and-coming scholar, occasioned for Rosenzweig a thorough review of German idealism, particularly as represented by Hegel and Schelling. As a student, Rosenzweig was drawn to the Hegel renaissance that took place in the first decade of the twentieth century at the University of Heidelberg and the nearby University of Freiburg where Rosenzweig was pursuing his studies in philosophy and history. Rosenzweig himself would write a doctoral dissertation on Hegel under the supervision of the famed historian Friedrich Meinecke (1862–1952). Submitted in 1912, the dissertation was later expanded and published in 1920 as a highly acclaimed book, *Hegel und der Staat* (Hegel and the State).[8]

While working on the dissertation, Rosenzweig joined a group of young scholars who had gathered in January 1910 at the resort city of Baden-Baden—halfway between Heidelberg and Freiburg—to found a society dedicated to the Hegelian ideal of promoting a historical consciousness appropriate to the epoch now emerging with the advent of the twentieth century. This new historical consciousness, in which the self will realize itself as the subject not only of its own destiny but preeminently that of the *Zeitgeist,* would allow one to overcome the false subjectivity that characterized the previous century. This neo-Hegelian society envisioned at the Baden-Baden conference, however, was aborted at infancy. Even as they gathered in Baden-Baden, Rosenzweig and at least some of his colleagues had incipient doubts about Hegel's absolute idealism with its doctrine that "truth is in the whole," namely, that truth is ultimately grounded and rendered manifest as the "whole" of world history is unfolded; accordingly, in one's quest for enlightenment, one is to identify with the "Spirit" as it unfolds and reaches fullness with the denouement of history. In a letter to a fellow participant in the ill-fated Baden-Baden conference, Rosenzweig observed that Hegel erred in ascribing an ontological status to history. For, he exclaimed, history is not the unfolding of being, rather it is but the discrete act of men (*Tat der Täter*): "We see God in every ethical event, but not in one complete Whole, not in history."[9]

At the Baden-Baden conference Rosenzweig made the acquaintance of Eugen Rosenstock (upon his marriage, Rosenstock-Huessy; 1888–1970) who had then just completed a dissertation on medieval constitutional law.[10] Rosenstock would play a decisive role in shaping Rosenzweig's spiritual and philosophical horizons. Rosenstock shared with Rosenzweig a conviction that Hegel's absolute idealism was amiss and that its failure (not to mention that of all other current philosophical schools) had led European civilization to a profound impasse.[11] Moreover, both men shared the conviction that the relativism in effect recommended by the prevailing mode of academic scholarship was inherently unsatisfactory and only served to deepen the malaise. The rational quest for truth now seemed futile and the spiritual fullness promised by the attainment of enlightenment, alas, remained elusive. As a way beyond the impasse Rosenstock had adopted religious faith.

Rosenstock's religious faith was based on what he called *Offenbarungsglaube*—a faith based on revelation. Genuine religious belief, Rosenstock held, affirms the reality of revelation—both the factual reality of historic revelation and the possibility of its renewal as an existential event in which God turns to an individual in the here and now.[12] Rosenzweig was initially puzzled by Rosenstock's faith; he was perplexed how a man of culture could affirm a position presumably eclipsed by learning and reason. In the spring and early summer of 1913, when their friendship began in earnest, Rosenzweig and Rosenstock met frequently to discuss questions of faith and reason. Slowly Rosenstock led his friend to the realization that a votary of culture and reason could with integrity affirm faith in revelation, and that indeed it was the only sensible way of overcoming the philosophical and historical relativism of the day. On the night of 13 July Rosenzweig yielded to Rosenstock's arguments and declared that he would adopt Rosenstock's *Offenbarungsglaube*.

Rosenstock's affirmation of religious faith led him to renounce his ancestral Judaism and convert to Christianity—as did Rosenzweig's cousins, Hans and Rudolf Ehrenberg (1893–1958; 1884–1969), who were close to Rosenstock and who participated in the Baden-Baden conference. Rosenstock and the Ehrenbergs had assumed that Rosenzweig would follow them to the baptismal font and to a genuine spiritual life that they assumed was no longer available in Judaism.[13] Rosenzweig, however, hesitated. He explained that he wanted to enter the Church as a conscious Jew such as Saul of Tarsus. Thus, in preparation for his conversion, he attended that au-

tumn the Jewish High Holiday services, finding his way for the Day
of Atonement to a traditional synagogue in Berlin. At the conclusion
of the day of fasting, prayer, and repentance, he wrote his cousin Rudolf Ehrenberg:

> I must tell you something that will grieve you and may at first appear incom-
> prehensible to you: after prolonged and I believe thorough, self-examina-
> tion, I have reversed my decision. It no longer seems necessary to me, and
> therefore, being what I am, no longer possible. I will remain a Jew.[14]

Having witnessed, perhaps for the first time, a traditional Day of
Atonement service, Rosenzweig concluded that Judaism was not
spiritually moribund as he and his friends had assumed. Reversing
his decision to enter the Church, he thus affirmed that a meaningful
life of faith may be pursued within the precincts, as he put it, of the
Synagogue.

Having made this decision, Rosenzweig set out with his characteristic diligence and attention to nuance to appropriate the spiritual and religious heritage of the Synagogue, a heritage that had
been neglected in his parental home of self-conscious assimilation.
He sought to immerse himself in the spiritual reality of traditional
Judaism, especially the prayer book and the liturgical calendar. He
studied Hebrew and the other requisite languages for the life of an
informed and pious Jew; he studied the literary sources of the tradition, Bible, Talmud, rabbinic commentaries, the medieval philosophers and poets, and even, it appears, some Kabbalah.[15] Gradually
he observed more and more of the ritual commandments incumbent
upon a faithful Jew. From the threshhold of baptism, Rosenzweig
had become a deeply pious, learned, and passionate Jew.

Rosenzweig became the focus and, indeed, fulcrum of a dramatic
spiritual and cultural renaissance of German Jewry in the Weimar
period. He became both the symbol and guide to a generation of
German Jews eager to break the spell of assimilation and to reinte-
grate their lives in the fabric of Jewish tradition. He taught this generation of post–World War I Jews how to read the sources of Jewish
tradition, to encounter these sources without surrending one's intellectual integrity, and to engage them as religious texts that speak
to one's soul. He also taught them that in order to reclaim the spiri-

tual reality of Jewish tradition one had to know it from within, that is, as he once put it, to know it "hymnically." [16] Intellectual acquaintance, hence, of and by itself is insufficient. For Judaism, after all, is a mode of life, and as such it entails the praxis of Judaism, the life of prayer and its mitzvoth (commandments). To be sure, Rosenzweig conceded, from the perspective of the observer, traditional Jewish religious practice may seem to be but a heteronomous legalism—impositions, as Martin Buber, for one, contended in a debate with Rosenzweig, that shackle the Jew's spontaneous relationship to God. [17] But as experienced from within its "hymnical" reality, the world of prayer and mitzvoth may in fact quicken the Jew's relationship to God—this was the challenge that Rosenzweig posed before his generation.

The experience of God's revelatory Presence, he held, is at the heart of Judaism—and it is this experience that must be placed at the center of the Jew's religious imagination, otherwise one courts the danger of perpetuating the absurdity of nineteenth-century liberal theology, which Rosenzweig characterized with the oxymoron "atheistic theology," a theology that fails to take God and revelation seriously. [18] Attendant to his affirmation of revelation, Rosenzweig also reasserted the centrality of creation and redemption—again categories that modern religious thought tended to ignore or, at best, treat poetically, that is, as metaphors bereft of genuine theological content. Each of these concepts—revelation, creation, and redemption—teach us, according to Rosenzweig, not only about God's gracious involvement in the world but also about the structure and meaning of existence. It is thus the exigent task of theology to rescue the phenomenological and existential significance of these concepts as well as the ancillary and, alas, similarly obfuscated notions of miracle, providence, and divine love.

In clarifying his newly won theology and its relationship to the larger questions of culture—which neither he nor his friends ever abandoned—Rosenzweig had recourse to Schelling, especially the writings of his so-called late period. In this period, stretching from 1809 to his death in 1854, Schelling struggled to find room in the philosophical horizon of idealism for the concrete existence of contingent, finite being. In pushing the boundaries of idealism to accommodate the irrefragable "factuality" (*Tatsächlichkeit*) of existence, Schelling broke decisively with his erstwhile friend Hegel, in particular with the latter's totalistic conception of reason as comprehending all of reality. Existence, Schelling insisted, is prior to thought, it is *unvordenklich*—it cannot be thought prior to thought's actual encounter with it, and therefore it should be regarded as autonomous of thought alone. Knowledge must start with existence itself, an objective given, a "that." [19] With respect to the "that" of existence, Schelling held, philosophy must abandon its "negative" posture of regarding the world as a "naught" whose reality is conceptually determined solely by the speculative activity of the rational mind; philosophy must assume a "positive" method in which the "that" of existence is acknowledged and its reality is merely "narrated" by reason. [20] Schelling would accordingly reject Hegel's supposition of a fundamental homology or identity between reason and existence. Hegel's "law of identity," which he, Schelling, held, had a baleful effect on German philosophy. In perhaps his last public lecture, delivered at the Academy of Sciences in 1850, the then seventy-five-year-old Schelling formulated his position in Nestorian terms: "Once you begin with [conceptual] content divorced from existence, you discover with consternation after an interval of intoxication that you have no vessel to contain this content." [21]

The philosopher Eduard von Hartmann (1842–1906) described these words as "Schelling's legacy to the German people." [22] Disaffected by Hegel's absolute idealism, Rosenzweig and his friends—and many others of their generation—were ready to accept this legacy and to heed Schelling's call to secure the integrity of existence—finite and autonomous—in face of the imperious rule of reason governed as it is by logical necessity. [23] To be sure, Schelling noted, "the whole world lies, as it were, in the nets of understanding or of reason, but the question is how it came into these nets, since something else and something more than mere reason, indeed, even something striving beyond these limits, is evidently in the world." [24] Schelling's legacy, which, by virtue of the insistence of the priority of existence over thought, has been construed as anticipating modern existentialism, [25] was not a celebration of the irrational. He in fact sought to retain the program of idealism to establish a system of philosophy (which he was the first to outline, according to Rosenzweig, in the "Oldest Program of German Idealism"). As a "system," philosophy is to provide from the perspective of reason, wedded as it is to a universal conception of truth, a comprehensive and coherent account of the unity of all knowledge and the intelligibility of the finite world. For the late Schelling, this account must acknowledge the inherently suprarationality of finite existence. Accordingly, philosophy must establish a unity in dualism, a unity between reason, girded by rationally constructed concepts, and the suprarational, grounded in the contingent reality of finite existence. Only in such a unity, Schelling held, is truth manifest. The search for the transcendental source of this unity distinguished the thrust of the late Schelling's work. He discerned this transcendental source of unity in the concept of God—a concept that required in his judgment a radical revision of the Hegelian conception of God and religion. In such works as *Die Philosophie der Mythologie* (The philosophy of mythology; 1847–52) and *Philosophie der Offenbarung* (Philosophy of revelation; 1841–42), he challenged Hegel's thesis that reason in time ultimately absorbs and refines the revealed truths of religion. For Schelling God is an autonomous personality whose will is refracted in human moral freedom. Specifically, Schelling averred, God realizes his will in human religious consciousness—from mythology to its "completion" in the historical monotheistic religions and the evolution of an "invisible church" in which God's will will be unambiguously one with human sensibility.[26] Further, only when religion—or rather man's evolving religious consciousness—becomes its object will philosophy advance from its negative to its positive phase, and thereby achieve the goal as a "system" to provide the world of reason and existence with a common unity. For Rosenzweig and his friends this envisioned alliance between philosophy and religion would inspire their own conception of their intellectual task. Rosenzweig himself would speak of the need for a "new theological rationalism" sponsored by a new type of thinker, "situated between theology and philosophy."[27]

This new type of thinker would perforce require a "new thinking," a new mode of philosophizing. Borne by a sense of urgency,

Rosenzweig and his friends—four of whom were of particular significance for his intellectual development, Rosenstock, Hans and Rudolf Ehrenberg, and Victor von Weizäcker (1886–1976)—resolved to determine the mode of philosophizing now needed. For them Hegel marked the *finis philosophiae*—for with Hegel, they contended, the millenial attempt of philosophers to comprehend the world on the basis of reason alone had exhausted its logical possibilities. As Rosenzweig put it, "from Ionia to Jena" [28]—from the seat of the pre-Socratic philosophers to the University of Jena where Hegal developed the foundations of his system—philosophy (and they had in mind specifically idealistic philosophy that views itself as a system illuminating the unity of reality) had endeavored to comprehend all of reality in terms of its "essence," one overarching principle. Hegel had identified the various efforts to define this principle—constituting the history of philosophy—as the dialectical necessity of reason as it unfolds in time and reaches its fullness. Rosenzweig and his friends were convinced that philosophy, at least as traditionally conceived, could not proceed beyond Hegel and his conflation of reason and the history of philosophy, and since it had manifestly failed to comprehend all of reality, philosophy grounded in reason alone could no longer be of avail. To philosophize *post-Hegel mortuum* thus required a new mode of philosophizing, specifically, it required that philosophers abandon their single dependence on reason that had reigned from Ionia to Jena, and allow themselves to acknowledge religious faith as having distinct cognitive import. In these gropings for a new mode of philosophizing, Rosenstock developed a concept of speech-thinking (*Sprachdenken*) that would exercise a decisive influence on Rosenzweig's thought. [29] In contrast to the timeless logic of reason of the "old thinking," speech—the genuine exchange between people that takes place in time and is nurtured by time—is the organon of the new thinking. Truth, Rosenstock taught, is revealed through the spoken word, and since speech or dialogue is forever protean in consonance with the existential reality and situation of its participants, the truth it bears is forever unique. Bound to speech, truth is grounded in contingent, temporally discrete experience (*Erfahrung*).

Rosenzweig discerned in Rosenstock's novel doctrine a clarion echo of Goethe's verse on "understanding in time":

> What is the truth so woefully
> Removed? To depths of secret banned?
> None understands in time! If we
> But understood betimes, how bland
> The truth would be, how fair to see!
> How near and ready to our hand![30]

Integrating Rosenstock's speech-thinking into his own thought, Rosenzweig developed his own distinctive conception of the new thinking.

On his road to crystallizing his own philosophical position, Rosenzweig was destined to make the acquaintance of Hermann Cohen (1842–1918), one of the most esteemed philosophers of his day. They first met in Berlin in November 1913, one month after the Day of Atonement service that had led Rosenzweig back to Judaism. The twenty-seven-year-old Hegel scholar and the septugenarian philosopher soon became intimate friends. Rosenzweig discovered in Cohen a "great soul," a "philosopher and a man." Rosenzweig also felt an affinity to the celebrated founder of neo-Kantianism as a fellow *baal teshuvah*—as one who from the pale of assimilation returned to religious faith and Judaism.[31] Upon retiring from his professorial chair at the University of Marburg, Cohen came to Berlin where he devoted himself to Jewish education, taught at the city's academy of Jewish studies, and employed his prestige on behalf of oppressed Jews, particularly in Eastern Europe. Rosenzweig was also undoubtedly enthralled by the fact that when Cohen befriended him, Cohen was in the midst of an intellectual upheaval in which he sought to reassess the relation of philosophy and religion. In his seventies, Cohen had the rare intellectual courage to revise long-held positions, which reflected his Kantian predilection to delimit religion at best to the role of handmaiden of moral consciousness; now he attributed to religion qua ritual and prayer a more substantial philosophical value. Rosenzweig would even detect in the elderly philosopher's ruminations intimations of a religious existentialism. Perhaps even more inspiring to Rosenzweig was Cohen's unapologetic reference to the literary sources of Judaism as relevant texts in the developing of his argument.[32] Cohen clearly represented for his young colleague and friend a paragon not only of the new type of thinker, but also of an individual who was both a philosopher and a passionate, learned, and pious Jew.

Similar to Cohen, Rosenzweig resolved to devote his energies to the Jewish community. He was instrumental in the founding in Frankfurt of the Freies Jüdisches Lehrhaus (the free Jewish house of learning), an unprecedented experiment in adult Jewish education that opened its doors in the autumn of 1920 and quickly became the focus of a veritable renaissance in German Jewish spiritual life. In a letter, dated August 1920, to his former teacher Friedrich Meinecke, Rosenzweig had the occasion to explain why he, a promising scholar, would devote himself to Jewish communal life. On his own accord, Meinecke had arranged for Rosenzweig a university lectureship, the dream of every young scholar and then a rare opportunity for one of Jewish provenance. Declining the opportunity, Rosenzweig wrote his incredulous teacher:

> The one thing I wish to make clear is that scholarship no longer holds the center of my attention, and that my life has fallen under the rule of a "dark drive" which I am aware that I merely name by calling it "my Judaism." . . . The small—at times exceedingly small—thing called by [Goethe] the "demand of the day" which is made upon me in my position [as director of the Freies Jüdisches Lehrhaus], I mean the nerve-wracking, picayune, and at the same time very necessary struggles with people and conditions, have now become the real core of my existence. . . . Cognition [*Erkennen*] no longer appears to me an end in itself. It has turned into service, a service to human beings.[33]

Meinecke regarded his former student's affirmation of Judaism as an expression of despair, a retreat from culture and universal fidelities in the wake of the First World War to what might indeed be an existentially pleasing community of "his blood" but, in the end, one that perforce remained a parochial cloister.[34] Meinecke had profoundly misunderstood the nature of Rosenzweig's Judaism, however. For Rosenzweig the affirmation of religious faith and Judaism did not constitute an abdication of the quest for truth and its universal promise. As with his mentor Hermann Cohen, for Rosenzweig Judaism as a living religious reality was of utmost relevance for the general enterprise of humanity. Accordingly, Rosenzweig maintained that his magnum opus, *The Star of Redemption* (1921), in which he presented his views on Judaism, was not as a philosophy of Judaism, or even of religion in general, but a "system of philosophy."[35]

Yet, in seeming contradiction to this claim, Rosenzweig took great pains to arrange that *The Star of Redemption* be issued by the publishing house of J. Kaufmann of Frankfurt, a firm specializing in Judaica and works of Jewish interest. By insisting that this ponderous and, indeed, rather esoteric philosophical disquisition appear with a Jewish publisher, he did not, however, at all wish to suggest that the volume's specific Jewish message rendered it parochial. On the contrary, he maintained that if Jewish religious life is to be true to its pristine calling, it must have a bearing on the most ultimate questions of human existence; accordingly, the conjoining of the Jewish and the universal—the theological and the philosophical—should be self-evident to Jew and non-Jew alike. This fact he sought to exemplify by the publication of his book, whose Jewish and universal significance he regarded as coterminous, under a Jewish imprint.

To Rosenzweig's distress his initial audience was primarily limited to Jews. But this disappointed him less than the fact that although often citing *The Star of Redemption*, his many admirers actually had seldom read it. The volume's prestige, he felt, was thus vacuous. As he ironically observed: "Precisely the thing I hoped for when I insisted on a Jewish publisher has happened, while the thing that I feared, and that made me hesitate to publish it during my lifetime, has not happened: it has made me famous among the Jews but has not obstructed my influence with the Jews. And the reason for both is that they haven't read it. Again and again I am amazed at how little its readers know it. Everybody thinks it is an admonition to kosher eating."[36]

Rosenzweig took solace, as he confided to a friend, in applying the "beautiful phrase of my Catholic name-saint: *tantum quisque intelligit, quantum operatur*"—one acts to the extent that one understands—"to the passive *intelligitur*" (is understood), that is, "one acts to the extent that one is understood."[37] He thus confined his efforts to two brief attempts at explaining his "system of philosophy" in terms more accessible to laymen—his essay of 1925, "Das neue Denken" (The new thinking), and in his lifetime an unpublished booklet, *Understanding the Sick and Healthy* (*Vom gesunden und kranken Menschenverstand*)—and devoted his efforts largely to the translation of sacred Jewish texts and to adult Jewish education, specifically through the Freies Jüdisches Lehrhaus.[38]

Indeed, few of Rosenzweig's many admirers and disciples actually read *The Star of Redemption*. It presents a daunting challenge even to the professional philosopher. Yet recognizing his brilliance, an ever increasing number of philosophers and intellectual historians, Jewish and non-Jewish, have accepted the challenge and have read Rosenzweig's *Star* with systematic care. On the occasion of the fiftieth anniversary of his death, the Fourth Jerusalem Philosophical Encounter, sponsored by the S. H. Bergman Center for Philosophical Studies of the Hebrew University, brought many of these scholars together in the spring of 1980 to assess Rosenzweig's contribution to general philosophy and modern Jewish thought. The present volume is but a selection of the more than twenty-five papers and comments presented at the conference.

This volume is inaugurated with an essay by the late Gershom Scholem, who for a time taught at Rosenzweig's Lehrhaus in Frankfurt. Scholem's chapter is an English adaptation of an address he originally delivered in Hebrew at a memorial service held at the Hebrew University of Jerusalem in January 1930.[39] Feeling that this essay represented his definitive view of Rosenzweig, Scholem requested that we include it in this volume rather than the oral statement he made at the conference. Unfortunately, he passed away before the translation was completed; the editor therefore bears responsibility for the adaptation and translation, as well as for the notes.

In addition to providing a personal testimony to the impact of Rosenzweig the man and the religious teacher on his contemporaries, Scholem, with his typical rhetorical grace and analytical nuance, reviews the major themes of *The Star of Redemption* and places Rosenzweig's endeavor within the historical perspective of both general philosophy and Jewish religious thought and spirituality. Scholem highlights Rosenzweig's critique of German idealism, especially as embodied in Hegel's "system," and its pretense to arrive at a timeless, universal conception of truth. Rosenzweig's ultimate significance, Scholem concludes, was to restore the mystery of creation and the Divine Presence to the center of both general and Jewish discourse.

Scholem's tour de force is followed by two essays that explore key concepts in Rosenzweig's "new thinking." Focusing on Rosenzweig's effort to develop a "time-bound" theory of knowledge that would acknowledge the contingent, multiple, and open character of reality, Reiner Wiehl seeks to clarify Rosenzweig's unique conception of *Erfahrung* (experience). He also offers insights into Rosenzweig's understanding of a "system of philosophy" (in contrast to Hegel's, which he criticized) and "miracle" as a boundary concept that connects and separates the respective domains of philosophy and theology. Nathan Rotenstreich considers Rosenzweig's crucial but often misunderstood use of the prefix *meta,* in his delineation of the metalogical, metaphysical, and especially, the metaethical. Rotenstreich shows that Rosenzweig does not employ *meta* as denoting that which is above but rather that which is outside or before. The individual metaethically conceived is, thus, not above ethics but distinctively independent of ethics and its universal precepts. The *meta* thus challengingly demarcates the limits of the all-comprehensive "totality"—"the All" (*das All*), as Rosenzweig was wont to designate it—of philosophical idealism. Further, as Rotenstreich emphasizes, Rosenzweig's conception of the metaethical was decisive in his attempt to render the individual's existential and ontological "self-enclosure" so radical that only revelation and miracle could "rescue" him from the anguished isolation implied by it.

Touched by revelation—the experience of being loved absolutely and infinitely by God—metaethical man emerges from his self-enclosure and "defiant" but vain self-assertion of his self. He is now "ensouled" (*beseelt*), and uniquely capable of what Bernhard Casper calls in his chapter "responsibility." Cognizant of God's revealed love of him as a distinctive, unique being, the individual obtains a "freedom," ultimately denied him by idealism and its delusory "ethos of autonomy," and finds himself in a spontaneous, responsible relation to the other whom he now realizes to be a unique and irreducible other like himself. The experience of divine love is thus experienced as the commandment to love one's neighbor. As Casper points out, Rosenzweig developed this theme in a nuanced critique of ethical idealism, particularly of the Kantian position. Casper also argues that the restoration of the concept of responsibility perhaps constitutes Rosenzweig's most lasting contribution to philosophy and theology.

Rosenzweig's critique of idealism, particularly the notion of totality—of Hegel's *hen kai pan* (one and all)—raises the question of Rosenzweig's relation to Hegel, to whose philosophy, as previously noted, he devoted his doctoral dissertation of 1912, later expanded and published as a two-volume book, *Hegel und der Staat*, in 1920. As Otto Pöggeler shows, Rosenzweig found it more difficult to break with Hegel than he himself perhaps knew. His "new thinking," which marks a radical break with Hegel's idealism, can only be truly understood in light of Hegel. The inflections of Rosenzweig's thought, as Pöggeler clearly demonstrates, remained "decisively influenced" by Hegel. More specifically, Pöggeler argues, Hegel's overarching problem of finding a resolution between the tension of the Enlightenment, which sought to subject all political and religious experience to reason, and romanticism, which acknowledged the uniqueness of every historical experience, also preoccupied Rosenzweig. From this perspective, Pöggeler indicates, Rosenzweig's affirmation of Judaism may be viewed as a dialectic attempt to overcome the limitations of the Enlightenment.

Rosenzweig was initially attracted to Hegel's conception of history as a meaningful process. His disenchantment with Hegel's panlogism obliged him to reconstruct a new view of history. Whereas Hegel subsumed revelation in the historical development of reason, Rosenzweig retained revelation, particularly as embodied in the Synagogue and the Church, as a central and autonomous axis of history. In contrast to Hegel, for Rosenzweig God does not become in history, but rather history unfolds as a meaningful process by virtue of God remaining outside of history. Alexander Altmann, whose chapter is a reprint, traces this distinctive understanding of history to the influence of the notion of the Johannine church, one of the leitmotifs of the Enlightenment and German idealism, especially as expounded by Schelling.[40]

Rosenzweig's struggle with the meaning of history was shared by his generation, a struggle often known as the crisis of historicism. On the basis of until recently unpublished manuscripts—written prior to Rosenzweig's clarification of his theological position and the composition of *The Star of Redemption*—the chapter by Paul Mendes-Flohr reconstructs Rosenzwieg's experience of that crisis, and shows that he first formulated his notion of a dialectic between a metahistorical reference and history proper in decidedly nontheological terms. In these early manuscripts the metahistorical reference generating the ontological possibility of history as a meaningful process was a purely philosophical construct; as his theological understanding matured he affirmed that the Synagogue and the Church, in covenantal conjunction, embodied the concrete reality of such a reference beyond history, vouchsafing to history a goal and genuine hope.

Rosenzweig's theology, as Scholem notes in chapter 1, exhibits many affinities to Jewish mysticism. Moshe Idel considers these affinities as well as the extent to which Rosenzweig was actually familiar with Kabbalah. Idel concludes that Rosenzweig had at least a rudimentary familiarity with the principles of Kabbalah and, more significantly, had a profound appreciation of kabbalistic spirituality, as expressed in its intensely personalistic view of the divine and its hyperbolic "anthropomorphism," as containing elements that may possibly revivify a Judaism spiritually desiccated by modern rationalism.

In more immediate terms Rosenzweig sought to adumbrate a strategy for the spiritual renewal of modern man in general through a revaluation of speech—the faculty that man shares with God. "The ways of God are different from the ways of man," as he succinctly put it, "the word of God and the word of man are the same." [41] Speech binds man both to God and his fellow man; it is the bridge that arches between the life of the spirit and the realm of humanity. As such it provides, according to Rosenzweig, the crucial link between theology and philosophy. Indeed, grounded in the concrete, time-bound reality of human discourse, speech—as opposed to abstract, timeless reason—is the central epistemological category in Rosenzweig's "new thinking." Through a careful reading of *The Star of Redemption*, Nahum N. Glatzer—a close associate and biographer of Rosenzweig—offers a "contextual clarification" of his conception of speech and the cognate categories of "language," "the word," and "silence." Glatzer delicately illuminates Rosenzweig's understanding of man's spiritual development through his relation to speech, from his emergence as a "speechless introvert" to a "speaking soul,"[42] to one beloved by God, who has addressed him as a Thou, and granted him the grace of addressing his fellow man and God as Thou.

The volume concludes with two retrospective appreciations of Rosenzweig. The first by Stéphane Mosès reviews Rosenzweig's last—and only recently published—diaries, written in 1922 shortly after he had learned of his affliction with a terrible disease (amyotrophic lateral sclerosis) that left him totally paralyzed and that at the time he felt would soon lead to his death. In these diaries, written with a sense of urgency, Rosenzweig critically reflected on some of the major themes of his thought: inter alia creation, revelation, history, and messianism. Mosès discerns in these reflections a tension between the Rosenzweig of *The Star of Redemption*—rigorously philosophical and systematic—and the later Rosenzweig, who though facing a horrible paralysis and death, was increasingly committed to a life of piety and service to others. "Beyond the systematic, almost dogmatic construction of *The Star of Redemption*, we have here [in Rosenzweig's last diaries] a living tension between opposite poles: contemplation and experience, eternity and history, mysticism and life."

In his reflections, Rosenzweig's beloved disciple and intimate friend Ernst Akiva Simon detects a similar tension. Referring to three concentric circles of those influenced by Rosenzweig—philosophers struggling with the tattered heritage of German idealism, Jews eager to reappropriate Judaism, and Rosenzweig's disciples—Simon notes that there was a basic tension in Rosenzweig between his contrasting proclivities to systematic philosophy and, what Rosenzweig calls after Kant, the rhapsodic; Simon suggests that it was by virtue of this rhapsodic power that Rosenzweig exercised his most enduring influence.

I

# Franz Rosenzweig and His Book
## *The Star of Redemption*

*Gershom Scholem*

Wenn aber stirbt alsdenn,
An dem am meisten
Die Schönheit hieng, daß an der Gestalt
Ein Wunder war und die Himmlischen gedeutet
Auf ihn, und wenn, ein Rätsel ewig füreinander,
Sie sich nicht fassen können
Einander, die zusammenlebten
Im Gedächtnis . . .
    selber sein Angesicht
Der Höchste wendet
Darob, daß nirgend ein
Unsterbliches mehr am Himmel zu sehn ist oder
auf grüner Erde, was ist dies?

Es ist der Wurf des Säemanns, wenn er faßt
Mit der Schaufel den Weizen,
Und wirft, dem Klaren zu, ihn schwingend über die Tenne.
Ihm fällt die Schale vor den Füßen, aber

Ans Ende kommet das Korn.
Und nicht ein Übel ists, wenn einiges
Verloren gehet und von der Rede
Verhallet der lebendige Laut.

Hölderlin

But when he then dies,
To whom beauty clung most,
So that a miracle was wrought
In his form and the heavenly pointed at him,
And when, an eternal enigma for one another
They cannot grasp
One another, who lived together
In memory . . .
Even the Highest averts
His face, so that nowhere again
An immortal is to be seen in the skies
Or on the green earth, what is this?

It is the sower's throw, when he holds
The wheat in his shovel,
And throws, towards the open, swinging it across
The thrashing-floor. The husks fall at his feet,
But the corn reaches its end.
No harm, no evil it is if some of the speech
Is lost and
The living sound subsides. . . .[1]

In his short life Rosenzweig accomplished much. He came from the desolate Jewish wasteland in Germany, of which the word *assimilation* gives only the slightest hint, and grew up and developed his vast talents without Judaism and without Torah. His first accomplishment was in philosophy in the academic sense. Wholeheartedly he entered the grove of German idealism, wherein he came upon one of the decisive discoveries in the history of its development— the discovery of the earliest outline of the idealist system, namely, a manuscript in the handwriting of the young Hegel but which according to Rosenzweig actually recorded the ideas of the young Schelling.[2] It was to Hegel that Rosenzweig devoted his first major book, *Hegel und der Staat* (1920; *Hegel and the State*), a book that superbly combines a profound descent into the world of dialectics with strict philological work. Hegel, who laid the cornerstone of idealistic philosophy and who became the standard (and at the time the stumbling block) for the philosophizing of all those who came after him, drew Rosenzweig too into his charmed circle. Even after Rosenzweig freed himself from the spell of Hegel's philosophy, it left its impress on him for a long time, as the form and inner style of his second book, *The Star of Redemption* (1921), testify.

It was Hermann Cohen, Hegel's *locum tenens*—even if unwittingly and unwillingly—who drew Rosenzweig to Judaism, or more precisely, who led him to the great awakening for which a language was found in his book *The Star of Redemption,* about which I shall have more to say later. The chance meeting between these two men— as Rosenzweig related it, he went to one of Cohen's classes at the Hochschule für die Wissenschaft des Judentums in Berlin merely out of curiosity and without any vital interest—led not merely to a friendship, but to a richly consequential love between the old man of seventy who was then about to rediscover Judaism, and the youth of twenty-five, who had then only just begun to formulate his view of the world. That encounter became a great event along the road of the Jewish people's spiritual history. Cohen's noble personality, which had as if transmigrated and reached us from the days of antiquity (all of us who still sat at his feet felt that way), and his talks—not Cohen's philosophical system but, if I can be precise about the intention of this word, the system or method of his thought, its inner flow and flux—made a deep impression on Rosenzweig, which is discernible in everything he wrote subsequently, up until his very last days.

During the First World War, while serving on the Macedonian front, Rosenzweig issued his famous appeal for the establishment of an Academy for the Science of Judaism as an organon for the renewal of Jewish life in Germany. All of us who were then in Germany remember how great a resonance the appeal, contained in his open letter to Hermann Cohen, which appeared under the title "Zeit ist's" ("It Is Time"), had for many.[3] He called for a new form of Jewish education and for an institution that would engage in the training of teacher-scholars who would combine precision of discernment and depth of knowledge with an alertness to the contemporary demands of a living education. The Academy for the Science of Judaism that was founded in Berlin in 1919 was the fruit of this first call by Rosenzweig, even though he tended to disavow his creation after it had strayed from the path he regarded as its very raison d'être: the path of a bold association between pure scholarship and the work of educating the Jewish public. In the last years of the war, as a soldier on the battlefield in the Balkans, he began his great book, the formulation of his *Weltanschauung*—*The Star of Redemption;* after the war he searched for a new way to fulfill his longing to study and teach. Cohen's spiritual heir, whose later introduction to Cohen's writings taught us to see and understand the fundamental revolution that had occurred in Cohen's spiritual world in his last years,[4] became once again a pupil and learned Talmud from the late Rabbi Nehemiah Nobel,[5] the "kabbalist" among the rabbis of Germany. Rosenzweig then founded the Freies Jüdisches Lehrhaus in Frankfurt, where, as director, he was the first of its pupils and where I and many of my early colleagues at the Hebrew University had our initial experience as teachers. About all of this— his activity and great influence on our elders and youths in Germany, who at that time flocked to the rooms of his school from all camps and all parties in Jewry—much can be said, but it is not in this that his greatness should be seen. Nor do I have anything to say in explanation of the secret of his personality and the attractive force that emanated from him then, in the brief days when he had his health. His books will testify for him; I have already dressed my feelings in the words of the great German poet Hölderlin, with which I have prefaced my remarks. We who had the privilege of knowing Rosenzweig regarded him as one of the most sublime manifestations of the greatness and religious genius of our people; he already exemplified for us the truth of the sages' definition of religious genius: "For wheresoever we found his greatness and majesty, there we found his humility."[6]

I set out to address myself to what I called Rosenzweig's distinctive activity in theology. This theology was indeed new, and if I add that in his article "Das neue Denken" ("The New Thinking"),[7] one of his most distinguished pieces, he called the content of *The Star of Redemption* a philosophical system, it will be appreciated that we must establish the place of this great book, which appeared two years after the conclusion of World War One, in relation to the spiritual world of the generation that experienced that war. *The Star of Redemption*, written with an exemplary precision of thought but nevertheless in the style of that generation, was considered in Germany among Jews and Christians, believers and apostates, to be one of the most difficult books in the philosophical literature; one can be certain that Jewish theologians (if there be such) either have not read it or, if they have, have given up on it. This book, which tries to set out a new way of thinking, is not one of those books of which one can readily say, I have understood it. There is no hope of encompassing the content of a book as rich and profound as this in a brief essay, and certainly no hope of interpreting it; all I try to do is outline some of its major features. As for the historical status of the book, it can be grasped from three perspectives: philosophy, the general situation of theology in Rosenzweig's day, and the status of theology among the Jewish people in that period.

In reference to philosophy, Rosenzweig himself described his point of departure and formulated it very sharply in his lengthy introduction to the first part of the book, called "On the Possibility of Knowing the All" ("Über die Möglichkeit das All zu erkennen"), which was intended as lethal criticism, as a war to the finish against idealism. For that is the demand and pretension of philosophical thought—to know the All, or the Whole. That was the demand from Parmenides to Hegel, "from Ionia to Jena," as Rosenzweig put it. Never in the history of philosophy did this aspiration receive more extreme expression than in the doctrine of Hegel. It and all those resembling it, including the teachings of Hermann Cohen, were considered ripe fruit on that Tree of Knowledge called independence or "autonomy" of thought. When, in Hegel, philosophy encompassed its own history and made it too a part of the system of pure thought, when it also included God in the Whole, in the one All of its own thought, it reached its summit and came to its end. For in truth, what step could it still take without falling from its haughtiness? Pure autonomous thought brings forth (*erzeugt*) its content by itself and from itself, and this content is being (*das Sein*); the thought that thinks itself thinks the world, thinks the Whole. The unity of the Whole, the wholeness, is assured by the unity of thought. For, asks Hegel, what assures us that there is only one wholeness in the world? And Hegel replies, only the presupposition that the world can be reckoned in thought. Over against the multiplicity of contents of cognition, the unity of thought maintains its identity with pure being. This indeed is a very proud and distinguished world: *hen kai pan* (one and all). Philosophy pretends to know the essence of the world and does not admit that something is missing from the wholeness it thinks. But can everything be grasped by thought? Is that philosophy's consolation to a flesh-and-blood individual who trembles with the fear of death, that it says to him we have already prepared for death and have overcome it by thinking? Does this consolation of Plato's really console us? Is not that answer a deception? It is this question of death that Rosenzweig placed at the very opening of his book, and truly there is no more apt point of departure than that for theology. This was, of course, not really the beginning of the rebellion against idealistic philosophy initiated by Kierkegaard's opposition to Hegel, and Nietzsche's objections to Schopenhauer, a rebellion later extended by Leo Shestov, who, when Edmund Husserl—perhaps the keenest mind to emerge from Germany Jewry—raised the Hegelian banner in his famous article "Philosophy as a Rigorous Science," came forward with his "Memento Mori," his remarks cutting to the very core of idealism.[8] It is not at all surprising that Rosenzweig and Shestov produced their works at the same time, during the First World War. The living present *I*, not the I of the doctrine of the transcendental subject of idealistic deduction and not the general I, the idea of the I, but the empirical I occurring in experience, the I that has a first name and a last name: that man Søren Kierkegaard and that man Friedrich Nietzsche asked about their place. For their very real afflictions, which idealism denies by not acknowledging them, there is no remedy in the system that is in a great hurry to pass from the wretched I that is no more than a "given" to the loftiness of the ideal subject. I wonder if anyone can read the modern idealists on the "given" as no more than a methodological principle, without despairing over the extent of this deception. In the world of idealism nothing is more contemptible than this "given," which, as it were, comes to the idealist as a reminder of sin, of the conjoining of being and thought involved in a rape, the groaning of the ravished I disturbing the repose of the noble philosophers. This empirical I has stepped outside of the philosophers' "Whole," finding itself beyond all-embracing thought, or more precisely: in the thought by which it thought itself it could not think anything else, not the world and not God. The unity of thought, and within it the unity of being, the All or Whole of philosophy, were shattered. And along with the I's departure from the fortress of the All, the divinity too left, and among the broken fragments of the panlogical cosmos, among the "breaking of the All," philosophy searches its way. This "breaking of the vessels" of idealism is what Rosenzweig came to repair in his book.[9] Theology builds for him this restored world. The autonomy of thought has broken down, and henceforth it, thought, will not create its subjects but will find them. This heteronomy of thought has other aspects as well: although each thought will think its own "Whole," it cannot link the various Wholes it will think. I will return to this topic later.

As for theology, the discipline—I dare not say science—that deals with man's innermost and darkest needs, that seeks to bare the riddle of his concrete existence and to show him the deed he must do in order to uncover the path leading from creature to Creator: theology is not a science of the essence of the divinity beyond creation but consists rather of the eternal questions of love and will, wisdom and ability, judgment and mercy, justice and death, creation and redemption. Theology has concrete questions. In time this theology took on an alien cast, in our times astoundingly abstract and pallid, as if abandoned by its subjects which went off in search of another field. The weakness of theology in our time, of which everyone is aware, undoubtedly has deep roots, but this is not the place to examine them at length. Theology became impoverished when in the last century it consented, equally among Jews and Christians, to position itself at philosophy's furthest boundary, a kind of ornament bedecking the roofs of philosophy's vast structures, rather than insisting on its own; so theology suffered the same dismal fate as philosophy, its most important issues abandoned by it. These issues were to find refuge for themselves elsewhere, I will not say forever but certainly for a long time. In sociology and psychology, matters of the divinity and of man, theology's eternal subjects, assumed a secular form. What was left as theology's legacy was what no one else wanted, and theology itself (disgracefully) was ashamed to inherit it and instead of extolling it concealed it in back rooms and clothed it in the tatters of scandalous allegory and embarrassing prattle. I am referring to the doctrine of miracle, which forms the mainstay of the second part of *The Star of Redemption*. The categories of faith hid themselves from the categories of science in the nineteenth century: the latter demanded for themselves the right of the mysteries of creation and the wretched experience of the "disenchanted" world, which they called *Erfahrung* (experience), set itself up as eternal.[10] All of us know how feeble were the protests of theology, which is only now beginning to stir, now that physicists in our generation have for their part, five years after the publication of Rosenzweig's book, come upon miracle as a possible category and leading scientists have begun to debate whether or not to allow miracle a place among the fundaments of physics.[11] The stone the builders spurned is become a cornerstone!

Is it at all surprising that with theology's status at its nadir, even problems no one could doubt belong to it have fled and have ensconced themselves in art and literature? Dostoyevsky was already well aware of this in *The Idiot*. And if we consider undertakings of a clearly theological nature such as Marcel Proust's *A la recherche du temps perdu* or Franz Kafka's *The Trial* or *The Castle*, it is amazing that the theologians had no feeling whatever of *tua res agitur*—that their concern is taken up here—but rather have allowed this discovery to be made by discerning critics. It is obvious, then, that in our time theological issues have vanished from sight, have become concealed—lights that cast their light inward and are not seen from outside. The divinity, banished from man by psychology and from the world by sociology, no longer wanting to reside in the heavens, has handed over the throne of justice to dialectical materialism and the seat of mercy to psychoanalysis and has withdrawn to some hidden place and does not disclose Himself. Is He truly undisclosed?

Perhaps this last withdrawal is His revelation. Perhaps God's removal to the point of nothingness was a higher need, and He will reveal His kingship only to a world that has been emptied, in the sense of "I gave access to them that asked not, I was found by those who sought me not." That is the abandonment and the question from which *The Star of Redemption* appeared to Rosenzweig, and to him as a Jew it appeared in its Jewish form, as a Star of David.

And what of the state of things in the Jewish world? We all know: ever since Judaism's association with and rootedness in the Eternal People was loosened in the decisive historical encounter between it and the riches of Europe in the last century, ever since the sorry attempts to turn its substance into nothing, to lead our reality into oblivion, ever since the ground of the people was taken from it, Judaism, having placed itself in a hopelessly vulnerable position, has of course suffered great damage. The fortification and forbearance needed today to read one of the theological works produced by the great thinkers of Western Jewry in the nineteenth century is well enough known. It is not for lack of ability to think precisely or lack of awareness of theology's unique perspectives, for it must be admitted that Reform Judaism certainly does not lack this ability, and undoubtedly the day will yet come when the life of thought buried in forgotten books such as Ludwig Steinheim's *Die Offenbarung nach dem Lehrbegriff des Synagoge* (Revelation according to the Doctrine of the Synagogue) or Moritz Lazarus's *Die Ethik des Judentums* (*The Ethics of Judaism*) will be discovered.[12] But this life is concealed, for it has no homeland or ground beneath it; it cannot be revealed because willingly and intentionally the authors of these books excised from themselves the life arteries of a full Jewish existence. As for the Orthodox theology constructed at that time by that exceptional person within Western Jewry, Samson Raphael Hirsch (1808–1888), the power of thought it contains is slight and frail. That can readily be appreciated if we descend one more rung in the analysis of this Jewish reality: if we ask what Jewish theology was, and where a full Jewish religious reality found living expression in thought during the centuries preceding the emancipation. The inescapable answer—so much to the displeasure of Liberals and Orthodox, secular and religious, that they fled in all directions so as not to hear it—is: in the Kabbalah. The Kabbalah in its last dialectical form is the last theological domain in which the questions of the Jew's life found a living reply; but in the period when panlogism totally overtook Western Jewry, this precious possession—a pitiful possession, perhaps, but a living one!—became a source of shame to those who inherited it, even in Orthodox Judaism.

This Samson Raphael Hirsch, whose opponents were very much on target when they said of him, in derision, that as a mystic who did not make it to mysticism (*ein verhinderter Mystiker*) he kept himself from taking nourishment from its spheres and chose to create a new mysticism—unwittingly—so he would not be associated with any trace of Kabbalah. The Orthodox too severed the continuity with the most powerful religious forces at work in the preceding period, and the Kabbalah was forgotten among Western Jewry. The mark of this historical amnesia—induced by fear, opposition, as well as will—is impressed on all the attempts to express Jewish reality in the last century. Mystery does not sit well with the *derekh eretz* with which Hirsch enlightened (and some say deceived) Orthodox Jewry.[13] Mystery, the most national of all the domains of Jewry that Reform Judaism sought to "rectify" by a universal, abstract and allegorical language, did not at all suit its aspirations. Finally, in our generation, the generation of Rosenzweig, this "amnesia" had already begot a new reality: it was no longer necessary to turn a blind eye to the reality of such a force, for it was not at all known to be such a "force," and it is not surprising that even Rosenzweig's remarks on the Kabbalah are like the words of a babe held prisoner among the Gentiles, unaware that his life is endangered.

This neglect of mystery as the ground of Jewish thought was shared by the early generations of the Zionist movement. And not only for the reasons I hinted at earlier, but also because the remedy of Zionism is itself the rub. The stirring new discovery that the nation has a reality and the rediscovered link between the individual and his world, namely, his people, have as it were drawn unto themselves all the problematics. The forgotten base level sometimes easily becomes the most important of things: here great problems have been uncovered that have not yet been solved because the ground from which they sprung was missing. The creation of the doctrine of Zionism, the attempts to portray the new world we Zionists have entered—the world of the living Jewish people and the land of Israel and all the new riches we discovered in them—these have attracted and absorbed the best of our people's spiritual forces. Theology stood, as it were, outside the bounds of this new world, and as it is written, the poor man's wisdom is despised. Nobody needs it, and why should we, who in our new discovery of nationhood are making Judaism secular, who are taking the path of *saecularisatio*, have any need of it? However, questions about the eternal life of the Eternal People before the eternal god are not of the sort that can be forgotten. After the Zionist movement has set itself to the work of implementation, the question must arise with redoubled force and with the almost frightening vitality that attaches to every authentic question, that is, a question that time makes pressing, the old question that the Jewish people are not free to rid themselves of or ignore: Where are we headed? And with it comes the old answer: toward "the star of redemption."

In the generation before World War I, one person did awaken and discover this world from which both philosophical thought and the concatenation of our people's history had banished us. It was Hermann Cohen, who in his last book, *Religion der Vernunft aus den Quellen des Judentums (Religion of Reason)*[14]—written when he was seventy-five—broke through into that world here called theology and established the heteronomy of thought, not because he wanted to take this step but because he was led to it by the idealistic dialectic of independent thought. What Rosenzweig said about Cohen's book was indeed apposite: today we all know of the errors in the plan Columbus presented to the professors of Salamanca, but America was found by means of this plan; until his dying days Columbus thought he had reached East Asia, but he had "only" discovered America. Cohen, for his part, thought he remained on the ground of the German idealism that had so thoroughly suffused its perspectives in his system. He believed that his last book was no more than an embellishment to his idealistic philosophy, especially to his ethics; he did not even acknowledge the systematic independence of religion, but merely accorded it a unique character (*Eigenart*). He did not know that he had discovered the paradise from which we had been banished because of the rebelliousness of autonomous thought. Others too, among them the great of our generation, have discovered the way of the Tree of Life, although not in the language of Jewish theology; here it suffices to mention two Jews who have done so, Martin Buber and Lev Shestov, the great Jewish-Russian philosopher. But this new thought, the thought of the generation that experienced the hell of the First World War, is nowhere expressed with such full awareness and clear grasp of the perspective that had here opened up as in Rosenzweig's book, which expresses it in the old words of the Torah of Israel.

Rosenzweig's book is a philosophical system, as can be seen from its form—its architectonic, tripartite division, the classic trichotomy that Kant established for a system. But how different this threefold division is from that found in any "proper" philosophical system: logic and the theory of knowledge, ethics and political philosophy, aesthetics and the theory of art. We vainly search for this division in *The Star of Redemption,* a book that begins with death and ends with a theory of knowledge. The subjects of the standard parts, logic, ethics and aesthetics, are discussed here, with much attention paid especially to logic and aesthetics (where Rosenzweig made particularly important discoveries), but according to a new methodological principle expressed in the astronomical image of the book's title, and in the three-part division it presents: The Elements, the Course, the Configuration (*Elemente, Bahn, Gestalt*). The theology appears here at the heart of concepts familiar to all of us. "The theological problems," says Rosenzweig, "seek to be translated into human terms and the human problems seek their way into theology's domain. The problem of the tetragrammaton, for example, is but a part of the logical problem of names in general, and an aesthetics that has no ideas on the question of whether artists may attain salvation may well be a decorous science but is certainly incomplete." [15]

We saw above how the All or Whole of idealism was shattered. Philosophy was left with three separate and distinct "wholenesses" given to it in the reality of experience since time immemorial: God, the world and man, and to them the first part of *The Star of Redemption* is devoted. Three sciences—theology, cosmology, and anthropology—dealt with these separate "elements" until philosophy and its criticism came along and proved to us that our knowledge of them is—nothing. The negative theology of Nicholas of Cusa, the negative cosmology of the sophists and of Spinoza, and the negative psychology of Kant with the misgivings about the I it uncovered—these are the product of reason's criticism of the living content of experience. Faith saw the world, man and God, and what it took for granted was stamped by knowledge as absurd. This threefold nullification of the elements is the point of departure for Rosenzweig's analysis, which does not maintain the negation of knowledge as a conclusion, but turns it into a springboard from which to leap into existence, into affirmation. God, world and man—the three cannot be proven, every proof leads knowledge toward negation. They form the triaxial system, the coordinates, from which knowledge cannot escape, within which all its lines are drawn. In the first part Rosenzweig tries to show that these three subjects, the first and last of all philosophizing, are not to be set alongside one another and cannot be reduced to one another, that the old game of philosophy, which teaches that everything is "really" "in its essence" something else, is baseless and futile, and that in fact it is the game of the wholeness we have left behind: that God is "really" the self or that the self is the world and the rest of these combinations and permutations called standpoints (*Standpunkte*), which are no more than the deception of the one cognized wholeness. In the thought that thinks the world, nothing but world will be found. No matter how far one burrows, how deep one penetrates, and how many divisions one makes, the world will not stop being the world and turn into something other than itself. Thought seizes upon objects given to it in their experiential context, in living reality, and sets them up in their elementary isolation, turns them into essences, into substances. Into such an essence thought may descend and gaze upon the holiest of holies—for God as an essence, not the living present God, is no more hidden from thought than the "essence" of the world or of man. How profound was Rosenzweig's observation of these essences, which he found to be the elements of the world as conceptualized in the three chapters titled "God and His Being, or Metaphysics," "The World and Its Meaning, or Metalogic," and "Man and His

Self, or Metaethics." But pure thought cannot escape its isolating wholeness and link essence with reality, that reality of our experience within which the elements combine and where they appear only so combined. A phenomenon has no essence! Immersed within their infinity and mute, without outward expression, the essences develop, each of these elements from its negation and from the negation of its negation, which determines its "beingness." The unprovable dialectic process that shows us the way from an "absence of knowledge" to the factuality of the fact of the body of the essence never leads us out. This world of the mute elements, that cannot project its voice outside, is called by Rosenzweig "the ever-enduring proto-cosmos" (*die immerwährende Vorwelt*). The organon for attaining it, the guide with whose aid we descend, like Faust, to these "Mothers" and lift up the depths of their nothingness, is mathematics, the language of mute symbols. With the help of this protolanguage, which precedes all language, we bring to expression these mute symbolic essences. From the three "primal words" that are not yet a language—from *yes, no,* and *and*—Rosenzweig extracts with both mystical and mathematical precision the secrets of the nothingness that stirs in these words and arrives at the existent in all three of the elements: the living God, who is nothing but living; the specific plastic world in nature; and "defiant" man enclosed within a substance, in his self (*Selbst*). This protoworld, which contains all the objects we also find in our world, but contains them with a disiccative strangeness, in a mute isolation, Rosenzweig recognized as the world of the pagans. In their world, and especially in Greek antiquity, he found these elements, fragments of the broken Whole, as forms of life and as a living reality, and he presents them to us here as the elementary forces of the Greek world: the living god of myth, the plastic world of art, and the defiant hero immersed in the muteness of tragedy.

Using these deductions, the first book offers what Rosenzweig calls a "philosophical defense of paganism" (*eine Philosophie des Heidentums*). The living god of myth is not the God of Creation, and however deeply we delve into his essence, layer after layer, we will not find the Creator, for that god is fully absorbed in his life, in his self-radiant timeless youth; the mute man of tragedy, who is not permitted to express himself in speech but is seen and heard from within his muteness, is not the speaking soul, the living man created in the image of God; and the specific plastic world enclosed in its display is not the work of creation. These are in fact elements, but our world, our reality contains something more. If thought will not link them, take them out of their isolation, and create an idiom for them, where shall we find them bound together?

The second part of *The Star of Redemption*, called "The Course or the Always-Renewed Cosmos" (*die allzeiterneuerte Welt*), proposes an answer. The orbit within which the elements are joined in reality cannot be formulated by pure thought, that pretentious thought whose concepts are not time-dependent. To know the orbit is to know their course in time and through time. Thought that wants to know the orbit must get up from its haughty chair and find for itself a new way; henceforth all of its concepts shall include concrete time, which cannot be turned into something else—and what appears absurd to autonomous thought is precisely what is taken for granted by theological thought, by the thought of belief whose classic terrain we enter here, by what is nothing other than natural thought uncorrupted by the conceit of the dream of its independence, thought that knows it is created thought and the thought of a creature—"creaturely thought," as Rosenzweig calls it (*kreatürliches Denken*). In the broken Whole, in the world of the "shattering of the Wholes," each fragment has its virtual time from which it cannot escape, and only in existing time, historical time, which is the Day of the Lord and is divided into its periods—the morning of creation, the noon of revelation, and the evening of redemption—do the elements leave their isolation. Upon departing from their muteness and submersion for the orbit, the forms of the ancient world of paganism of which I have spoken are transformed, and from this transformation and turning (*teshuvah*, a Hebrew theological term not chosen idly by Rosenzweig) a new wholeness develops, the world that belief had always seen and that theology described as creation, revelation and redemption—these regions into which Rosenzweig penetrates here constitute the Star's orbit.

If the language that preceded language, within which the elements of the Whole's silent departure from the depths of their isolation was expressed, was, as I said, the symbolic language of mathematics, the order of creation must be developed from ordinary language, that which is spoken and heard. If mathematics served as a guide to the "Mothers," the "higher mathematics" of theology, which is language, will act as the guide for discerning the Star's orbit by the movement of the elements' return; for while the idealist world was born and created in thought by thought, the existing world was created by speech. On the gates of this theology I would inscribe the profound words of Johann Georg Hamann: "Language is the mother of reason and revelation." True, Hamann was a mystic and Rosenzweig did not have high regard for such—the great introduction to the third part of his book bearing the motto *in tyrannos* (against the tyrants) is directed against them, and generally, there is a marked attempted by many associated with the philosophy of the "new thinking" to draw a sharp line between themselves and the world of mysticism. However, we can reply with another Latin phrase, *amica veritas* (truth is friend), and the truth is that in his comments both on language and on time-bound thought, Rosenzweig is in very close agreement with the disdained Kabbalah.

As for language, it is well known that the theory of language is, in the words of one of the early luminaries of Kabbalah, "the wisdom of the inner logic";[16] as for time, it is worthwhile recalling the remarks of Rabbi Isaac ibn Latif, one of the foremost kabbalists, who, writing on the essence of mystical thought, said the following: "Whatever be in the heart of a wise man and is without duration and without time, that is called wisdom, and every picture of a genuine thing that does not occur of itself without time—that is not wisdom and he who puts his trust in it is not a wise man, he is a Kabbalist."[17] This kabbalist had already attained to the secret of time-bound thought, and the minor difference between him and Rosenzweig is that what Rosenzweig and others call experience these earlier figures called—Kabbalah!

But let us return to the matter at hand. Through that transformation by which the elements enter reality, by which they arise in experience, every interior side becomes an exterior. When the mute elements are given language, everything is reversed, and Rosenzweig, who came out of Hegel's world, twisted the formation of the content of the existing world of religion by dialectic antitheses. By this dialectic, however, he gained something that would have been difficult to extract by any other means, namely, the deduction that Islam is that conception of reality in which the elements go into their orbit without any transformation of the constitutive structure they had in their isolation. Alas, according to Rosenzweig, Islam knows of no interrelationship between the elements; God, man, and the world remain locked in mutual isolation.

Acknowledging reality to be time bound, genuine biblical faith (embodied in Judaism and Christianity) does, however, affirm a vital interrelationship between the elements. To be sure, "the times of reality," says Rosenzweig,

cannot be exchanged. The elements we found in their isolation have no order, among them there is none that came earlier and none that came later. But just as an isolated event and occurrence has its own present, past and future, and without them cannot be known or understood, or if so only in a distorted way, so too the generality of reality, which is the course. It too has its past and its future, albeit an eternal past and an infinite future. To know God, the world and man—that is but to know what they do at these times of reality and what is done to them—what they do to each other and what is done to them by each other. It is quite clear that their pure "beingness" is distinct, for if not—how could they act on each other? Who benefits when I am enjoined to love my neighbor, if I love not my neighbor but myself, and what that I do not already know can a god tell me who is nothing but my "higher self"? They are distinct, and in the world of the shattering, the world of the "elements," we knew them in the distinctness of their essences. But in reality, and it alone and not essence is what arises in our experience, we bridge this distinctness. Every attempt of ours is an attempt at such bridging. We try to attain God and He is hidden, man and he is closed, the world and it is an open riddle. Only in their interrelationships, only in Creation, Revelation and Redemption, do they open up.[18]

"Philosophy as narrative" is Rosenzweig's name for what he is doing in this part, which begins with a new theory of miracle ("über die Möglichkeit das Wunder zu erleben") and establishes a new philosophical and theological attitude. The highest point of the book is reached in this part, in the chapter "Revelation, or the Ever-Renewed Birth of the Soul" ("Offenbarung oder die allzeiterneuerte Geburt der Seele"). I am not ashamed to say that I regard this chapter in particular as one of what may be called Judaism's "definitive statements" on religious questions. I cannot describe here the details of his "narrative" which explains to us how the living god of myth becomes the God of Creation who creates the world anew every day, and how the mute stubbornly self-absorbed object that is tragic man becomes the speaking and hearing soul, loving and beloved, that has been opened by ever-renewed revelation ever since God called to Adam and said to him: "Where are you?" and ever since the words of the poet about man were fulfilled: "Going forth towards you, I found you / Coming towards me." [19] The story also explains how the plastic world of art, which became the work of creation by the speech of creation, will be restored to *malkhut,* that is, will become God's kingdom, in the redemption that is always to come—not idly did the kabbalists interpret the "world to come" as the "world that is always coming." Here, from a comprehensive philosophy of language, a veritable fountain of concepts of belief is developed and the system of philosophy becomes a prophecy of revelation. Had Rosenzweig appeared in our world to do no more than reinstate belief and restore miracle, the divine sign concealed in letters, to show us that and no more—that would have been enough. At the end of this part we understand how the restored world, which the kabbalists call the world of *tikkun,* is made, in redemption, and we have departed from the world of the shattered Wholes we have left. "Only in redemption, God becomes the One and All which, from the first human reason in its rashness has everywhere sought and everywhere asserted and yet nowhere found because it simply was nowhere to be found yet, for it did not exist yet. We had intentionally broken up the All of the philosophers. Here in the blinding midnight sun of the consummated redemption it has at last, yea at the very last, coalesced into the One." [20]

We have passed through two worlds: the world of concept and muteness and the world of reality and language. The historical forms of revelation have not yet been spoken of. There are no fixed configurations (*Gestalten*) in the course. It goes on, continues and changes. In the world of living reality, according to Rosenzweig, there is only the present moment, every past merely has been, and every future will only come; there is no time in the living sense other than the present. But just as forms of the past, forms of the world of elements of paganism to some extent still reach into the present, so too, by eternal forms, we anticipate the redemption that is to come.[21] This anticipation, this bringing of redemption into the present via the fixed cycle of days of the religions, creates a new dimension in the world, its last dimension: truth. Revelation takes on a historical guise: time, the "river which flows and issues from its source," extracts from its three hidden fountains, which we called elements, luminous and enduring forms (*Gestalten*). These forms, Judaism and Christianity, and their relationship to the truth, are taken up in the third part, entitled "The Configuration or the Eternal Hyper-Cosmos" ("Die Gestalt oder die ewige Überwelt"). This part, a logical further step in the system's development, searches once again for the eternal present, after the one eternal Being of idealism had shattered in our hands, the remaining temporal reality being, after all, time and not eternity. Rosenzweig, the sworn enemy of philosophical irrationalism in whatever guise, scoffs at the desperate suggestions that we hurl ourselves into the stream of life, indeed at all suggestions and slogans of that sort. He is in search of the eternal that does not need thought in order to be. The necessary anticipation of redemption in revelation, according to its two worldly forms in Judaism and Christianity, provides Rosenzweig with what he wants: the form, or more precisely the forms, for these two are but forms, configurations of the one eternal truth, the truth that bears witness unto itself—the seal of God.

Judaism and Christianity are conceived here as two different rhythms by which time in its worldly course—creation, revelation and redemption—takes on a fixed form in accord with the respective type of anticipation of redemption each embodies. To present and portray them as fulfilling this vital role, Rosenzweig does not consider differences in their dogma but rather the materialization of each of these religions, the guise they actually assume in the cycle of life. The order of prayer in the traditional Jewish prayer books and in the Catholic liturgy—that is the organon acting as guide to Rosenzweig in the third part of *The Star*. Prayer, by which man anticipates redemption in his life and for that moment sets up God's kingdom, is the language of the heavenly world, the hypercosmos. The depths of Judaism and of Christianity are bared to us by considering the order of their prayers. Here what they share can be discerned, as can the profound differences between them, especially in the doctrine of redemption. Rosenzweig describes Judaism at length in terms of the category of eternal life or the fundamental fire burning within the star—a world reality of the Jewish people founded on the natural reality of their life as the eternal people—and he describes Christianity in terms of the category of the eternal way or of the rays of light emitted by the star. The Jew is always at home, in the sense of "among my people I dwell," because he and his faith are rooted in the fertile and constant soil of the people; the Christian is always on his way, for he has no refuge in this world save for the Church founded on the one event, which being an event is not enduring and which the Church is always having to renew and become what it once was. Jew and Christian stand before God; to both of them eternity within time has been revealed by means of the division of the cycle of their life in the liturgical year of Sabbaths and holy days; both partake of the one truth, each having the part that has become for it the principle of time's rhythmic division. To this, the one truth, and the possibility of change and variance in it in revelation, the last chapter of *The Star* is devoted, which includes Rosenzweig's theory of knowledge. Nothing illuminates the unique structure of this system more than this situating of the theory of knowledge at the end and not at the beginning of the book, as is ordinarily done in philosophical systems.

A "messianic theory of knowledge" is what Rosenzweig calls this theory. The one truth—that is his final conclusion from long debates on the place of truth and on its bearer, after it turned out here that it too requires a bearer—is truth only for the One, for God. And if truth has only one bearer, one subject, our truth is not truth, is not *the* truth. Truth bears witness to itself. But our truth requires existence. Our truth has more than one face, is variable, like the two elements other than the Creator: man and the world. This variability, necessary for flesh and blood, does not—not in Judaism and not in Christianity—place its bearers at a disadvantage, and it is in it that Rosenzweig finds the principle that explains the unfolding of the difference in the conception of redemption in Judaism and in its rival. Our partial truth is not had by logical acumen; the truth theology speaks of is not a conditional truth, like that of mathematics, dependent on its axioms. The existence of our truth depends on the price we paid for it and pay for it daily, and the existence of the Jew's truth depends on his acceptance of the yoke of the kingdom of heaven in his daily life.

Here the book ends, and I could do no more than try to compress within my remarks a faint reflection of its brilliant light and abundant ideas, for the entire Jewish world is as if folded into this book. The system is not autonomous, does not stand on its own. It has been completed but has not come to an end, for at the end its gates open onto life, simple concrete life in which it must find its justification and existence, for it does not stand on its own.

The book was created and behold it is very good—and that *very* is death, thus constituting an affirmation of death and human finitude in general as an essential aspect of existence. Rosenzweig's book became a prophecy of his life, and he was compelled to pay for its truth in a most awful way. The life he went into from the gates of his book was soon to be death. After he had devoted only a small measure of time to Torah, he was stricken with a terrible disease and for more than seven years he lived among us in death's clutches. One after another, movement and speech were taken from him, the power of movement and the power of speech. Totally paralyzed except for two or three slight movements with his head and slight movement in one of his fingers, totally paralyzed in speech—that is how this man lived. Were it not for the absolute devotion of his wife, who, with an inestimable intuition born of love worthy of being called the holy spirit, understood his thoughts from hints and the faintest of cues, the divine voice echoing from the living soul in this dead body would never have reached us, that voice from the life of a soul that remained full and radiant as on the day the star of redemption was revealed to him. He became mute, and everything in the poem by Hölderlin with which I prefaced my remarks came to hold for him: the living sound was taken from his speech, but his seed was sown and from the fire of his muteness we heard the sound of the words of the living God. Whoever once was in that room in Frankfurt and heard his questions answered and heard the eloquence of that mute saint, surely he knows what a miracle happened to us here. Rosenzweig hardly stopped working at all, and he bestowed upon us very important gifts, among them the precious delight of his lengthy and profound comments on the poems of Judah Halevi, which he translated into German—theological and aesthetic comments illuminating for us the world of Judah Halevi in light of the star that shone for him. For four years he worked with Martin Buber translating the Bible, applying a linguistic principle that can be formulated in the biblical phrase "A [sky] light [*tsohar*] shalt thou make to the ark [*teivah*]," [22] which the kabbalists interpreted as follows: Make *zohar* (brilliance, splendor) for every word (*teivah*) until it shines like the noonday light. [23]

In his death he fulfilled his truth, and not for naught did he request that words from Psalm 73 be engraved on his tombstone, the same psalm in which it is said:

> For all the days have I been plagued
> And my chastisements came every morning
> If I had said I will speak thus
> I had been faithless to the generation of thy children
> And when I pondered how I might know this
> It was wearisome in my eyes
> Until I entered into the sanctuary of God
> And considered their end.

## 2

# Experience in Rosenzweig's New Thinking

*Reiner Wiehl*

## The Contradiction between the Messianic Theory of Knowledge and the New Thinking

In his postscript to *The Star of Redemption*, entitled "The New Thinking," [1] Rosenzweig protested against the view of his thought as a religious philosophy, characterizing it instead as a "system of philosophy": "To be sure, it deals with Judaism, but in no more detail than Christianity, and in little more detail than Islam. Moreover, it does not claim to be a religious philosophy; how could it, seeing that the word 'religion' does not even occur in it. It is merely a system of philosophy." [2] At the same time, Rosenzweig explicitly differentiates between his new concept of a system and Hegel's old one, invoking as a precedent the views of his friend Victor von Weizsäcker (1886–1957), who at the time was developing a philosophical anthropology of medicine. Thus he writes in a letter to Rudolf Ehrenberg (1884–1969) on 1 December 1917:

His [Weizsäcker's] concept of a system—which for me is the main thing—is indeed mine, and probably also Rosenstock's. I formulate it thus: System is *not architecture,* where the stones compose the building and are there for the sake of the building (and for no other reason); system means that every particular has the drive and the will toward *relation* to all the other particulars; the whole lies beyond the periphery of its conscious vision, it sees only the chaos of particulars, into which it sends its feelers. In the Hegelian system every particular position is anchored only in the whole (that is, by two others, the one preceding and the one following).[3]

Rosenzweig mentions language, in which system and subjectivity hang together in a manner not thus conceived by Hegel: Thus the speaker is, on the one hand, the ideal center of the system "language," which from the standpoint of the person who actually speaks presents itself as an infinite multiplicity of *and,* his conjunction denoting for him the relation of one autonomous subject with another. Rosenzweig stumbles here upon a new complex of problems: the constitutive connection between the concept of the system and a principle of relativity. Thus in the earlier-mentioned letter he goes on to ask:

But what becomes then of the absolute, which is indispensable to philosophy? Weizsäcker asks this question, and I ask it too; I say, when the whole is no longer the content of the system, then it must be the form of the system, or in other words, the wholeness of the system is no longer objective, but subjective. I myself, I the world-viewer, am the limiting ether for the content of the world which I view. Limited and turned toward the interior, toward the content, toward the world, the philosopher is the form of his philosophy.[4]

But how does Rosenzweig here link system and subjectivity in the "new" thinking, as distinguished from the corresponding linkage in the old thinking, for which Hegel's thinking stands as a paradigm? What does it mean to conceive the subject as the boundary of the world, as the form of philosophy?

Now it is the concept of experience, of an "experiencing philosophy," that is supposed to make an answer to that question possible. "More likely, this very point, where traditional philosophy comes to an end with its way of thinking, is the beginning of philosophy based on experience [*erfahrende Philosophie*]."[5] But how does experience connect system and subjectivity? How is this connection conceived in the new thinking? The concept and theory of experience are unquestionably among the principal items of the "old" thinking, as

Rosenzweig calls it. Must he not, then, if he is to be consistent, rethink the concept of experience itself, in order to make it usable for the new task of making the aforesaid linkage? Rosenzweig's effort of rethinking moves in two directions. Experience is no longer to be indissolubly bound to objects, nor yet to the thinking, conscious I. Thus he writes concerning the former: "For experience knows nothing of objects. It remembers, it senses, it hopes, and it fears." And,

It is only a prejudice of the last three centuries that the I must play a part in all cognition: that a tree cannot be seen by me unless my self sees it. As a matter of fact, that ego of mine is present only—when it *is* present, when, for example, I must emphasize that I for one see the tree because someone else does not see it. In that case, my cognition shows the tree certainly associated with me, but otherwise I know only about the tree, and about nothing else. Philosophy's claim that the self is omnipresent in all cognition distorts the content of this cognition.[6]

One must ask: does not this new concept of experience exacerbate the problem of the constitutive connection between system and subjectivity? What after all is the subject of experience, if it is not I, if it is not at least occasionally and contingently I? Is it the "It," the "unconscious" of which Freudian psychoanalysis speaks and of which V. v. Weizsäcker also occasionally spoke? Rosenzweig is not so much intent on defining what this self, this experiential subject between the soul and the I, really is as he is on making clear that just as, for the person who speaks, language is set into a multiplicity of *and*. Accordingly, the experience of the human being, placed before the multiplicity of particular facts, is set into the multiplicity of factuality itself, a multiplicity of the *and* that constitutes the condition of experience:

If something is to come out of knowledge, it means that—exactly as with a cake—something has to be put into it. What was put into *The Star of Redemption* was, first of all, the experience of factuality that precedes all facts of real experience, the factuality that forces thinking to apply (instead of its favorite term "actually") the little word "and," the basic word of all experience, the word the philosopher's tongue is not used to. God *and* the world *and* man! This "and" was the first word of experience, and thus it must also be the last word of truth. Even in truth itself, in the last truth which can be a truth for *us,* there must be an "and."[7]

Here, it seems to me, Rosenzweig's thinking consciously departs from the classical philosophy of modern times, in a new direction: The multiplicity of the *and* means not only the multiple data from which human experience proceeds; nor does it mean merely the multiple objects of experience, which experience forms out of its preliminary data. The multiplicity of the *and* is, finally, not even only that multiplicity of conditions on the basis of which human experience is possible at all. This multiplicity is finally that of the I itself—multiplicity that finally continues to exist when human experience believes it can ascertain its own ultimate, primal conditions. For this reason Rosenzweig says: "Unlike the truth of the philosophers . . . this truth must be truth for someone."[8] The truth of the philosophers, which Rosenzweig distinguishes from the truth of the new thinking, is represented, paradigmatically, by the truth of absolute cognition in speculative philosophy: truth in and of itself in its absolute exclusiveness is the idea of philosophical knowledge. Rosenzweig's "new thinking" presented a radically different conception of truth.

The Star of Redemption has been aptly called a transitional work.[9] It is characteristic of such works that they dissolve the familiar contours of tradition without yet being able to cast in clear and definite forms the new thing they anticipate. This seems to hold good especially for the new thinking's concept of truth. Rosenzweig says: "And that is why our truth must become manifold, and why 'the' truth must be converted into 'our' truth. Thus truth ceases to be what 'is' true and becomes that which wants to be confirmed as true. The concept of confirmation [Bewährung] becomes the fundamental concept of this new theory of knowledge."[10] What does this mean, truth as confirmation? Wherein lies the novelty of the new theory of knowledge with respect to this concept of truth? The novelty indeed is not evident if one understands confirmation in the sense of verification. For this view of truth is one of the most widespread and accepted in philosophy. It is found among the most heterogeneous positions. For speculative philosophy, just as for modern pragmatism and logical empiricism, truth is verification. What, then, distinguishes Rosenzweig's theory of confirmation from the modern theory of verification? Does the emphasis on the multiplicity of truths suffice to characterize this distinction? Or does the peculiarity of the confirmation theory only become understandable from the concept of the radical subjectivization of truth? If we make the latter assumption, must we not inevitably recur to transcendental idealism's attempt at solution if we are to avoid pragmatism, even skepticism? The key to understanding the peculiarity of Rosenzweig's theory of truth as confirmation lies in the concept of the "messianic theory of knowledge." But here, also, lies the basic problem of the new thinking itself. Rosenzweig speaks of the way that leads from the trivial truths of science "over those truths for which people are willing to pay, on to those that he cannot confirm save at the cost of his life, and finally to those that cannot be confirmed until generations upon generations have given up their lives to the end." [11] In this characterization of the messianic theory of knowledge we recognize without difficulty a continuity with the introduction to the first part of *The Star of Redemption,* where reference is made to the interrupted tradition of belief in miracles and the relation of this belief to prophecy and sacrifice:

In earlier times . . . the skepticism about miracles was not directed, as it is today, against their general possibility, but rather against their specific reality, against the credibility of the individual miracle. Miracle had to be proven, not like a general proposition, but as a particular occurrence. It required witnesses. The necessity of proving this and this alone was always acknowledged and so far as possible satisfied. We encounter every form of judicial proof here: from the weakest sort—circumstantial evidence—to the most substantial—the sworn witness and the trial by ordeal. Even in law, circumstantial evidence did not come into favor until very late, and for miracles too it plays only a slight role. . . . Thus the proof of miracles must basically fall back on eyewitnesses. . . . Only the testimony that is maintained through the tortures of an inquisition provides absolute certainty. The Satan of the Book of Job already knew this: only he is a true witness who testifies with his life's blood. Thus the most cogent proof of the miracle is the appeal to the martyrs. [12]

But how are we to conceive this problematic connection between the messianic theory of knowledge—the confirmation theory of truth—and the testimony of the miracle? How does Rosenzweig think of truth and miracle in one thought? And where lies the problem of the connection? Surely it is above all at the point where we inquire into the differences in degree of witnesshood between the unjustified and the justified, the voluntary and the involuntary sacrifice; moreover, along with these distinctions we must inquire into the conditions for making them, the right to make them. But most of all, the problem lies at the point where we must ask who sets the appropriate price for truth—whether it is man, whether man can or may be the one to set the price, and what becomes of the truth and the possibility of its confirmation if we must answer the latter question in the negative? But the problem may also be depicted from another angle. Rosenzweig not only designated his new thinking by the concepts "confirmation theory" and "messianic theory of knowledge," he also called it a "philosophy of sound common sense": "What the new philosophy, the new thinking, actually does is to employ the method of sound common sense as a method of scientific thinking." [13] The method of sound common sense—this seems at first to mean, in agreement with the phenomenological theories of this epoch, to hold onto that which is in plain sight, to not always look behind what everyone can see for something "actually" (*eigentlich*) other, a hidden Being-in-itself or essence.

Sound common sense never bothers to ask what a thing "really" is. Common sense is content to know that a chair is a chair and is unconcerned with the possibility that it may, actually, be something quite different. It is just this possibility that philosophy pursues in its inquiry into the essence of things. Philosophy refuses to accept the world as world, God as God, man as man! All these must "actually" be quite different from what they seem. [14]

The new thinking here criticizes philosophical thinking insofar as it is guided by the ancient Platonic inquiry into the essence. But this does not yet characterize the specific quality of the new thinking as such. For many, before and since, have criticized Platonism as such and its consequences. Rosenzweig is interested in another characteristic of common sense: not only does it keep to what is, but above all,

Common sense waits, goes on living; it has no fixed idea; it knows: time solves all problems. This is the secret that constitutes the wisdom of the new philosophy, which instructs us to think what Goethe had in mind when he wrote his lines on "understanding in time." . . . The new thinking, like the age-old thinking of sound common sense, knows that it cannot have cognition independent of time—though heretofore this was one of the highest distinctions which philosophy conferred upon itself.[15]

Let us, following Rosenzweig, allow common sense this newly bestowed distinction of patience and serenity. If it truly earns this distinction, then it is certainly not to be unreservedly identified with that common sense with which pragmatism operates. Of course, in the context of pragmatism, too, common sense is bound up with time. But it is precisely in this boundedness that it lacks that higher virtue of patience and serenity: it wants to do something, and to wait until all the questions have settled themselves of their own accord is precisely what is impossible for it. Our question, however, is directed to the connection between the confirmation theory of truth, that is, the messianic theory of knowledge, and the philosophy of common sense as Rosenzweig understands it. What becomes of the need to confirm the truth, what becomes of the will to testify to the miracle, before the bar of that patience and serenity which the new common sense professes? Does not the latter demand that one leave to truth its own time of confirmation, and to the miracle its own time of fulfillment? Is the effort toward confirmation and testimony not the helpless impatience of an attitude in comparison to which the old impatience of philosophical knowledge is true serenity?

## The Singularity of Experience

One of Rosenzweig's most important theses on "experiencing philosophy," as he alternately called the new thinking, is defining experience itself by the characteristic of nonobjectivity. The sense of this characteristic only emerges with its full trenchancy when we consider its connection with a second characteristic: defining experience by the characteristic of singularity. Only through this second characteristic does the definition of nonobjectivity take on the specific features of the new thinking. If we ask how we are to make these two characteristics understandable to ourselves, we first encounter the nonobjectivity and singularity of the experiencing subject. We are led one step further by a remark Rosenzweig makes at the beginning of *The Star of Redemption*, where he points out the particular meaning of Schopenhauer's philosophy for his own thinking:

Schopenhauer was the first of the great thinkers to inquire, not into the essence but into the value of the world. A most unscientific inquiry, if it was really meant to inquire into its value for man, and not into its objective value, its value for "something," the "sense" or "purpose" of the world, which would after all have been only another way of saying an inquiry into its essence. Perhaps it was even meant to inquire into its value for the man Arthur Schopenhauer.[16]

But what does this view of the world as value mean for the view of experience as nonobjective and singular? How does the world as value relate to experience? Is it the object of experience, or is it rather the nonobjective foundation of experience? To contemplate these questions more closely, I return once more to Rosenzweig's affinity, which he himself noted, to the thinking of Victor von Weizsäcker. This affinity shows itself not only in the similarity of their concepts of system, but also in the similarity of their concepts of experience. For the one as for the other, what is experience if not systematic experience, and what is a system, if not the experience of one subject? Weizsäcker goes beyond Schopenhauer's definition of the world as value, by defining the human being as value:

The existence of man is taken here to be a *quaestio juris* [question of law], not a *quaestio facti* [question of fact]. I do not dispute that there are also factual things to be ascertained about a human being, such as the color of his eyes or the length of his body. But what is human about him can be judged only from the perspective of certain wishes. I do not say that these wishes are always the same—or need always be idealistic. But one cannot say who or what a human being is, what people are, what man is. Always, one can only say what he should be. Another way of expressing this is to say that a human being is a thing with a subject. It is subjectivity which prevents objective assertions, or at least so relativizes them that one cannot see where it ends.[17]

For Weizsäcker, the human being as value is first of all the human being as object of medical anthropology. He stands here primarily in the value space "Health—Sickness." But how does the human being as value enter into experience? Is he the object of experience or its nonobjective foundation?

In another context Weizsäcker introduced the concept of "pathic

existence" with respect to all living things in general and interpreted our existence by analogy: "If I consider myself or another
living being, then my life is much more important than my existence. As a living being I do not say 'I am,' but I would like or I will,
or I can, must, may, ought; or I will not, may not, etc., do any of
these things." [18] This sounds very close to vitalism and the existentialist theory of knowledge, but it also sounds similar to Rosenzweig's confirmation theory of truth. To be sure, Weizsäcker speaks
of the necessity of introducing morality into nature and the knowledge of nature, but with this not unproblematic formula he means
something similar. He is concerned not only with setting up a heuris-
tic maxim that demands we orient ourselves in the knowledge of nature by the paradigm of living behavior and limit the claim of the
theory of nonliving particles of matter to universal validity. Here
subjectivity is declared a fundamental category of the knowledge of
nature and a universal basic value of that which is. Accordingly, consideration of the basic relationship is decisive for all knowledge of
nature. "A concrete growing-together and working-together of singular elementary subjects in the unity of a context of experience
which is singular each time." [19] From this basic relationship we can
discern the basic traits of experience, its nonobjectivity, its uniqueness, and its openness. Not only in the concept of the system but
also in the concept of experience and in the confirmation theory of
truth, as well as in the way all these elements hang together, Rosenzweig's thinking is contiguous with Weizsäcker's. What they have in
common is underlined by a comparable orientation of both to the
concept of experience in the classical philosophy of modern times.
Both of them here invoke theories of the rationalistic type. Whereas
Weizsäcker names Leibniz's "monadology" as its preferred source,
we find in Rosenzweig repeated references to the classical theories
of Kant, Hegel, and Schelling. What both have in common is the attempt to give the traditional concept of experience a new formulation under changed theoretical-practical conditions and to adapt it
to a new way of thinking. Both employ similar coefficients of refrac-
tions, derived above all from Nietzsche's thought. Common to both,
finally, is a certain imperfection in the success with which what is

received from tradition is updated—a certain lack of transparency in the relation of the "new" to the old thinking.

The affinity of Weizsäcker's and Rosenzweig's concepts of experience must not, however, be allowed to obscure the important differences. In itself, the fact that they prefer different philosophical sources suggests material disparities. In Weizsäcker we observe an updating of the romantic philosophy of nature, particularly regarding the universal application of the principle of subjectivity. This philosophy points in the general direction of the thinking of vitalism and the philosophy of values. The aim of thinking here is the foundation of a philosophical-medical anthropology. In contrast, Rosenzweig's formulation of the question is not anthropological. Unlike Weizsäcker, and in emphatic contradistinction to the philosophical speculation of idealism, the principle of subjectivity appears in his work in a multiple fragmentation. Whatever sounds close to vitalism and the philosophy of values here points unmistakably in another direction of thought, namely to a new definition of the relationship between philosophy and theology, to a new distribution of tasks between the two disciplines, in the conceptualization of the way God, the world, and man hang together. In *The Star of Redemption* we are continually stumbling upon traces of the traditional classical concept of experience. These traces are not always explicitly registered by Rosenzweig himself; often they serve to describe the continuity, or else to mark off the critical distance, between his thinking and that of his predecessors. Rosenzweig's new experiential thinking can be understood only in connection with his criticism of philosophical idealism, of its "one-dimensionality" and its narrowness as a theory of consciousness. His *Star of Redemption* offers a significant methodological alternative to the dialectical method of Hegelian speculative idealism. This method of the new thinking does not start from Being as the simplest, most abstract and general thought of the absolute and unique totality. Rather its movement begins with the thought of Nothing: of Nothing in a threefold sense, in a threefold form. The starting point is given here by the threefold Not-knowing in the face of the three primal elements, the three "factualities" of a philosophy of experience: God, the world, and man. And to the fundamental difference in starting points corresponds a fundamental difference in the methodological movements that proceed from them. In place of the uniform, homogeneous movement of the self-unfolding of the Absolute, which, like a circle, anticipates its completion at the starting point and at every further moment of movement in the same way, we now find a nonuniform movement of the three primal elements, which are fundamentally different one from another. These move toward one another, each on its own different path. Here are fragmentation and interference. In these veerings, there is no homogenous anticipation of perfection, but a marvelous formation of the ultimate Form of the path of the Star. Unlike the circular movement of speculative thought, this methodological movement is not the same at every moment of movement. As a methodological multiplicity whose unity appears only in the idea of its completed form, it corresponds rather to a method of experience than to that of pure, self-enclosed thought. Rosenzweig's criticism of the one-dimensional character of idealism is thus above all a criticism of the one-dimensional character of its methodological movement, of the linearity of successive negations of negations.

But how, in contrast to speculative idealism, are we to think of philosophical experience under the conditions of a multiple, multidimensional methodological movement? To be sure, the classical theories of experience, as was seen from the traditionalist formulation of Weizsäcker's concept of experience, are as a rule all aligned with the normative principles of nonobjectivity, uniqueness, and incompleteness. But these principles do not stand alone. Rather they are embedded in higher principles that are binding upon all knowledge, upon every kind of cognition, and thus also upon experiential knowledge and experiential cognition. I mean the fundamental principles of unity, universality, and necessity. These principles bind cognition and knowledge, generally and fundamentally, to the idea of science. Experience, too, stands here under the conditions of such a binding. Classical theories of experience link the general principles of knowledge and cognition with the particular principles by attempting to clear away, insofar as possible, the discrepancies and contradictions that arise. The construction of this connection occurs, as a rule, with an eye to the facts of perception. The concept of experience thus formed is then carried over by analogy to other domains of experience and other types of experience. How does the image of an experience thus projected look? All experience starts from perception. Sense perceptions comprise the material from which experience is formed. Outer and inner perceptions make available a multiplicity of phenomena. Experience is a specific form of processing this multiplicity, which requires for its success certain conditions: it is a conditioned synthetic unity of the multiple. Experience is to be distinguished from perception; the latter relates to a singular object, a particular concrete thing, that, grasped from a certain point of view, is perceived in a certain perspective, which last is objectified, through a projection, to a property of this thing. An individual thing is—with or without quality—never given by itself. It stands in a larger, comprehensive context, which perception, even if vague, encloses like a horizon. For this reason there is always a nonsensual component associated with perceptual knowledge, namely, a noetic knowledge that the perceived thing could also have other qualities, and the perceived quality could pertain not only to this thing, but also to other things. Therefore perception is impressed not only with the knowledge value of the particular, but also with that of the relatively general. Experience then differentiates itself from perception, out of which it takes shape, above all by its objectivity and its cognitive and assertive values. Experience is not concerned with the individual thing and its specific quality. Its object, in the face of the given multiplicity of perception, is something general—whether it be a form or a law—that has validity, under the given conditions of this multiplicity, for all possible things of this context. Finally, the particular perception has the character of contingency. This means that neither its occurrence nor its holistic constitution could ever be adequately explained from any previously given data. With experience it is otherwise: its conditioned synthetic unity contains, in the form of the conditions of this unity and the multiplicity of what is given, the conditions of the possibility of its explanation. Thus experience, in contrast to perception, is, at least potentially, conditionally necessary.

The classical theories of experience thus demonstrate, by the theoretical connection of perception with experience, the constitutive linkage between the universal principles of knowledge and cognition, on the one hand, and the particular principles of experience, on the other. At the same time, they also distinctly show, by this paradigm of a specific experience, the fundamental difficulties of the coordination of these general and particular principles. For all the difference in detail, the theories of experience in modern philosophical rationalism, in which we include the theories of experience held by Leibniz, Kant, and Hegel, agree on one point: in all of them, for every conceivable human experience, the specific principles of experience are definitively subordinated, even beyond the relationship of objective perception and experience, to the universal principles of knowledge and cognition. This means that multiplicity is founded upon unity, particularity upon generality, and contingency upon necessity; this relationship in which the second term is the foundation of the first enjoys unequivocal ontological and epistemological priority over every conceivable possibility of its reversal. How, then, does Rosenzweig's new conception of experience differ from that of modern classical philosophy? How does the alleged multidimensionality of the methodological movement precipitate itself in the concept of experience, with respect to its form or its content? What does it mean for experience that the presupposed ontology distinguishes itself by multidimensionality? It cannot be said that Rosenzweig has definitively given up the principles of cognition and scientific objectivity in favor of an unscientific experiential thinking, that he has completely lost sight of modern philosophy's great task of linking and coordinating those principles with the principles of experience. Rather it is clearly evident that, precisely in *The Star of Redemption,* he is very well aware of the danger of a subjectivist and ideological "*Weltanschauung*" (worldview) philosophy and that out of this awareness he takes pains to maintain the connection between philosophy and the scientific form of thought.[20] Yet there remains a chasm of difference between his new concept of experience and that of modern classical philosophy. In the face of this difference we may speak of a downright reversal of the values of cognition and experience. The basic principles of cognition and science no longer seem to be placed above the principles of experience, nor are the latter conclusively defined by subordination to the former. It would seem that in the new thinking abundance and multiplicity are rated far above unity, that the new and unique have unequivocal priority over the universal, and that contingency has become more primal and more fundamental than necessity and law. Experience as such in its independence, in its difference from scientific cognition, in its inexhaustible abundance, in its singularity and uniqueness, in its unprejudiced openness to the wholly other, seems to have freed itself from the spell of scientific thinking. The phrase "transvaluation of all values" must, however, not be misunderstood here. Rosenzweig is not interested in reducing science to mere empiricism, or its philosophical concept to positivistic notions, any more than he is interested in taking leave of scientific form in philosophy. On the contrary. Rosenzweig's idea of the scientific approach in philosophy remains oriented to the concept set up by modern classical philosophy. He is merely interested in limiting, out of consideration for the giveness of experience, the claim of scientific thinking to universal validity.

## The Multidimensionality of Experience in the *And* Form

What does this limitation of science by experience mean in Rosenzweig's new thinking? It leads, first of all, to the modification of the classical concept of the system as described at the beginning of this chapter; to the binding of this concept to a subjectivity external to it; to an insight into the necessity for a multiplicity of philosophical standpoints; and to the recognition that philosophical insights are subject to revision. But this is only a first step in the interpretation of this limitation. Through the transvaluation of the values of its relationship to science, experience gains, in the face of science, independence and independent value. We may express it thus: Besides scientific experience, there is nonscientific experience, and the latter cannot be reduced to a function of some prescientific experience, Nonscientific experience cannot be subsumed in prescientific experience; it is something different. This is true for everyday experience and for interpersonal experience, as well as for artistic and religious experiences. But this transvaluation must be considered from one further point of view: There is no satisfactory and adequate analysis of experience into components of cognition alone, even if we are talking about an analysis into esthetic and noetic, or prescientific and scientific components. In every single experience the given component of cognition must be imagined as complemented by a corresponding component of belief. This necessary complementarity of belief and cognition in all experience is, however, not to be understood as a plea for a purely empiricistic theory of knowledge, in which the possibility of general and necessary cognition is replaced by the contingent evidence of belief. It is not that Rosenzweig carries out a change of position from philosophical rationalism to empiricism. His experiential thinking, for all its distance from philosophical idealism, still keeps to the paths of philosophical rationalism. This complex attitude is bound up with the striking peculiarity of his style of thinking, which is always farthest away from Hegel just when its formulations suggest the greatest proximity. This peculiarity may be exemplified by three aspects, among others: First, Hegel in his theory of perception and experience speaks of the determining form of the *also*,[21] while Rosenzweig instead prefers to speak of the logical-grammatical form of the *and*. Second, in Hegel we find the famous remark about "God's thoughts before Creation,"[22] intended to describe the pure Being-in-and-of-itself of the categories as mere logical forms independent of their defining and noetic function in the real world of experience. Rosenzweig instead says that God's creation (considered as Providence) "in this world . . . pertains directly only to the universal, to 'concepts' and 'kinds.' It pertains to things only 'each after its own kind,' to the distinctive, therefore, only by means of its universal character and in the final analysis only by means of universal existence altogether."[23] And third and last, we find in Hegel a "science of the experience of consciousness,"[24] which is related to the new thinking about experience in Rosenzweig by the fact that in both cases mundane, human, and divine experience are brought into direct connection with one another.

In all these central theses and theorems, what connects Rosenzweig's thinking with that of Hegel lies very close to what separates them. Thus the categorical form of the *also*, expounded by Hegel, pertains to the way in which the qualities of a thing are linked together in its specific unity. As this form of thought it determines sense perception and the experience based upon it, as well as every analogous relation of knowledge. Part of its determining function is to remind us that the unity it effects, which is found in perception and experience, is in certain respects imperfect and in need of improvement. This imperfection and need for improvement become evident when one measures the unity at hand by the principles of cognition and knowledge, by ideal unity, universality, and necessity. The function of the *and* in Rosenzweig's theory of experience is altogether different. Here this form is not the basis for definition of a context of perception and an experience that builds upon it; rather it describes the relations among experiences in general. Thus what it reveals is not a certain lack in a certain type of experience, but the true essence of experience as such: its multiplicity, its contingency, its openness. Thus this descriptive form is as valid for the relation between experiences of the same type as between experiences of different kinds. It describes an essential characteristic of the way objects of experience are connected one with the other, as well as of the different subjects of experience and finally of the relation of the former to the latter. Thanks to the validity of that form, these relations cannot be fused, whether by empirical general concepts or by specific categories, into a more or less seamless and uninterrupted unity of consciousness. Rather the breaches, the points of irruption, remain despite all efforts toward a synthetic unity. Above all, the logical-grammatical form of the *and* is valid for the ontological-methodological multidimensionality of that which is, as impressed upon the particular elements of experience. Every particular experience participates in the ultimately primal three-dimensionality of that which is. Through this participation, it is primally divine-mundane-human experience in the form of the *and*. Or, seen from another perspective: Every particular experience occupies a specific place in three-dimensional "logical" space, which extends through the primal elements God, world, man and through the trajectories drawn through them. The *and* form as primal form of the three-dimensional multiplicity of that which is, is not exhausted by the function of determining three different classes or kinds of experience. More primal than such a constitution is, rather, the constitution of every possible experience as divine and mundane and human; or, to express it with a formulation from *The Star of Redemption,* in all experience it is "impossible not to hear, as undertones, the timbre of the three-part bass of our world-symphony."[25] This metaphorical periphrasis makes clear how Rosenzweig actually conceives the nonobjectivity and unconsciousness of experience. God, the world, and man, as "factualities," as primal givens of experience, are given in experience before all objectivity, before all consciousness of them. Precisely as such preobjective and preconscious preconditions, they penetrate experience more strongly than every conceivable objectivity and consciousness. Therefore they also mean for experience something more and other than the undefined horizon in which particular objects of perception and perceptual experience are situated and to which phenomenological theories, above all, have called attention. Nor are the primal elements God, the world, and man to be understood as products of categorical functions and effects. The reverse is true. Only where the primal elements begin to move toward one another do the categories acquire their specific four-dimensional meaning as functions.

In Hegel's famous remark about the thoughts of God before creation we find the same situation. Its meaning is vastly different from that of Rosenzweig's similar-sounding statement. Hegel's remark means that the logical forms must be thought in their absolute being-for-themselves if their defining and founding effect in experiential reality is to be understood. The transparency of their own inner continuity corresponds to the transparency of divine comprehension to itself. This clarity sets standards for the knowledge of reality. First of all, it creates the necessary precondition for the possibility of an adequate experiential knowledge in the philosophical sense. The continuity of the divine thoughts in their purity anticipates by its order the order of reality. From the former we understand the latter. Thus from the former an unambiguously defined, straight way leads step by step through the ordering of experiential reality to the perfection of the knowledge of it. By virtue of the "pure" thoughts—and the context of logical forms that they constitute—everything in general is thought and said beforehand, a priori; by virtue of these "pure" thoughts, everything which is to be thought, said, and known essentially in light of the unity of experience is in principle anticipated. What remains to be done to the divine creation in its actualization, beyond this a priori thinking and speaking, is the positing of this thinking and speaking as knowledge. This positing may be labeled as the subsumption of the given under the concept, as the specification of the universal, and as the manufacture of a thoroughgoing analogy between the order of thoughts and the order of things. By philosophical thought's action here in subjecting the living creation to purely formal operations of thought whose products are bound to the principles of unity, universality, and necessity, this creation is sworn in to the highest dictum of science. According to this dictum the particular as such is neither sayable, nor thinkable, nor knowable as such in its particularity. By the force of this basic assumption the infinite abundance of the new, of births and rebirths, the originality of individual experience, as well as what is unique and unexampled about the particular—all this remains excluded from creation. Rosenzweig's new experiential thinking emphatically takes a stand against this uncreative concept of creation, against the notion of creation as a basic operation in logic. Rosenzweig's new thinking endeavors to make room for the abundance and uniqueness of the particular. From here the proximity to and distance from Hegel's thinking which we have observed becomes understandable. From the methodological perspective of the multidimensionality of what is, the idealistic concept of creation turns out to be an abstraction, the reduction of a complex, multidimensional creation to a one- or two-dimensional logical space.[26] In this space spontaneity and activity are reduced to logic; action is reduced to general cognition. The absolute totality of created reality is, from this point of view, no different from creation as mere providence. Of course—says Rosenzweig—the world, seen from the perspective of the initial creation, has emerged from the total darkness of premundane existence; of course, the two primal elements, God and the world, have begun to describe their orbits, so creation is bathed in the light of a first revelation. But the clarity of this light is imperfect. The world appears at first in mere chiaroscuro, which seems to correspond to the gray-in-gray with which Hegel's idealistic philosophy describes its own coloration of reality. But these two colorations are after all different. This chiaroscuro is the color of the dawning day, while that gray-in-gray was the color of the evening twilight.

Rosenzweig's new experiential thinking wants to let creation appear in the radiance of a new light. The chiaroscuro of the first revelation waits for the luminary of a second revelation, by which the creatural human being becomes an independent partner in dialogue with God and the world. But even this first chiaroscuro bathes the logical operations in a certain light, transforms its mathematics into a hermeneutics of mathematical symbols. Here room is made for birth and rebirth, for abundance and uniqueness of event. If it is true that each particular concrete experience contains, besides a component of cognition, a component of belief, then it is also true that this belief here acquires a new independence. It no longer presents itself as mere defective appearance of an element that is totally different, nor as blind, deceptive, and insufficiently founded cognition. Rather these components of experience develop their own sensorium for the particular in its primal particularity, a specific sense for its presentness and novelty, its unexampled uniqueness. In Weizsäcker's concept of experience it is above all this fundamental trait, this connection between belief and sensitivity to what is original, that is emphasized as the essence of pathic existence: "Everything which is original possesses a priority and a surpassing credibility which cannot be deduced from any superordinate interest. We have complete faith only in that which we have seen only once. Every repetition weakens this faith and arouses the suspicion of a legality, not a reality. Thus sense perception, and action too, demonstrate their genuineness by their unmistakable and irreplaceable originality."[27] In this description the new values of experience, which had been suppressed in the idealistic theory of experience, are given their due. Here experience is seen altogether differently, that is, not with a view to the evidence of theoretical cognition, but with a view to practical certainty. Experience here constitutes itself not in stages of knowledge, but in the concrete reality of living and acting. The shift in viewpoint is mirrored by a shift in the assignment of sense perception, which functions here not as the beginning of cognition, but as the organ of living and acting. In the one case and in the other, gain and loss are measured by opposites: here by repetition, there by unrepeatability. But Rosenzweig's new thinking goes beyond the shifting of the weight of values, beyond an ontological transposition of the basic definition of experience. Let us describe the methodological demand of multidimensional contemplation in our context by means of the logical-grammatical basic form of the *and:* Experience is the elementary behavior of living organisms in the space of creation, in the space of the relation between God and the world; *and* experience is the distinguished mode of the dialogical, partnershiplike encounter between human beings in the space of revelation, of the relation between man and God; *and* experience is that practice of life which is specifically human, the form of human activity, of the way man affects the world, in the space of redemption.

The third aspect in which the proximity and distance between Hegel's and Rosenzweig's thought becomes clear has already been implicitly considered. The criticism of speculative idealism, the methodological-ontological multidimensionality opposed to idealism, operates above all in the concept and theory of subjectivity. In his criticism of the narrowness of idealism as a theory of consciousness, of the uncritical overestimation of the principle of subjectivity and the too-great demands placed on it, Rosenzweig anticipated many later developments of philosophical criticism. This criticism is concerned less with the expansion of the space of consciousness than with the manifold inner space of the unconscious. The multiplication of spatial dimensions is something altogether different from the enlargement of a space of so-and-so-many dimensions. This holds true as much for logical spaces as for "metalogical" and real spaces. In Hegel's theory of experience, the whole manifoldness of possible human experience is imagined as bound up in the supreme unity of an absolute consciousness. This unity of the manifold is developed in a science of the experience of consciousness in the form of a system. The form of the system adopted as a basis here is given in advance in the shape of a systematic order of categories that anticipates the order according to which the scientific presentation of the whole proceeds. This scientific systematics—or method of classification—makes it possible to unite hierarchies of objects of experience, modes of validity, and cognitive values with the stages of development of a cognizing subject, concluding in the highest unity of an absolute experiential cognition. This unity then forms an absolute maximum with regard to the possibility of human experience: a maximum of mutual interpenetration of subject and object, a maximum of universality, and a maximum of consciousness. The invocation of the logical-grammatical *and* form, which Rosenzweig sets up in opposition to philosophical idealism, may suffice by itself to raise doubts concerning the meaning of such a positing of a maximum and the possibility of its concretization in experience. The far-reaching methodological demand for multidimensional contemplation of that which is, concerns, however, not only the multiplicity of human experience, but also, and not less, the principle of human subjectivity that is definitive here. This subjectivity, too, must put up with having the *and* form applied to it. Thus we must, with Rosenzweig, answer the question of the nature of human existence in this *and* form: Man is in the first place a creature among creatures, a finite and dependent creatural being, which distinguishes itself from other creatures by such-and-such shortcomings, such-and-such advantages. All those qualities, dispositions, and competences determine his nature in general, in particular, and in the individual case, in contrast to other beings. *And* this human being in his individuality reveals himself as a genuine self in the dialogical encounter with other selves, whereby he relates in such-and-such a manner to the other. *And* finally, man contributes actively and passively, for good or will, to the transformation of the world. The stamp of the *and* form enables man to know his own fragmentary being in each of his experiences. His self-understanding always reveals to him only a fragment of his possible wholeness.[28] And where he thinks he see light, he is also simultaneously made aware of his own closedness and unfathomability.

## Miracle as a Boundary Concept in Philosophy

Rosenzweig's speculative empiricism aims at regaining for philosophical thinking the abundance of singular life- and self-experience, which philosophical idealism had suppressed in its striving for scientific form.[29] But this apparent gain brings with it the burden of other, hardly soluble questions. With especial emphasis the question of the possible integrality of the individual human being and of the possible nonambiguity of his experience and action arises here once more. The expansion of the domain of experience and the gain of particularity as particularity must here, it seems, be paid for with the insight into the impossibility of an ultimate integrality of existence and nonambiguity of action. In the new thinking the human being seems destined always to remain a fragment, to experience in his "pathic existence" his own closedness to himself and unfathomability and to feel in every one of his experiences, unconsciously, his own edges and corners. Is the question of the possible unity and integrality of human existence, the question of the possible nonambiguity of his speaking and thinking, the question of the concord of his lived life, a meaningful question? Is it a philosophical question, or does it go beyond the possibility of philosophical thinking and human insight? In which domain of thought does the idea of redemption belong? Does the hope of redemption mean primarily this, that the fragments of each singly lived life finally fit together into an ultimate totality and form of meaning; that the unfathomable ambiguity, the "hermeneutic ambiguity" as it has been called,[30] of all human action and passion finally transforms itself into something unambiguous, so that a Yes will at last be a Yes, a No finally a No; so that all life-lies fall away from life? This is the question of the ultimately valid truth. In Rosenzweig's remarks on the new thinking, this question is given an abbreviated answer that is extremely easy to misunderstand. The phrase "confirmation theory of truth" and its conceptual exposition hardly do justice to what is said in *The Star of Redemption* on the question of truth; "messianic epistemology" is a somewhat better expression. For every imaginable confirmation of truth as human action, exclusively human action, remains in the realm of possible ambiguity and dubiousness. A confirmation theory of truth, as Rosenzweig conceives it, belongs in the realm of redemption, in its metalogical, metaethical, and metaphysical space. Such a theory can have validity only on condition that the truth of redemption prevails. Truth and experience belong together, generally and in every conditional relation, in the new thinking. It is the thought of their belonging together that places Rosenzweig's thinking at an unbridgeable distance from Hegel's. Hegel saw their belonging together as absolute knowledge; Rosenzweig saw it as a miracle. To have revived in thought "the possibility of experiencing miracles" is among Rosenzweig's greatest philosophical audacities.[31] Miracle here becomes a boundary concept that connects and separates the topical domains of philosophy and theology. Both domains are thereby not so sharply demarcated one from the other that one must leave the field of philosophy and enter that of theology in order to glimpse the notion of miracle. Rather, by virtue of its belonging together with experience on the one hand and truth on the other, miracle is a concern of philosophy too.

But how can one philosophically comprehend the notion of miracle without at the same time renouncing the ideal of philosophical rationality? Do not belief in miracles and rationality stand in irreconcilable opposition? The experience of the miraculous and of miracles is an experience in the most eminent sense of the word. It is an emphatic intensification of usual and everyday experience. For this reason the basic characteristics and the basic values of all experience, seen in the perspective of this intensification, stand out with all possible clearness: the nonobjectivity and singularity of experience, its property of being one of a kind and occurring once only, its contingency and openness. But on the other hand it is also true that the miraculous and the miracle are only inadequately defined in their essence when defined as such intensifications. What is miraculous about the miracle is something more and incomparably different; its nonobjectivity is something wholly other than nonconcreteness; its one-time occurrence is something wholly other than the nonrepeatability of the transitory; its unfathomability and inexplicability are something wholly other than randomness and contingency. The forgetfulness of self in the experience of miracle is profoundly different from the unconsciousness of daily life. The experience of the miraculousness of the miracle is, in the face of all familiar experiences that move in the orbit of the already known, including the experience of the relatively new, something wholly other. Rosenzweig rightly proceeds from the assumption that the miraculousness of the miracle is not based on its "deviation from the course of nature as this had been previously fixed by law"; its unusualness is not what draws our attention.[32] The notion of the miraculous and the belief in miracles are thus quite compatible with the scientific recognition of nature's universal conformity to law. The miraculousness of the miracle can by no means be understood as a contentual deviation from the rule and from the accustomed, not even as the maximum of such deviation.

For every conceivable miraculous phenomenon, our imagination can invent a fantastic world that is fantastic enough to outstrip and trivialize the miracle. And conversely, in the face of a world that is felt to be chaotic and anarchic, the outward nature, which is familiar to us in its orderliness and conformity to law, may be experienced as a genuine miracle if one orients oneself by the criterion of the unusual and not self-understood. And indeed human beings have marveled, over and over, at the orderliness of the cosmos in its beauty. But the miraculousness of the miracle surpasses all that is marvelous and thus transcends the limits of the possibility of marveling. The experience of a miracle cannot develop out of the comparison of different contents. Miracle is not at all a matter of content, and therefore it is not at all comparable. Hence Rosenzweig characterizes it, in consideration of its outward inconspicuousness, as a sign. But what kind of sign is the miracle, and for what is it a sign? Can any arbitrarily chosen content of experience become the sign that we call a miracle? In what does the miraculous aspect of such a sign consist? Is it not necessarily different, even as a sign, from all other signs, something wholly other than a novel use of signs, that is, a unique, incomparable, miraculous sign?

In *The Star of Redemption* Rosenzweig directly connected miracle with prophecy, equated the one with the other: prophecy is the authentic and true miracle, and this miracle is nothing other than the miracle of the promise. But what distinguishes prophetic signification from the sign interpretation of scientific prognosis? Both posit signs for what is to come. But the one signification is an explanation that points forward, while the other stands outside all possibilities of explanation; the one measures its explanatory content by degrees of probability, while the other would fundamentally fail if it tried to measure off levels of the miraculous by degrees of credibility or incredibility. Prognosis and prophecy are therefore not to be compared. What is miraculous about the miracle cannot be differentiated either by degrees of probability or by levels of credibility. It is either simply true or simply false, like prophecy and prophethood. To this extent it stands outside all hermeneutic ambiguity. Rather it presumes, like the "confirmation theory of truth," like the messianic theory of knowledge, the prevalence of an ultimately valid truth, the truth of redemption. In *The Star of Redemption* Rosenzweig speaks of freedom as "the miracle in the world of appearances." [33] This turn of phrase directly recalls the basic thought of Kant's critical philosophy, which requires that cognition be limited in order to make room for the possibility of belief; above all it recalls the fulfillment of this requirement by the specific definition of the relationship between the laws of nature and freedom. Considering the unlimited prevalence of the laws of nature, it is quite possible to designate freedom as a miracle. To be sure, this does not yet apply to "freedom in the negative understanding," which is on the one hand something unexplainable, but on the other something entirely thinkable. What is a miracle is freedom in the positive understanding, a primal fact, a final factuality, of which all humans are conscious, though only very indistinctly. But Rosenzweig's concept of freedom, and thus his notion of the miracle, goes further. According to his thinking, freedom belongs in the three-dimensional space of the world, man, and God, in the space of creation, revelation, and redemption. The experience of the miracle cannot be adequately understood either as something unexplainable or in contrast to the general prevalence of the laws of nature. The experience of miracle must be located equally far beyond the domain of moral order, wich is also an order of universal laws that orients itself by the principles of unity, universality, and necessity. And as we have seen, even the domain of art is not the domain of the experience of miracle since fantasy as the organ of artistic shaping outstrips every notion of the marvelous and the miraculous. The experience of the miracle necessarily lies beyond the domains of validity of logic, physics, and ethics. But it also lies, as Rosenzweig emphasizes particularly strongly, beyond the realm of aesthetic experience and art. Is there, then, such a thing as the experience of miracle? Is this at all a possibility of philosophic thought? Do we not inevitably depart here from the ground of philosophical rationality?

If we are to seek for the experience of miracle anywhere, then it must be where expectation and disappointment, hope and fear are not far away, in the proximity of ecstasy and despair. The belief in miracles will make a space for itself where it is no longer possible, or fundamentally impossible, to count on deliverance and liberation. The experience of the miracle and the belief in miracles belong in the realm of religious experience. As already stated, such experience is placed, in Rosenzweig's philosophical-theological thinking, under the condition of the truth of redemption. And yet, with this condition the concept of miracle does not necessarily drop completely out of the realm of possibilities of philosophical thought. For among the most important tasks of philosophical thinking is the investigation of the reasonable and its boundaries with the unreasonable, and this implies the task of defining the boundaries of philosophical reason itself. But every drawing of boundaries requires certain general and particular boundary concepts and a procedure for defining their function of demarcation. Rosenzweig's discovery that the concept of the miracle is not only a religious concept, but also henceforth a valid philosophical concept, entails such a task of regarding this concept as a boundary concept of practical reason. This concept is thereby referred to the domain of all those concepts that attempt to grasp the idea of the absolute, the true, and the purely good. Like all these concepts, the concept of miracle demands its philosophical analysis and definition of function. And just as philosophical thinking conceptually distinguishes between the true and the untrue, the good and the bad, so it must also distinguish conceptually among belief, unbelief, and superstition, not only in general, but also with regard to the idea of miracle. On the other hand, with this demarcation a glance is cast across the boundary, and this glance across the boundary allows us to see that the boundary cannot be drawn as unambiguously as it seemed at first. The demarcation between the reasonable and the unreasonable always requires a notion of the latter. Boundary concepts not only contain guidance for meaningful demarcation. They also entice one to an exorbitant transgression of boundaries into the unbounded. This danger exists not last with regard to the boundary concept of miracle. Here the only immediate help comes from the general rule for boundary concepts: that the demonstration of a possibility does not yet imply the demonstration of a corresponding reality; and that where the demonstration of the possibility is lacking, one cannot necessarily conclude the absolute impossibility. Thus the possible demonstration of the concept of miracle as a boundary concept in philosophy must not mislead us into wanting to fill this concept with a definite content or into trying to define the origin and the place of the possible entrance of a miracle into human experience.

# 3

# Rosenzweig's Notion
# of Metaethics

*Nathan Rotenstreich*

I

Before analyzing Franz Rosenzweig's concept of metaethics, we
should consider the meaning Rosenzweig attached to the notion
and position of *meta* in general. He refers to *meta*physics in the
context of his discussion of God and His being, to *meta*logic in the
context of the world and its meaning, and to *meta*ethics in his consideration of man and his self. By examining these three terms we
should be able to clarify Rosenzweig's notion of *meta* in general.

*Meta*physics in the traditional sense connotes what is beyond,
outside, or above physics, and we may take Rosenzweig's use of
*meta* as deriving from that sense. To be sure, while retaining that
connotation in his own derivations of the notion of *meta,* he gave it
a specific meaning or meanings that we will have to extract from his
specific usages of the term.

First, it should be stressed that the notion of *meta* is an ontological reference that, as such, cannot be subsumed under any broader
sphere or dimension. Thus, for instance, when in referring to man's

metaethical position Rosenzweig says that man will always be under the spell of the fear of death (8;4),[1] he sought to emphasize the irreducible ontological position of man. That again comes to the fore in his statement that the All could not die and nothing could die in the All (8;4). The All designates the broad sphere in which man is included or immersed, but once Rosenzweig introduces a demarcation line between man and the All, the aspect of man's irreducibility is highlighted. Negatively speaking, not only idealism—with its denial of everything that would distinguish the singular from the All— is rejected, but positively speaking, the position of an independent and even secluded ontological status becomes central.

That Rosenzweig points here to the ontological status of man is significant not only for understanding the concept of metaethics, but also as a kind of paradigm for his variations on the theme of *meta* in general. When he says, for instance, that the philosopher as a particular individual ceases to be a negligible quantity for his philosophy (15;9f.), the position of the philosopher vis-à-vis philosophy is only an example of something more general, that is to say, that man has to be seen not only in intellectual terms (*geistig*) but also as endowed with a soul (*beseelt*). In this context the notion of soul is meant to imply something more specific and thus more individual than the concept of spirit (*Geist*). Thus, metaethics would be more related to the position of the individual and the soul than to the relation of the All and the spirit. This applies, generally speaking, to Rosenzweig's critique of traditional philosophy, for instance, his critique of Schopenhauer, when he says: "He [Schopenhauer] made will the essence of the world and thereby let the world dissolve in will, if not will in the world. Thus he annihilated the distinction so alive in himself, between the being of man and the being of the world" (17;10f.).

We can sum up this preliminary analysis by noting that the point of departure of Rosenzweig's analysis appertaining to the concept *meta* is the emphasis on fundamental distinctions in terms of the position of man as well as the position of the spheres to which man could be, or to which he has been, viewed as belonging and which thus eventually absorbs him. The criticism of the notion of the All or the totality is the guiding principle of Rosenzweig's variations on the *meta* theme. This is expressed in his statement: "The All can thus no longer claim to be all [*Alles*]: it has forfeited its uniqueness (18;11). Hence we can make a further step in our preliminary presentation by observing that the notion of *meta* is introduced in order to save the irreducible ontological position and thus the uniqueness of the respective sphere to which it refers (viz., God, world, and man).

Both historically and systematically Rosenzweig presupposes here certain philosophical approaches that are based on identities between comprehensive spheres, for instance, the sphere of thinking and being. In his critical remarks he points to what can be called the hidden or presupposed dialectical nonidentity, which in the dialectical systems eventually leads toward identity—"Thus the identity of reasoning and being presupposed an inner non-identity" (19;13). Any synthesis overimposed on the primary nonidentity is, as a matter of fact, a deus ex machina. Thus any systematic attempt toward an inclusiveness defies the trend toward the *meta* and, by the same token, undermines the nonidenticalness of what must be seen as irreducible. Rosenzweig himself mentions that he adopted the term *metalogic* from Hans Ehrenberg (21;14), but in interpreting it Rosenzweig was most probably following the traditional understanding related to *metaphysics*. It is also possible, however, that he was following the concept of metacritique as we know it from the philosophical tradition, mainly from Johann Georg Hamann and Herder.[2]

## II

It is not by chance that Rosenzweig started his own exposition of metaphysics in this sense from an interpretation of negative theology, that is, from the theory of divine attributes that deliberately tried to show that God's essence cannot be expressed in positive statements. The negative attributes are meant to indicate more adequately the transcendence of God than any positive description of God. He thus saw the possible affinity between the theory of negative attributes and metaphysics as he understood that notion: "We seek God, and will presently seek world and man, not as one concept among many, but rather for itself, dependent on itself alone [the original has *Gestalt*] . . . in its absolute actuality . . . precisely in its positiveness" (33;23). The notion of "for itself" with all its Hegelian associations does not connote here what is related to reflection or self-understanding, but what is detached and thus, as it were, self-enclosed. That indeed is Rosenzweig's meaning of *meta*. When Rosenzweig points to the traditional connotation of metaphysics, he deliberately introduces the concept of physics and even plays on the terminological differences when he says, "for he keeps his physics to himself, and therefore remains what he is: the metaphysical" (the original does not have "therefore" but the emotive particle *denn*, "then" (54;40). At this point Rosenzweig anticipates in a way what will follow in his system, namely, that the revelation of God is a special act and is not a continuity of the essence of God. Nevertheless, as long as the unique essence is present, the metaphysical impact, in his sense, becomes central, and all the ways in which the historical religions maintain the bridge between God and the world or God and man cannot uproot the metaphysical dimension proper. Here that term denotes the unique essence that is nonidentical with the essence of any other sphere, namely, the sphere of the world and the sphere of man.

### III

Irreducibility is the negative presentation or assertion of the particular and unique sphere with which the system is concerned. With respect to the world, the core of metalogic is thus that "disconcerting fact about the world" that, after all, "it is not spirit" (60;45). While the emphasis here is clearly anti-Hegelian, Rosenzweig nevertheless is anxious to emphasize the uniqueness of the sphere of the world; it, as such, cannot be made to be related, let alone identified, with any other concept or sphere. Spirit is an example of a candidate for identification and also represents a given historical philosophical system that entertained the notion of the spirit of the world.

One method Rosenzweig employs to establish the self-enclosed character of the world or the worldly plentitude is use of traditional terms rendered according to his own philosophical orientation, for example the term *naught*. He speaks, for instance, about the emergence of the worldly plentitude from naught, which sets off that idea from the emergence of the world from Logos (60;45). He also hints at the Platonic myth or metaphor implying that the world cannot be seen in a context broader than itself, for instance, the relationship of the world to the idea of Good. Irreducibility applies both to the world and to the knowledge of it. Thus: "The sun is no less a wonder than the sun-like quality of the eye which espies it. Beyond both, beyond the plentitude as well as the arrangement [*Ordnung*] there is immediately the naught of the world" (60;45). The naught appears here as a metalogical notion in the strict sense of the term as lying above and beyond the locus in which we can discern only that the world is, in the Parmenidean interpretation, identical with thinking. The reference to the Platonic myth is meant to emphasize that the world is self-enclosed. The idea of the Good as the comprehensive sphere in which both reality and the knowledge of it are placed runs counter to the notion of the self-enclosed character of the being of the world; Plato's idea of the Good points to the essential reliance of the world on an idea beyond and above itself as well as to the essential openness of reality to the knowledge of man.

Rosenzweig's emphasis is thus on the irreducible character and position of the unique and is again expressed polemically in what he says with reference to the great systems of the German idealism— and this has a bearing on metaethics proper: "The individual is not derived immediately from the whole, but rather is developed through its position between the next highest and the next lowest in the system, as for example, 'society' for Hegel in its position between the 'family' and the 'state.' The force [*Kraftstrom*] of the system as a whole courses through all the individual configurations as a one and universal current" (69;52). However, when we place that which has to be seen as unique, and thus as irreducible, within a context that shows, as it were, the continuity between that thing and a whole beyond it, we undermine irreducibility. To put it in broader terms, we may say that any continuity vis-à-vis God (e.g., that implicit in the employment of positive attributes) or vis-à-vis the world (e.g., possible primary relationship between thinking and being) or vis-à-vis the individual (e.g., man seen in the context of society or state at large), all these attempts have to be negated because eventually they lead to reducibility. The notion of the *meta* is meant to negate that philosophical or systematic trend. This is expressed by Rosenzweig when he says that metalogical refers to something that has its own basis and base, is inspired with its own spirit, and is resplendent with its own splendor (*in eigener Fulle prangende*). This is what is meant by *metalogical,* that is to say, what the world should be (81;61).

## IV

The common denominator of Rosenzweig's two usages of the term *meta* seems to suggest that the term is meant to connote the aspect of transcendence,[3] either transcendence applied to God or transcendence applied to reality of the world. God transcends any positive attribute or proposition meant to designate his essence. World transcends any attempt to identify it with propositions, in more general terms with the Logos. To be sure, the term *transcendence* has a different meaning in the two contexts. Vis-à-vis God it connotes the basic impossibility of finding an expression that would be adequate to the essence of God. Vis-à-vis the world *transcendence* connotes the fundamental lack of identity between the position of thought and the position of being in the sense employed by Hegel—that it is impossible to find that identity within the realm of being and to understand thought as the self-understanding of reality.

When we come now to consider the third application of the term *meta* in Rosenzweig's presentation, namely metaethics, we may wonder whether the term retains some of the previous connotations. We may even ask why Rosenzweig applied that transformation of the term *meta* when he addressed himself to man and his self.

One may wonder at this point whether Rosenzweig's statement— that one of the most noteworthy achievements of Kant was to have turned the most self-evident (*die Selbstverstandlichste*) quantity, the I, into the most questionable object—represents an adequate interpretation of Kant. According to Kant, as Rosenzweig interprets him, the cognitive I can be recognized only by its fruits, by its relation to cognition and not per se (82;62). We may question this understanding of Kant. For Kant the position of the I, which has to accompany all our representations, is primarily one of reflection; it cannot be known per se because it is not a reality, nor does it have an existential connotation. But just the same, Kant refers to the transcendental apperception that is the very essence of the I; the I, then, is totally independent of the "fruits" of its cognition.

What Rosenzweig wanted to prove, if that term is at all applicable, is what he himself says, namely, that man's individual being is not subject to proof. In this sense, the position of man is parallel to that of the position of the world and of God (83;63). What he wanted to show is that knowledge cannot be the instrument or bridge for proving the reality and the primary essence of those self-enclosed spheres of reality. Once knowledge attempts that, it necessarily loses itself in the naught; it loses its very legitimacy because it attempts to refer to a sphere of reality and by the same token loses that sphere from its horizon. Hence, Rosenzweig also tries to find a way to establish man's irreducibility, and according to his basic methodological approach this can only be done, as it were, from within. He takes several steps in that direction, which are eventually summed up in what is to be seen as metaethics in his particular or peculiar sense.

Rosenzweig's first step in establishing the fundamental position of man is to note the basic relationship appertaining to man and what he calls "existence in the distinctive" (*Sein im Besonderen*) (84;64). We may come closer to the meaning of Rosenzweig's phrase by trying to understand it as denoting being in its "uniqueness," as that which cannot be encompassed by any general or universal context. That uniqueness or particularity is related to man's ephemerality. It is man's essence to be of this transitory ephemeral character as compared with God. It is of the essence of God to be immortal, eternal and unconditional, whereas the essence of the world is universal and necessary. According to Rosenzweig, existence in particularity apparently bears on inherent relation to the ephemerality of that particularity as exemplified by its death, because death is an occurrence related by definition to the single individual and cannot be understood in its particular, *experiential* dimension as being of a general or universal character. In other words, even when we accept the traditional expression or definition that man is mortal and deduce from that statement the mortality of Socrates, in its experiential character that mortality is *particular* to Socrates; it is not Socrates' particularity that can be nominally derived from the definition of man qua man, that is, man in general. It is clear, therefore, that in his anthropological approach Rosenzweig tries to deal not with the characteristic features of the human race or of mankind, but with the position of the individual qua individual. Thus, his anthropological exposition takes a view different from the anthropological trends that stress inter alia human historicity, human linguistic capacity, the human's distinctive "upright posture." The significance of that shift to the individual as such will come to the fore in a subsequent part of our analysis.

Rosenzweig's attempt starts with the position of the individual and leads to a second step: negatively speaking, man qua a particular individual cannot be seen as belonging to a universal sphere, of which by definition he is not a part. The self-enclosed character of man as an individual is expressed both negatively and positively in the statement that man is individual and nevertheless universal [*Alles*] (85;64).

Rosenzweig seeks to expose the ontological position of the human individual from several additional perspectives. According to the programmatic point of departure, the human individual has to be seen from within, as a being that cannot be immersed in a totality outside itself. This comes to the forefront in Rosenzweig's attempts to characterize human will or freedom. The axis of this analysis is the notion of finitude. He elaborates that notion and its relation to human essence in several ways. According to Rosenzweig, the finiteness of human freedom is inherent in freedom itself because that freedom is freedom of volition and not—like the freedom of God—freedom of action. It is free will in the strict sense of the term, but not free power: "Human freedom in contrast to divine freedom is denied capability in its very origin, but its volition is as unconditional, as boundless, as the capacity of God" (87;66). The reference to God in this context is obviously for the sake of comparison and not for the sake of trying to establish a basic or primary relation between man and God. God's freedom is an original synthesis between will and might—what is translated in the text before us as "capability." As a finite being man cannot be endowed with that primary synthesis. There is a rift in his existence. His freedom as the freedom of will may be boundless, but the execution of that freedom is limited, that is, it is restricted by the surrounding reality. While that emphasizes the primary difference between man and his circumstances, it also highlights one of the meanings of finitude, namely, the limitation in terms of the boundless desire or freedom and the restricted execution of that desire.

Rosenzweig enlarges the scope of that finitude when he stresses in addition the difference between man and God in terms of essence. Here freedom amounts to the willing or the wanting of one's essence. God's freedom amounts to his wanting his own essence. Since he too wills his essence, man from this point of view is architectonically, as it were, similar to God. His essence, however, is finite, and therefore, what his freedom can refer to is finitude (88;67). Whether that parallelism between God's freedom and man's freedom is apposite in this context may be questioned for two reasons: (a) Rosenzweig's statement that God's freedom amounts to wanting his own essence can be viewed as founded because God is described as a totally self-enclosed entity. Therefore, his freedom is but an expression of his essence, and nothing that can be seen as surrounding it can be viewed as present on the horizon at all. But this is not so with human freedom. Once Rosenzweig related that freedom to finitude, he saw that finitude not from the standpoint of volition as such but from the standpoint of dependence upon circumstances, even of the very presence in the circumstances. Hence, (b) God's freedom cannot mean any attempt to change or shape circumstances, while man's freedom means indeed an attempt to shape or change circumstances. The very distinction between volition and might or capability presupposes, in a way, the duality between inner will and circumstances. Hence, from that point of view, the parallelism as presented does not totally suit the basic features of Rosenzweig's own position.

The next step taken by Rosenzweig in describing the irreducible condition of man qua a unique individual is in the introduction to his notion of the self—the self being a function of the individual's "defiant will," which is the very ground of his self-consciousness or "character." As Rosenzweig puts it: "The self is utterly self-contained, owing to its being rooted in character" (89;68). (The German here is stronger: "Das verdankt es seiner Verwurzelung im Charakter.") In his various elaborations of this thesis Rosenzweig seeks to highlight still further the self-enclosure of the self, as for instance, in his discussion of the natural death of man. At death the ultimate solitude of man becomes absolutely manifest; as Rosenzweig observes, there is no isolation like that which appears on the countenance of the deceased (94;72). To emphasize this self-enclosure Rosenzweig even says of the self that it does not "become" or form itself. "One day the self [simply] assaults man like an armed bandit and takes possession of all the wealth in his property" (93;71).

Before proceeding with the analysis of Rosenzweig's position it should be stated that he is concerned with establishing the ontological status of the individual human being who cannot be viewed as immersed in the human race at large, let alone in the surrounding world or universe. Accordingly, Rosenzweig emphasizes the finitude of man, the distinction between his essential self-awareness and any particular content that can be seen as grounded in that self-awareness and the distinction between man as an individual and the surrounding circumstances; he also emphasizes the difference between man and his qualities. To highlight that difference he negates one of the features brought to the forefront by anthropological thought, namely, that man is a self-forming being. According to Rosenzweig the self is not formed; it is there in the first place. In Rosenzweig's metaphoric presentation, man is not forlorn but *befallen* (overtaken). Similarly, the event of death is significant not only because it emphasizes finitude, but also because it emphasizes the self-enclosure of the self. It is only man as an individual who is exposed to the particular event and experience of death. The fact that mortality is a common feature of all human individuals does not negate the individuality of the experience, but on the contrary reinforces it. The consequences of that description or analysis lead to the understanding of the concept of the metaethical—and that is now our concern.

V

The description of the position of the self is reinforced by two additional nuances or, we may say, anticipating the following critical analysis, interpretations. The first refers to what Rosenzweig calls *der Trotz,* translated into English as "defiance." It is the position that can be described as one of "in spite." Let us quote at some length what Rosenzweig says about the context into which the concept of defiance is introduced. The finite being wants nothing other than what it is: it wants its own essence—and here Rosenzweig adds, "like God's freedom."

But this own essence that it wants is a finite essence. . . . Still entirely within its own realm, then, but already sighting its objects from afar, free will recognizes itself in its finiteness without, however, in the least surrendering any of its unconditionality. At this point, still entirely unconditional and yet already conscious of its finiteness, it changes from free will to defiant will [*zum trotzigen Willen*]. Defiance, the proud *withal,* is to man what power, the lofty *Thus* is to God. The claim of defiance is as sovereign as the privilege of power [*Recht der Macht*]. The abstraction of free will takes shape as defiance. (89;67−68)

It may be noted that Rosenzweig relates defiance to self-awareness: man aware of himself in his finitude somehow responds to the circumstances surrounding him and his response ensuing from his inspired position; Rosenzweig even adds that that position itself bears the aspect of pride. Hence the self is not just given but is endowed in the first place with self-awareness referring to itself or reflecting upon itself. By the same token, that self-awareness is an awareness of finitude, which here means awareness of the restrictions imposed by circumstances. The self relates to the circumstances even as it emphasizes or establishes itself in its self-sufficiency. As Rosenzweig describes it, self-reliance becomes or is defiance once self-awareness is present. Here we may wonder whether the previous description of the self as something "befalling" man can really be maintained. For he says: "The 'self' is what originates in this encroachment [*Übergriff*] by free will upon peculiarity as the And of defiance and character" (89;68). In any case, Rosenzweig here relates the position of defiance to character, though he earlier said that the character does not evolve but is there in the first place. Yet without this combination or integration of self-awareness in the reflective sense, awareness as a distinction between the self and circumstances, and the self-assertion of the self that finds its expression in defiance, we could not describe the position of the self as Rosenzweig has. If that indeed is so then the self-enclosed character of the self cannot be maintained—and this aspect is rather significant for understanding Rosenzweig's systematic view as well as its inherent limitations.

The second nuance—at this juncture we can say consequence—that Rosenzweig reaches from his description is that the world of ethical considerations is inherent in the self itself. "For the self, the world of ethics is merely its ethos; nothing more is left of it. The self does not live in a moral world: it has its ethos. The self is metaethical" (96;73). This statement makes it clear why and in what sense Rosenzweig used the term *metaethics:* since there is no primary relationship between the self-enclosed self and the ethical realm, the self, not being immersed in the ethical realm, is conceived as metaethical, in a mode analogous to the employment of the terms *metaphysical* and *metalogical*. The self is above or prior to the ethical realm and hence "metaethical."

Yet from this description Rosenzweig proceeded, or perhaps leaped, to an interpretation of man within the aesthetic realm. It is probably not by chance that he starts that part of his description by pointing to the position of silence, which is described as speechlessness, a speech before speech, the speech of the unspoken or the unspeakable (105;80). The world of art is described as a world of tacit accord "which is no world at all, no real, vital, back-and-forth interconnection of address passing to and fro and yet, at any point, capable of being vitalized for moments at a time" (107;81). Apparently, an attempt is made here to see the connection between the totally private world of the self in the speechless component of its essence and the world of art, since that world is grounded in the self and expresses it in its particular way, which is not expression in the linguistic sense, but still carries some message. Since art is the sort of expression that starts and leads from the self, it does not relate to the world outside the self. The self possesses the world within itself as a personal property and not as a world; "The only humanity of which it was aware was that within its own four walls . . . elevated above any world, fixing its own interior within a defiant gaze, incapable of sighting anything alien except there in its own sphere and therefore only as its own property, hoarding all ethical norms [*ethische Ordnung*] within its own ethos so that the self was and remained lord of its ethos. In short: the meta-ethical" (108;82). (What is rendered in English as "lord" is in the original *Freiherr*, a term probably associated with freedom.)

We are bound to observe here that Rosenzweig himself was somehow not satisfied with the variations on the descriptions of the independent position of the self. Hence he moved to the association of the self with the aesthetic component or with art and thus gave that position of man a normative or axiological connotation. He wanted to distinguish between the axiological dimension as related to art and the axiological dimension as related to ethics as he understood it, because of the traditional interpretation of ethics as referring either to man's benevolence and openness to his fellow man or, what is even perhaps more significant for Rosenzweig's understanding of the ethical realm, to man's ethical attitude toward the universality of mankind. The last point is significant because it may bring into prominence Rosenzweig's tacit rejection of Hermann Cohen's understanding of ethics as well as his interpretation of religion and the dimension of morality that, according to Cohen, religion brings into the horizon of human behavior. Hence our critical comments start with this aspect of Cohen's thought and the difference between his and Rosenzweig's position.

## VI

Cohen says that only from the perspective of the whole of humanity can the individual reach his moral salvation.[4] Cohen is here faithful to the Kantian legacy in the sense that the categorical imperative relates to mankind at large and to the recognition by the acting human being that mankind in its ethical position is represented by and in the individual encounter. In the language of ethics, the individual is recognized as an end and not as a means only, since the individual is grounded in mankind and represents mankind in his presence vis-à-vis the acting fellow individual. Kant's moral position, which has been reformulated by Cohen, has a factual aspect—that the individual inheres in mankind—and an ethical aspect proper, namely, that mankind is not only the factual sphere to which the individual or individuals belong, but also a kind of human *telos* that has to be recognized in every human individual. An obligation follows from that recognition. To put it differently, that recognition is both a factual cognition and a moral acknowledgment. This interpretation of the moral sphere, inherited by Cohen from Kant, has its descriptive basis in Kant's anthropology, namely, that the goal of the human race cannot be achieved within the limits of individuals but only within the scope of the race or mankind at large. Thus, as we know, for instance, from Kant's analysis of historical progress, human individuals or even generations should recognize the ethical priority of the goal of history, which is in the future, that is to say, beyond themselves.

Returning now to Rosenzweig, we realize immediately that Rosenzweig's description of the position of man, which he called metaethical, is meant to cut the basic tie between the human individual and the human whole or mankind. Since Rosenzweig accepted the interpretation of ethics as essentially the recognition of the whole or the recognition of the individual as a representative of the whole, the emphasis laid by him on the isolated individual can no longer be understood as an ethical interpretation of the ontological position of man. It becomes metaethical by being understood as referring to the self-enclosed individual, with all the reservations we have already noted about that self-enclosure. As metaphysics has been understood as the lack of identity between physics and the description of God, and as metalogic has been understood as the lack of identity between the logos and the reality of the world, so metaethics is understood as the lack of identity between man as a self-enclosed individual in the first place and the totality of human beings or the whole of them. Hence we have to understand Rosenzweig's concept of metaethics not only as a continuation of his presentation of the two spheres to which we referred above—God and world—but also as a hidden polemic against Kant's or Cohen's identification of the human individual and the human ethos that led them to the primary reference to mankind at large. Rosenzweig, as we have seen, applies the term *ethos*, but applies it not to the openness of the individual but to his self-enclosed character, in the strict sense of the latter term.

Rosenzweig's polemic with Cohen, which he never made explicit, was directed against Cohen's attempt to place the individual within the purview of morality, namely, via religion, the "Religion of Reason," specifically calling Judaism a source (*Ursprung*) of the latter. (Cf. Cohen's *Religion of Reason out of the Sources of Judaism*, New York, 1972.) Let us merely recall the well-known position of Hermann Cohen, that man becomes an individual through his own sin and that only through atonement with God do we see the sinning individual become a free self.[5] Cohen relates the position of being an individual to the position of sin because sin is antinormative behavior and as such removes the individual from his positive or affirmative relationship to the other human individuals or to their totality. Hence, antinormative behavior is the origin of the background for the emergence of the individual human being. Comparing this point with Rosenzweig's position, we would say that for Rosenzweig the individual's position is given in the first place and is not an outcome of a human act or performance. Hence Rosenzweig speaks about the self and not about the sin committed by the human individual. Moreover, Rosenzweig relates—or even identifies—that position of the self in its basic meaning as the position of a free self, though that freedom is accompanied by the awareness of finitude; for Cohen, on the other hand, the I becomes free only by overcoming his sin because through that he is recognized in God or by God. In these two points we see the difference between Rosenzweig and Cohen: while Cohen regards sin as the point of departure for establishing the position of the individual, Rosenzweig emphasizes the aspect of defiance, which is not an act of man or an omission, though one could interpret sin as a defiance of the divine commandment. For Rosenzweig defiance is placed ab initio vis-à-vis the surrounding world and thus is inherent in the very position of man. Hence Rosenzweig thought he could not, and did not have to, refer to a specific act of man, be it of a normative or antinormative character, but could describe the primary human position by a variation of the theme of finitude, that is, defiance. For Cohen, the position of the individual is not in the first place the position of finitude. For Rosenzweig the identity of man's finitude and ontological position is primary.

### VII

Rosenzweig, however, does not confine the individual to finitude and a self-enclosed sphere. In the latter two parts of *The Star* he asserts a relationship between the respective spheres of existence. It seems that first he attempted to overemphasize the separation characteristic of the spheres in order to reinforce the need and expectation for a relationship between them, which for him is grounded in revelation and thus in what he calls mystery. He says in one of his best-known statements that the everlasting birth is creation: "This becoming manifest [*Offenbarwerden*] of the everlasting mystery of creaton is that ever-renewed miracle of revelation. We are standing at the transition—the transition from the mystery into the miracle" (118;90). The use here of so many terms pointing to something outside the self-enclosed sphere—miracle, revelation, creation, mystery—leads us to surmise that, once at the position of the creation or revelation that is to come or to occur, Rosenzweig attempted to overemphasize retrospectively the secluded character of the spheres. The relationship between them is established in those mysterious events that fall under the common heading "transition." This last comment brings us to a closer critical examination of Rosenzweig's concept of metaethics.

The first question that must be raised is whether the parallelism guiding Rosenzweig in his presentation and analysis is really founded in the profiles of the spheres to which he addresses himself. To refer, in the first place, to the transcendence of God and the starting point of negative theology seems to be an established assertion, at least in the tradition of the historical religions and of theology and philosophy. If God is above the universe, as the position of the Creator implies, it may follow that there is no way to explicate God's essence by any positive attributes that apply to piecemeal realities or even to the universe at large. Rosenzweig does not attempt to prove the existence of God. He attempts to expose or to explicate, phenomenologically, the essence of God. Here the method he applies seems consonant with established notions, even when Rosenzweig brings these notions to their extreme conclusion or explication. With all the due systematic or phenomenological differences, the situation is analogous vis-à-vis the reality of the world. Knowledge guided by the Logos is by its own intentionality directed to a state of affairs, to that which is about to be known, and thus, in an amplified way, it can be shown that reality is different from the act of knowing or the sum total of knowledge. The very intentionality of knowledge points, at least initially, to a distinction beween knowledge and that which is known. When a systematic interpretation attempts to bring about the identity between knowledge and reality, it starts from this, not from a primary synthesis; at best, the synthesis is arrived at after considerable analysis or dialectical exposition. Hence the presentation of the self-enclosed and secluded sphere of reality seems to be justified, at least prima facie, even as a point of departure of an idealistic-systematic presentation, as we know it, for instance, from Hegel. And hence the parallelism, with all the due differences between the position of God and the position of world, seems to be grounded in the phenomena analyzed.

But this is not the case with the position of man, even according to Rosenzweig himself, because man himself starts with self-awareness that both constitutes the self and is its presentation or expression. Self-knowledge in terms of God and the world would upset the whole thrust of Rosenzweig's system; but obviously we cannot take over the position of God referring to his own essence, nor can we place ourselves with our thinking or knowledge within the sphere of reality, thus making reality not only open to knowledge but exhibited in it. Such is not the case with the self, that is, with man, since here we start with self-awareness. The leap performed by Rosenzweig can be seen as his way of understanding or presenting self-knowledge as self-enclosure. But the two are phenomenologically different, since the first points to awareness while the second points to an awareness of a position, and a position is, to say the least, relational. It is the position vis-à-vis free will, vis-à-vis the surrounding world and conditions. Self-awareness is present in any of these directions of awareness, but it is intentional or referential and thus man goes beyond himself in the first place: he is a self-transcending being from the very beginning and cannot be viewed as self-enclosed. This, the first phenomenological misreading in Rosenzweig's presentation, is probably motivated by his attempt to see the human being's position as transcending his own boundaries not as a primary datum but as a miracle, and so forth.

Let us consider a specific example from Rosenzweig's own exposition, namely, the attitude or phenomenon of silence. Silence presupposes language; it refers to it; it is an overcoming of the spoken language, but not the overcoming of the realm of meanings; to be speechless is not to be mute. If silence presupposes language, then certainly the self-awareness of silence, which is not bound to be expressed but is still there, presupposes language; it refers to it. The reference to language is a reference to a realm that is transindividual in the general sense or—when we refer to a particular historical language that is not language at large—in the historical sense. Chronologically speaking, human beings first acquire a historical language and then take the attitude of silence. Their attitude refers now to that language. If so, we encounter the self-transcending position of the human individual within silence itself; the individual can be silent only because that self-transcendence is presupposed.[6] But not only the transindividual position of language has to be brought into an adequate anthropological analysis of the individual and the human race: the whole aspect of man's position within the surrounding world must also be so introduced. Rosenzweig interpreted that position as related to the awareness of finitude; he did not, however, give proper attention to the societal aspect of human existence, which has been described by Adolf Portmann as the extrauteral position of the human being. Thus, whereas Rosenzweig's expositions of the sphere of God and the sphere of the world of reality could be considered at least seemingly adequate, his exposition of the position of man is from the outset inadequate.

The lack of adequacy is also prominent in the relation pointed out between the position of the individual and art—understood here as of an expressive character only. The shortcoming in the analysis of expression does not have to be spelled out here because expression is related, at least partially, to language and to its onto-logical position, to which we have already referred. But even when we grant different modes of expression, like that in colors or time, the very selection of colors, for example, presupposes the broader horizon of colors; the same applies to musical expression. Hence a horizon is present not only in the very restriction and limitation but also as a spectrum of possibilities out of which the selective attitude of expression chooses the proper medium for the particularity of the expression. It should be added that, though Rosenzweig tried through his concept of metaethics to reach a transnormative posi-tion, he certainly did not attempt to examine the proper relation-ship between the realm of art and the norm of beauty. An expression is gauged not only according to the built-in norm of sincerity (i.e., the genuineness of a given expression), which is indeed of an indi-vidual character and thus can be viewed as exhibiting a continuity from the individual to the expression. Once the notion of art is brought into context, expressions are also evaluated according to the norm of beauty, which is not of an individual character or posi-tion—whatever the specific meaning of the norm.

It is not by chance that these aspects are missing in Rosenzweig's exposition because his whole anthropological approach is charac-terized by an attempt to make self-enclosure so radical that only revelation and divine miracles can open the "doors" or the "win-dows." Yet once the implicit and explicit parallelism between the three spheres presented in the first part of *The Star* cannot be main-tained, we may wonder whether Rosenzweig remained consistent to his phenomenological approach and whether his primary presenta-tion is not tainted by the general thrust or bias of his system. Here we must recall our previous comments on his hidden polemic with Hermann Cohen.

A concluding comment about the difference between Rosenzweig and the philosophy of existence is appropriate here. The philosophy of existence places man, from the very beginning, within the broad scope of being, or of time and temporality, even if his position is that of a forlorn being. Finitude is understood mainly in terms of time and this has to be stressed, though both Heidegger and Rosenzweig, for instance, emphasize their awareness of that.[7] But Rosenzweig, who was not trying to identify the various aspects of the broader context in which human beings are placed or into which they are "thrown," emphasized mainly the distinction between freedom and the conditions in which freedom cannot be actualized. Hence if the concept of existence is to be employed as a proper characterization of Rosenzweig's philosophy, we should be cognizant of the basic difference between his thought and existentialism—the prevailing trend in that philosophical orientation that has placed existence at the center of its concern and to which Rosenzweig is understood to be in close affinity. This difference is probably ultimately grounded in Rosenzweig's presentation of his philosophical analysis with a view of the whole scope of existence as it is yet to unfold, while existentialism includes, at least implicitly, the broader coordinates of existence already at the very beginning of its analysis.

# 4

# Responsibility Rescued

*Bernhard Casper*

## I

"I believe that there are in the life of each living thing moments, or perhaps only one moment, when it speaks the truth. It may well be, then, that we need say nothing at all about a living thing, but need do no more than watch for the moment when this living thing expresses itself." [1] Thus wrote Franz Rosenzweig in a letter to Eugen Rosenstock-Huessy in December 1916. If this statement is true, it is also applicable to Rosenzweig's own life and thought, and an understanding of Rosenzweig should then begin with a careful search for the moment in which his life and thought expressed itself. What was Rosenzweig's basic principle, the principle prompting and directing his thinking? What princple gives Rosenzweig's thinking its unity and thus also its plausibility? The thesis I propose is that the basic principle of Rosenzweig's thinking can be grasped not only in terms of "revelation" and "temporality," but also, and most crucially, in how human responsibility as such is conceivable.

From the purely biographical viewpoint, the centrality of this question to Rosenzweig's thought is indicated, for instance, by his now famous letter to Friedrich Meinecke justifying his rejection of an academic career, which doubtlessly is one of the moments in which Rosenzweig's life and thought truly "expressed" themselves. "Cognition no longer appears to me as an end in itself. It has turned into service, a service to human beings (not, I assure you, to tendencies)."[2] As for the genesis of *The Star of Redemption,* one might refer to a letter to Hans Ehrenberg in which Rosenzweig claimed that the "primary conception" of *The Star* lay in the "concept of the metaethical."[3] Here one should also recall the conclusion of Rosenzweig's essay "The New Thinking." Referring to *The Star,* he says there that the responsibility for the new philosophy must be borne by the philosopher, that is, the individual himself—and in his everyday life. The thinking presented in *The Star* could only obtain its goal by virtue of such responsibility.[4]

But more important than such essentially external references is the very nature of Rosenzweig's question about how thinking can do justice to reality and to responsibility. A singular coherence issues from the very center of that question and pervades Rosenzweig's entire opus. This proposition appears enigmatic at first, and clearly is an exception to virtually all philosophical traditions—even of the twentieth century—and has so far found but few adherents.

## II

Inquiring about the context of Rosenzweig's initial philosophizing, we are led to the problem of historicism,[5] and to German idealism, both of which Rosenzweig encountered in Hegel—the subject of his doctoral dissertation—and in the teachings of Hermann Cohen.[6] Endeavoring to understand why Rosenzweig was so totally dissatisfied with German idealism,[7] we are led to the question of responsibility.

In the system of idealistic thinking, everything emanates from the One and is also taken back into the One.[8] The *hen kai pan,* "the one and all" of Hegel's "mad book"[9]—*The Phenomenology of the Spirit*—becomes a problem for Rosenzweig, just as for Kierkegaard, because thinking in which the One creates itself as the All must eliminate the distinctive Self within its own distinctive origin, and that in effect eliminates responsibility.

In his analyses of the idealistic ethos, in the second part of *The Star of Redemption*, Rosenzweig shows that for the individual who understands only the particular—deisgnated *B* from *Besonderes*, the particular, as opposed to *A*, from *Allgemeines*, the general or universal—only the formula of submission ($B = A$), which is also the formula of religion and of ethics, can correspond to the idealistic notion of a rational "generation" (*Erzeugung*) of our conception of reality. This leads to the idealistic world formula $A = B$. According to Rosenzweig, the ethos of idealism is one of submission to the universal, which Rosenzweig also sees in Kant's categorical imperative.[10] Individual will is subordinated and submits to the supreme law. The latter, however, in the final analysis can only be that of the absolute. Freedom, which originally was to be rescued in idealism by an ethos of autonomy, "disappears in the blinding ray of the supreme law." The self merges into the "uppermost universality of the law," which always was and always is.[11] Read with regard to responsibility, this means: the self, myself, who lives in relation to myself and thereby stands in a responsible relationship to the other, does not matter at all. Rather, whenever I seem to be acting ethically, I am only proving myself as a separate entity of the universal. The responsible act, for which I and only I can be held responsible, and which has its own time, cannot exist according to this understanding, which Rosenzweig reconstructs here as the self-understanding of idealism. The oneness of the totality of being, which through me takes itself back into itself, generates my action as a necessary action. Therefore, if responsibility requires that an act originate in the individual, there is no room for it here.

But when responsibility, the phenomenon that alone makes man really human, becomes an impossibility, there is clearly something wrong with the idealistic systematic thinking. The decisive question for Rosenzweig, casting his reflections in a philosophical mode, had to be: How is the totality of reality thinkable in such a manner that responsibility in its irreducible factuality is rescued and even becomes the center of what is to be penetrated and exposed by philosophical thinking?

### III

In light of this question, Rosenzweig's thinking as a whole gains a special coherence and plausibility. In particular, *The Star of Redemption*, with its complicated and rich structure, becomes intelligible and readable. Wondering about the meaning of the fragmentation of the totality undertaken in the first part of *The Star*, and of the singular phenomenology of the primal phenomena (*Urphänomene*), which with its intentional lack of coherence appears inappropriate to philosophical thinking, we must bear in mind that the whole first part of *The Star* is of a preparatory character. By completely separating the *Urphänomene*—God, world and man—it lays the ground for the development of Rosenzweig's basic insight. For man's own originality is only possible on the presupposition that man in his humanity is not conceived as dialectically dependent on God or on the world. Only on this condition can he be himself, without presuppositions, and only thus can he be held absolutely responsible for his actions. Those actions then cannot be explained as a mode of his being-in-the-world, nor can they be excused on the grounds that man is conscious of being the particular something in which the Absolute becomes manifest.

Observing how Rosenzweig in the "germ cell" of the *Star* struggled to free himself from idealism, one sees clearly that the experience of the individual's irreducible and irrevocable consciousness of self—which for that very reason is responsible—constitutes the superiority of the "new thinking" over the systematic thinking of idealism: "I, a quite ordinary private subject, I, having a given and a family name, I, being dust and ashes, I am still here. And I am philosophizing." [12] I am, Rosenzweig insisted, not reducible to Schiller's "man with his palm branch," that is, to the man who is defined throughout by ideals, whose paradigm, in Rosenzweig's view, is the artist. [13]

The reality of reason must be separated from the individual's consciousness of self (*noesis noeseōs*). Or, logically speaking: in reason there exists, beyond reason, "a unity which is not the unity of two." Rosenzweig calls this discovery, which reminds us of the beginning of Kierkegaard's *Sickness unto Death*, his "philosophical Archimedean point."[14] It is the discovery of the "facticity before all facts of real experience."[15] It is the discovery, too, of freedom, of which, according to Rosenzweig, only Kant has preserved a living anamnesis.[16] To preserve this discovery, Rosenzweig, in the first part of *The Star*, draws up each beside the other, explicitly unconnected,[17] a theogony, cosmogony, and psychogony. These processes, however, here represent nothing but the elements that are the course of reality as it takes place; they are, however, not reality itself. Through the analogy from mathematics, namely, the relation between element and course, Rosenzweig clarifies his basic insight that, although God, world and man occur in reality as it takes place, historical temporal reality—and only it is the whole reality in which man's responsibility plays a constitutive role—by no means merges in God or in the world or in man. God, world and man rather manifest themselves as clearly separate from one another. Therefore, there is no continuous logical connection between those three primal phenomena. Rather, experiential thinking is confronted by the fact that one can be disturbed and disappointed by others, a fact that points to the irreducible otherness of any other primal phenomenon,[18] yet that thereby, ultimately, points again to the irreducibility of myself as an entity bearing responsibility.

The separate essences of the primal phenomena, as Rosenzweig explains in "The New Thinking," must be presupposed in order that God, world and man may do something to each other in reality. That also means that the separation must be presupposed in order that I should be able to love the other in reality: "If the other were 'fundamentally' identical with me, as Schopenhauer would have it, then I could not possibly love him, for I would then love only myself."[19] The primal phenomena of God, world and man are conceivable only as separate, and yet by themselves they are unreal—or in Rosenzweig's sense of the abstract: pre-real[20]—that is, mere elements of a course. How, then, does the course—the whole reality as it takes place—become manifest?

The first part of *The Star* juxtaposes a theogony, cosmogony, and psychogony in such manner that the geneses of the phenomena in question seem plausible and may be taken as the abstract patterns of God, world and man, although their reality is by no means proven.

The second part of *The Star* brings the thinking to the unfolding of reality, which is now finally granted genuine autonomy. Here an attempt is made to illuminate what happens *between* God, world and man—in everyday reality, which, however, again can only be regarded from the viewpoint of the man who thinks and has to vindicate himself. The unfolding of this everyday and whole reality, as seen from the viewpoint of the thinking and accountable man, cannot, however, be deduced from "I think" and "I relate to myself." For essentially, it is the occurrence distinguished by the existential fact of being "disturbed and disappointed." Further, it is an occurrence distinguished by the overcoming of the perceived individuation and isolation of the primal phenomena of existence.

Someone reading *The Star of Redemption* for the first time may be inclined to regard this process of overcoming as a mere formal play or—as Walter Benjamin did—as a modification of Hegelian dialectics. As a description of the paradox, however, it is the only way by which Rosenzweig can discuss the occurrence of reality *as* an occurrence, and as one at the center of which stands the accountable man, namely, the man who is called by his name and who answers.

In the first book of part 2 of *The Star*, Rosenzweig shows that the reality of the world in which we find ourselves is only conceivable as the fruit of a happening that had already happened, namely as creation. The world as a formal phenomenon manifests itself as enclosed within itself and therefore requires no explanation. Yet in its existence, which "must continually become new in order to maintain itself" [21] (which is to be understood in light of the root word *good*, [22] the world appears as not being a matter of course. It appears as the fruit of something that takes place.

In the same book of *The Star*, Rosenzweig argues that the "scientific image of the world" appertains to being-already-in-existence, or what Aristotle calls the *to ti en einai* (what something is, i.e., essence). [23] He seeks to demonstrate that this manifestation of realtiy, anchored as it is in the past and thus subject to scientific exploration, is by no means the whole of reality. In the face of this reality— which theologically is to be understood as an already accomplished and existing fact of creation—there arises a decisive question for human existence: What is to be made of this reality by man, a creature created "in the image of God,"[24] that is, as a being endowed with freedom and called to freedom.

The notion that creation has a future—that there is the creation of something new—is conceivable, however, only if one relinquishes the idealistic notions of totality and generation and if our thinking proceeds from the radical separateness of God, world and man. Thinking, not the thinking of an outside observer but of one directly concerned, must then inquire how the evolution of reality into the future is to come about as an occurrence that can only be accomplished by man, and which at the same time is the only occurrence by which man becomes man.

Precisely when it is realized that creation as the "already existing" is incomplete and that the future can only take place through man, there arises the ethical question. For Rosenzweig it is the question about the orientation of the metaethical man. Man, as the creature existing in relation to himself, is as such a metaethical being. He is the "lord of his ethos."[25] He can want what he wants. But what should he want and how should he want?

The second book of the second part of *The Star* develops the thesis that this occurrence, in which the orientation of the *eo ipso* metaethical man takes place, that orientation through which the "lord of his ethos" becomes the responsible human being, is nothing less than the happening of revelation. For Rosenzweig the word *revelation* has so broad a meaning that it takes place in all serious speech in which a man really says something of his own. In this sense, then, it also shares in the Jewish and Christian understanding of the term, that is, as that linguistic happening in which we find the "word of man in the word of God."[26]

Why does the "orientation" of metaethical man toward responsibility require revelation? Or, in other words: Why can responsibility be rescued only through the event of revelation?

The answer is as follows: In my responsibility I am actually concerned not with myself, but with something other than me. However, if I give up the idealistic notion of generation (*Erzeugung*)—that is, the reality of the world is subject to the mind's rational conception of it—and proceed from the independence from me of the world in the process of being created and, even more so, of the other person who is conceived as self-originated and independent of me, I am faced by a seemingly impossible task with respect to my responsibility. For on the one hand I myself must act, and I cannot overcome this independence of mine, without what is called responsibility again collapsing. On the other hand, what I am concerned about is the other as other, and only through him about our living with each other. Yet how shall I find the way in this direction, when I am the "lord of my ethos" and as such am essentially self-enclosed vis-à-vis the other?

Rosenzweig shows that this can only occur in a *conversio* in which I experience myself as ultimately affected by the absolute Other, namely by God. For Rosenzweig, whose thinking takes many of its cues from the process of language, this *conversio* already takes place at the moment a man begins to speak truly as himself. For this speech act, in which he himself speaks, contains him in his own entirety. He reveals himself. Nevertheless he is concerned with that which is other than himself. In his speaking he experiences himself as affected by the other-than-himself—and therein by the absolutely other. This means that the fact that I begin truly to speak as myself already constitutes an answer—an answer to a voice that unconditionally calls to me and to everyone else.

Similarly, as later for Emmanuel Lévinas, God's question in the story of the creaton—"Adam, where art thou?"—becomes for Rosenzweig the biblical designation of man's primal situation in which man awakens for the first time to become a "living soul,"[27] namely, to become a man who speaks for himself and accounts for himself.. Seen from this perspective, the metaethical appears as a phenomenon of abstraction, which is attained at the cost of disregarding what is truly happening, that is, of disregarding the reality that takes place *between* me and the other. This abstract quality of the metaethical, however, is the precondition for responsibility, insofar as it evinces itself as paradoxical, that is, as a happening between "factualities" that are irreducible to one another, in which the isolation of these factualities is overcome. The essential effect of this happening is that I experience myself as infinitely and absolutely loved.

It seems to me that this dynamic is also manifest in the internal experience of responsibility. For wherever I seriously take upon my-self responsibility for the other person, I am aware that I am concerned unconditionally with what affects me in his act and with what I respond to. There is no act in which I could find myself more intensely concerned as myself and affirmed in my own originality. Referring back to biblical tradition, Rosenzweig goes on to say that even when I have to answer for my sins, I experience myself as my-self and in this too as unconditionally affirmed, that is, chosen[28]—namely, affirmed and chosen by God. No self-affirmation in the sense of the metaethical or mythical merging in the Godhead brings with it this experience of myself being unconditionally affirmed by the absolutely other-than-myself. This experience also appears to correspond to the fact of finding oneself responsible. For finding oneself responsible is conceivable only if, on the one hand, the Kan-tian postulate of autonomy is fulfilled, that is, if I myself in my own originality am the one who is creating reality here by speaking and acting myself. Yet, on the other hand, the concern of responsibility must be absolutely other than myself, and in such a manner that the other, for whose sake I am acting, has the character of the absolute that calls and affirms me.

Rosenzweig has described this relationship in his phenomenology of divine love, which is at the center of *The Star*. The "love of God" is to be read as an objective and subjective genetive, being loved by God and loving God. It shows itself as the loving one, in which God's enduring essence is in the present moment reversed to an original "meaning me."[29] By means of the phenomenology of the paradox of the reversal of the contents of the primal phenomena, which cannot be called a dialectic but rather a phenomenology of the paradox of the reality of responsibility taking place in time, Rosenzweig shows the interplay between the divine and human level that occurs at the moment one finds oneself acting responsibly. What Lévinas, using Kantian categories, called the "retournement de l'hétéronomie en autonomie" becomes visible here as love of the one who loves and at the same time of the one who is being loved. This "simultaneity" of the love of the loving one and of the beloved one—which alone is the whole of the present reality—is again read by Rosenzweig in the language that in its "real process of being spoken" reveals itself as "word and response,"[30] that is, as an ongoing dialogue.

Once it is presupposed that "that which is" reveals itself in an all-embracing way in language, it becomes evident that for Rosenzweig speaking always simultaneously reveals what is and what occurs. What occurs does so through the speaker who has to say something new on his own on the basis of what he is, but one's being, of course, is also incomplete. Further, Rosenzweig argues, language is the basis of dialogue by virtue of the absolute reality of the *proper* name. Although we speak responsibly, this fact in itself is not an absolute that renders dialogue possible. Dialogue is rather a reality by virtue of the name that "God himself created" for me.[31] My proper name is that by which I am "absolutely" called. This being called absolutely occurs preeminently through the divine commandment of love.

As Rosenzweig demonstrated in the most central passages in *The Star*, only love can be commanded. Love can only be commanded by the "One,"[32] whose concern for me must at the same time be a concern for fullness of reality. God's query "Adam, where art thou?" which bestows upon me my proper name and the possibility of acting responsibly, means at the same time the *commandment* of love. Rosenzweig sharply distinguishes this commandment from all laws, even from those general laws to which the categorical imperative leads. The law implies an anticipation of a definite time, a moment within man's reach. God's commandment of love, however, lives entirely in the today of the moment and is thus simultaneously open to all of the future.

But all of the future is, first, the future in which the other exists. "One proper name demands others."[33] In this respect the "Adam, where art thou?" which through the proper name constitutes responsible speech, implicitly also constitutes speaking vis-à-vis another and all others.[34]

Second, however, "all of the future," to which my responsible speech is open, is the hoped-for fullness of reality—that very fullness that Rosenzweig indicates through the biblical concept of the kingdom of God. By speaking responsibly, awakened by the love of

God, I cannot intend anything less than the absolutely true reality, which, however, at first remains the other in relation to myself and to my speaking.

Nevertheless, I can in a certain way anticipate this reality, to which I, having been taken hold of by the revealing love of God, was awakened from my metaethical imprisonment. I can do so in the act of loving my neighbor. As already stated in the title of *The Star*, redemption is reality proper. Yet redemption is conceivable only if we assume a state of nonredemption or lack of freedom, a state of imprisonment or bondage from which we should be liberated. In *The Star* Rosenzweig does not offer a theory of the state of subjugation. However, he shows how one can strive for redemption from the very heart of the self that has been awakened to the love of God; this striving is the essentially positive *constituens* of human history.

In other words, the discrete events of creation, revelation and redemption effect a temporalization of reality, and this temporalization allows Rosenzweig to conceive reality, as read from man's viewpoint, as incomplete. Although unconditionally founded in the existence of already accomplished creation, in revelation reality is entrusted to the man who "under the love of God" comes of age as eloquent soul,[35] and who has to speak and act on his own. The meaning of this coming of age, however, is responsibility for redemption. Hence, by understanding reality as essentially incomplete, and as entrusted to man "awakened" by divine love, one can conceive of the manifest unfolding of reality as something that occurs by virtue of human responsibility or of the shirking of such responsibility.

A closer examination of Rosenzweig's conception of responsibility shows it to be specifically the love of one's neighbor or rather, as Rosenzweig puts it, "the nighest" (*der Nächste*). This aspect of responsibility is considered in the third book of the second part of *The Star*, in which Rosenzweig demonstrates that the momentary love of God does not exhaust the abiding reality of divine love. For the love between man and God "longs to be founded in the presence of all the world," and not just in the soul's intimate experience of divine love. The love between man and God yearns for "matrimony," for "external fulfillment," which can only be the "realm of brotherliness." Thus revelation points to, indeed anticipates, redemption as "a future beyond the present revelation of love."[36]

Redemption, then, is the future that unveils itself at the very moment of the occurrence of the divine love. But this means that man, as the beloved one awakened from his metaethical imprisonment, is referred through the command of love to the whole reality that is other than him, that is, to the reality of all other human beings and of the whole world. The command of love is expressed in the biblical commandment "As he loves you, so shall you love."[37]

But this commandment can only be perceived by means of the "need for the other and . . . by taking time seriously."[38] Being awakened by the command of love, I can only turn to whoever happens to be my neighbor. And on the strength of having already been touched by God's love, I must turn to my neighbor ever anew. In doing so, I recognize him in his ever-new and unattainable otherness, as well as the contents of the world in their otherness, as the *conditio sine qua non* of my love of my neighbor. In contrast to an autonomously constituted ethics whose laws "lose all content, for any and every content would exercise a power disturbing the autonomy," the act of loving one's neighbor has as its content the inclination toward the other, whom I can by no means anticipate. This inability to anticipate the other leads inevitably to a "disappointment" in the other—a disappointment that reveals to me the "otherness" of the other and, as such, "keeps love in condition."[39] It is, however, precisely this content that turns the love of one's neighbor, that which was awakened by divine love, into responsibility, that is, into the deed by which I respond. In light of the divine promise of redemption, this deed is included in the love of God. At the moment of love, the neighbor, to whom I turn exclusively, is simultaneously "representative" and "locum tenens." Love goes out "in truth to the all-inclusive concept of all men and all things which could ever assume this place of being in its nighest neighbor. In the final analysis it goes out to everything, to the world."[40]

This understanding of responsibility as an act of love of one's neighbor cannot be reduced to a legal ethic because the love of one's neighbor has an "absolute presupposition beyond freedom," namely the love of God, understood in the sense of the *genitivus subjectivus,* that is, God's love *for* man. This presupposition is strengthened in that the loved neighbor is absolutely independent and that "love of neighbor is love of God's creatures."[41] Here again it becomes evident that the radical separation between the primal phenomena, which has to be accepted as the first premise, is constitutive for Rosenzweig's thinking. But precisely this separation permits us to conceive of the act of responsibility in greater detail, namely, as an act that (*a*) rests upon an unconditional preliminary concern with the other; (*b*) does not obtain what it "intends"; and (*c*) nonetheless "anticipates" its intended goal, namely, redemption grounded in divine love, and that is thus an act that takes its own temporality seriously.

The man who takes time seriously, whose time thus takes place in responsibility, that is, in the act of loving his neighbor, is—according to Rosenzweig—the saint, a true servant of God. He is not the "tragic hero" who remains secluded within his own self, nor is he the "otherworldly mystic." Rather it is the "whole man" who loves his neighbor in the light of the love of God and who, taking time seriously, becomes a witness to the hope for eventual redemption.[42] Such a holy life produces peace in the biblical sense and not acts of duty in the Kantian sense.

## IV

When Rosenzweig calls his thinking "absolute empiricism,"[43] he gives expression to the fact that he gains the right to his peculiar form of thinking by referring back to experience.

But what experience is intended here? It is reasonable to suppose that what is meant is not categorically conditioned experience in the Kantian sense, nor transcendental experience in the sense of Husserl. Experience here corresponds most closely to becoming involved or familiar with what Rosenzweig calls "absolute factuality."[44]

Thus because I myself constitute experience in that I obtain it from somebody other than myself, experience differs from the dream whose content is completely transparent to me. Moreover, I am engulfed by experience and carried by it—by virtue of this happening to me through the indisputably other—into the course of real events. That is why the principle of disappointment is the *conditio sine qua non* of the ever-renewed *becoming* familiar with such experience.[45]

It is also obvious that such experience is always only given in its happening, in its own temporality. Only by taking over the responsibility for the other as the other, only by letting myself be concerned with the one lying by the roadside as my neighbor, like the good Samaritan, do I experience what is responsibility and what is love of one's neighbor. I only experience it in the happening of becoming involved. Referring to the impossibility of anticipating the experience of responsibility, Lévinas observed that from my own viewpoint I represent being responsible as a "passivité plus passive que toute passivité."[46]

The experience with which we are concerned here does not depend a priori on the possibility of synthetic propositions. It is the experience that literally is given only "with time." It manifests itself as the experience by which time becomes "completely real" to man. my time becomes really time only as the time of loving my neighbor, that is, the time of responsibility.

Such experience is not random and ephemeral. Rather, it shows itself as continuous experience and, as such, as a continuous "*becoming* at home" within absolute factuality. That is so because while the experience takes place, it brings together those extreme and mutually separate phenomena whose combination cannot be achieved by an a priori construction.

Rosenzweig probably took over the term *factuality* from Schelling.[47] Here, as with Schelling, this term does not mean facticity of the individual, but the all-embracing and inalienable constituents that make such facticity possible. In the occurrence of responsibility, there is a simultaneous manifestation of the human, the divine, and the worldly. And this in such a manner that these three constituents—Rosenzweig calls them factualities (*Tatsächlichkeiten*)[48]—are nevertheless irreducible to one another in the experience in which they come together. The responsible act, or the act of loving one's neighbor, is human because it has its source in the originality of the self. Yet it is not only human. For man as himself only awakens to the love of his neighbor through the commandment to love God, who, to him, is the absolute other. At the same time, however, this act is also worldly. For by letting itself be concerned by the other, it turns toward a part of the world that thereby enters the light of the divine realm.

The idea of responsibility and of loving one's neighbor are another step forward on the road to the kingdom of God[49]—without it thereby becoming possible to anticipate the future steps on this road. As Rosenzweig explains in "New Thinking," in *The Star* the "day in the life of the universe" is traversed in ongoing reality— which is always simultaneously defined by the three primal phenomena—such that one's actions in everyday life may be acknowledged as demanding responsibility.[50] Modifying the well-known Kantian axiom,[51] one could say, therefore, that the primal phenomena have no other purpose than their application to the experience of everyday life, insofar as this experience is that of ongoing responsibility and of the love of one's neighbor.

Here, then, it becomes evident in what way and why this experience differs from concrete, categorically conditioned experience. It is intensively and extensively much more comprehensive than the latter in that it is nothing less than the experience of a life of genuine human responsibility, which unfolds temporally in remembrance, occurrences, hope and fear.[52] And as a matter of fact, *The Star* intends to deliver the reader to life.

It is an intensively comprehensive experience in that there is no experience for man more comprehensive than this experience of responsibility. And it is the most extensively comprehensive experience in that the road traveled here is directed toward the ultimate hope, to the kingdom of God. That, too, is why we pray for this experience. Everything that in the act of responsibility is my neighbor, represents to me, in hope and fear, "all the world." Therefore this experience may be called the experience of "absolute factuality."[53]

From this viewpoint it also becomes clear why objectivizing experience, that which takes place for example in the sciences, cannot be an experience in the sense of absolute factuality. For the laws of nature establish "only the inner interconnection of occurrence, and not the content."[54] The content only takes place in the occurrence of responsibility. It now also becomes clear why Rosenzweig, in all three books of the second part of *The Star,* counterposes the experience encountered in art, which is merely a preliminary experience, to that with which he is concerned. Though art may be deemed the only truly "necessary thing" among all that is "empirical," it is not to be understood as a step on the road of ongoing unfolding reality. In the empirical realm of art, creation, revelation and redemption coagulate into mere categories.[55]

Conversely, it also becomes evident that the experience of responsibility and love of one's neighbor involves more than the narrow experience of necessities of art; by virtue of the concomitant realization that the promised redemption remains unfulfilled, the experience of responsibility requires that we take compassionate cognizance of the needs of the other.

In his essay, "The New Thinking," Rosenzweig discussed the content of this ongoing experience under the title "messianic epistemology," especially in regard to the involvement of the man through whom the experienced truth comes up for discussion. I can prove the truth experienced in the most comprehensive sense only by putting my own life at stake. But this proof, being the realization of truth, is demanded by the truth that "can only be proven by all generations putting their lives at stake." The internal criterion of such a verification of the truth, that is, the criterion of its authenticity, consists in its ability to "establish a bond . . . between men."[56]

It may be asked whether Rosenzweig's thought would retain its plausibility were one to bracket the phenomenon of the metaphysical God and the occurrence of creation, revelation, and redemption and thus read it in strictly secular terms. Anyone even slightly acquainted with Rosenzweig's work will clearly see that this is impossible, and not for the external reason that the trinity of creation, revelation and redemption actually determines *The Star of Redemption* as a whole. It is impossible for the internal reason that unless responsibility is directed toward the absolute, it loses all orientation and thereby becomes void.

This claim is also made by classical metaphysics, which in one way or another has always connected ethics with the absolute. What is new in Rosenzweig's contemplation of the process of reality vis-à-vis all, if we may coin a term, "onto-theological" designs, is the attempt to conceive of God, world and man as having their own origins and to bring them, within the *Welttag des All*, into the process of events in such a way that their interaction does not take place "ever since" but "only now." In this context the proper object of thinking is the otherness of the other, which cannot be encompassed by thinking qua phenomenal knowledge and therefore by neither representative nor narrative language. At an early stage,[57] therefore, Rosenzweig already opposed any attempts within Judaism as well to conceive God reductionistically, that is, to identify God with such transcendental magnitudes as the soul or essence of a people.

But how then can one talk of God?

Only in such a way that thinking does not proceed from the previous unity of thinking and being within which the *Theion* (Godhead) is then conceived as the *ontōs on* (veritable being) or the *omnitudo realitatis* (total reality), but in such a way that thinking is rooted in the experience directly concerning it.[58] It is then swept by its own absolute otherness into the happening that reveals itself by itself in the factuality of responsibility as the happening of reality *quo maius cogitari nequit* (that something greater is inconceivable).

The reality of responsibility as the point through which the course of ongoing reality leads only becomes possible in its full factuality if God is thought of as absolutely not in need of anything. He needs neither the world as creation nor man as the metaethical creature.[59] In this respect, world and man have a thoroughly a-theistic character.[60] Precisely this absolute liberation from God, which had been postulated by the Enlightenment out of an entirely different, namely emancipatory, interest, is the precondition for man's coming of age, that is, his ability to respond freely, to be responsible.

But such responsibility occurs in the world that exists as an already created world, existing as such without "God's interference." This noninterference by God is also a *conditio sine qua non* for the possibility of man's responsibility being responsibility in earnest. Moreover, from the standpoint of the—incomplete—world which, having already been created, is left to his responsibility, man has no excuse for acting in a manner that eliminates his responsibility.

But insofar as he acts responsibly, the goal of his actions can only be redemption or the kingdom of God. Here, in the essence of concrete responsibility, which is always a worldly human action, man experiences the love of God, which directs him and which gives content to responsibility.

The only occurrence that completely rescues responsibility is revelation. And it is this occurrence of revelation that, according to Rosenzweig, brings with it a new concept of God, through which "God's relationship with man and the world is established in an unequivocal and unconditional manner wholly foreign to paganism."[61]

God no longer shows himself as the ground of the totality—no matter how conceived—but, as the voice that says "thou shalt love, as he loveth thee,"[62] which always reawakens the redeeming occurrence of human responsibility.

God shows himself as the *deus absconditus sed tamen non ignotus* (as a God who is hidden yet not unknown). Yet his becoming *tamen non ignotus* (yet not unknown) takes place in the occurrence of a revelation that cannot be anticipated. Thus, the whole of Rosenzweig's thinking, culminating in the rescue of responsibility, is decisively grounded in the occurrence of revelation.

# 5

# Between Enlightenment and Romanticism: Rosenzweig and Hegel

*Otto Pöggeler*

Franz Rosenzweig's book *Hegel and the State* is a milestone in Hegel research.[1] Everyone working on Hegel must examine Rosenzweig's chronology of Hegel's manuscripts and deal with Rosenzweig's interpretation; in the archives and in the discussion of the main problems in Hegel research the contemporary scholar must follow Rosenzweig's footsteps. Yet we do not find his book on Hegel in Rosenzweig's collected works. In countless remarks Rosenzweig himself attributes the book—his doctoral dissertation—to a world that collapsed, a world that Rosenzweig felt obliged to leave. Finding the book on Hegel in Rosenzweig's collected works would be like reading statements of Saul of Tarsus in the epistles of Saint Paul. To be sure, Rosenzweig in his *Zweistromland* included his essay on the so-called oldest program for a system of German idealism.[2] There his essay, however, represents the "old thinking" as distinguished from the "new thinking." In that essay Rosenzweig tried to demonstrate that a paper written by Hegel was actually drafted by

Schelling. For fifty years the history of ideas followed Rosenzweig's suggestion; today, however, we have come to believe that there is no reason to assume that Schelling (or Hölderlin) drafted this program and gave it to Hegel to copy. The program fits into the development of Hegel's thinking, but not into the development of Schelling's early writings.³ When in 1917 Rosenzweig expressed such a high opinion of this program, Hegel was obviously closer to him than he would concede. Now, after the recent publication of Rosenzweig's diaries and letters, it is obsolete to read the author of *Hegel und der Staat* (completed in 1913, but published in 1920) and the author of *The Star of Redemption* (1921) like two different authors. If we separate Rosenzweig's book on Hegel from his essential work, we render the Hegel book a mere academic exercise; the questions Rosenzweig has to ask about Hegel do not come into play. Or to put it the other way around: if we do not integrate the book on Hegel into Rosenzweig's collected works, we cannot see how important the confrontation with Hegel was for Rosenzweig's own development. For clearly Rosenzweig's "philosophy" was developed in the wake of Hegel.

In his introduction to Cohen's *Jüdische Schriften* (1923), Rosenzweig reports that during a trip to the Jewish communities of Russia the then elderly Cohen was hailed as a *baal teshuvah*, a repentant Jew who had "returned home." Playing on this theme, Rosenzweig pointed out that Cohen had now objected to the way of thinking begun in the name of Spinoza by Jacobi, Herder, and Goethe. In the end, according to Rosenzweig, Cohen remained loyal to Plato, Kant, and the Jewish prophets; therefore in his posthumous work he could, indeed, delineate "a religion of reason out of the sources of Judaism."⁴ Rosenzweig looked upon Cohen as an "unconscious Hegelian" who in his posthumous book broke with his earlier systematic convictions. In fact, the repentant Hegelian was Rosenzweig himself. To be sure, it is not justifiable to regard Rosenzweig merely as a Hegelian. His writings have their roots in a criticism of idealism; his "new thinking" is part of the protest against Hegel because it acknowledges not only the *I* but the *Thou*. In 1923, Rosenzweig reminded his teacher Friedrich Meinecke that the preface that he, Rosenzweig, had written in 1918 to his book on Hegel and the motto he then appended denied the hopes of the book, which he completed before the commencement of the Great War. Rosenzweig, in 1919, expected not a perfection of history, but a new Deluge.[5]

Perhaps in the twentieth century a confrontation with Hegel is creative only when it is no mere Hegelianism but a Hegelianism that "returns home" or goes unprotected and exposed into an open future. The Hegel renascence in Heidelberg at the beginning of the century may be typical. In this little university town the great sociologist Max Weber formed an opposition to the scholars of the circle around the famous poet Stefan George. In a liberality that made room for his opponents as well, Weber assembled young scholars for free discussion. But these young men committed what to Weber was an outrage: they studied Hegel, to the extent that in 1910 the neo-Kantian Wilhelm Windelband, in a now famous address, spoke about the renewal of Hegelianism. But this interest in Hegel was only transitional, a medium for the liberation from the scientific character and methodology of neo-Kantianism. The way through Hegelianism led to new orthodoxies: Julius Ebbinghaus (who, as son of the well-known psychologist Hermann Ebbinghaus, for a time saw in Hegelianism the dialectical opposite of his father's system) eventually returned to a strict Kantianism; Hans Ehrenberg (of Jewish origin) wrote *Die Heimkehr des Ketzers* (Return of a heretic) and combined an interest in the Orthodox church with a conversion to Protestantism; Ernst Bloch derived "the spirit of Utopia" from the mystical tradition; Georg Lukács took Hegel, together with Marx, as a model and so on.[6] When, in 1921, Rosenzweig read Weber's sociological analysis of Judaism, he discerned an affinity between his own work and Weber's sober-minded analysis of the facts and freedom from idealizing enthusiasm. But, he wrote, Weber himself would not have acknowledged the affinity: "He probably thought that he was still going about the business of the old ones."[7] "The old ones" refers to those humanistic scholars and social scientists who did not wish to be confronted with the question of meaning and the possibility of conversion and "homecoming." In fact, neither this homecoming nor any other could be Weber's concern.

The Enlightenment tested the strength of the knowledge that man himself can seek and find. Past and present political and religious affairs came before the bar of reason. But various romantic tendencies pointed out that it is the human condition to live historically in individual structures. Hegel tried to combine and reconcile the Enlightenment and the romantic tendencies; he wanted to bring all acquisitions of history into an all-encompassing system. Hegel's philosophy, as a so-called world philosophy and representative of German idealism, broke down under attack of the new specialized research in the fields of nature and history. But whenever the antagonism between the Enlightenment and romanticism became manifest, Hegel was called on for aid. At Berlin (in Dilthey's late works), at Heidelberg (in the circle around Max Weber), and at nearby Freiburg Hegel played the role of midwife: he gave decisive stimulations, but he was abandoned by creative thinkers as soon as they took their own stand. In a further phase, the protest against Hegel was credited to Hegel's thinking. For example, in the thirties Alexandre Kojève in his Paris lectures brought Hegel into existentialist philosophy and into the discussion of the relation between philosophy and history, and finally associated him with Marx and Kierkegaard. Heidegger, after his late "homecoming" to Hölderlin about 1929, increasingly took Hegel as a foe in his endeavor to overcome metaphysics. Philosophers in the United States were speaking of this kind of "Hegel" (Hegel and the protest against Hegel) when, after 1970 in a national crisis, they discussed, together with Hegel as it were, problems that had been banished from philosophy—the problematic relation between state and society, the role of art in our technological civilization, the importance of tradition, and so on.

When the young Rosenzweig wrote his book on Hegel, he did not repeat Hegel's idealistic solutions; he saw himself in the situation between Enlightenment and romanticism from which Hegel began his way. Rosenzweig, finding his own solutions, differed from all those who followed primarily the tendencies of the Enlightenment. Indeed, Rosenzweig's affirmation of Judaism may be regarded as a *dialectical* overcoming of the limitations of the Enlightenment. One reaction to Rosenzweig's stand is exemplified by Walter Regensburg, who in the United States became Walter Raeburn and consciously accepted the ideal of "mediocrity" and the "average man." In light of this ideal, he regarded his cousin Franz Rosenzweig (precisely at the time of his "homecoming") as an "absurd joke" and after a meeting in 1920 wrote to him: "I came with a violent preconceived prejudice against you—not, of course, on political grounds for I am not such a fool as that; but because I regarded you with a kind of horror as something morbid and uncanny, something which I had myself fled from becoming again and again in the years when I was entering adulthood. I have not got your brains unfortunately, but equally unfortunately I *have* your disposition; and your very morbidity has a siren-like fascination for me which forced me to tie myself, as it were, to my mast, like Odysseus."[8] Raeburn quoted what the Roman governor Festus shouted to St. Paul: "Too much study is driving you mad" (Acts of the Apostles 26:24). In reply, Rosenzweig rejected the "family legend" of "an unrealistic melancholia"; above all he pointed out that hatred against speculation as mere hatred remains bound to speculation and hence does not lead to freedom. Even in the manner of his return to Judaism, Rosenzweig differed from others. His friend Buber, for instance, sought to revitalize forthwith the Jewish mystical tradition that had been abandoned ever since Mendelssohn joined the Enlightenment. In contradistinction to Buber, Gershom Scholem wanted first to investigate this tradition historically. Rosenzweig differed from both Buber and Scholem, as witnessed by his approach to the translation of Jewish liturgical texts. In contrast to Scholem, he did not seek primarily to give an exact historical translation; cognizant of the risk of falsifying the tradition, he rather sought to transfer into the living present the spiritual reality of the text. Rosenzweig was of the opinion that Scholem combined scientific and "nihilistic" asceticism with "his central dogma" that Judaism was in a deathlike trance (*Scheintod*) and could be revived only "beyond," that is, after its reconstruction in the land of Israel.[9] "Judaism is for him [Scholem] only a cloister. . . . Perhaps he is the only one who has truly come home. But he has come home *alone*."[10] In his intention to reactualize tradition Rosenzweig was obviously following Hegel, and specifically the manner in which it was fashionable to interpret his thought at the beginning of the twentieth century.

Rosenzweig's great grandfather Samuel Meir Ehrenberg was an instructor at the Jewish Free School in Wolfenbüttel and the teacher of Leopold Zunz, one of the founders of Wissenschaft des Judentums. Rosenzweig wanted to preserve all the liberality and the standards of free, objective research that had been achieved by Wissenschaft des Judentums. He was, nonetheless, of the opinion that "short-circuited" efforts to achieve emancipation had led to a tragic loss of the very meaning of tradition and that only a return to Judaism could recover this meaning. With this return to Judaism, this "homecoming," Rosenzweig (after a short period of indecision) had to differ from those relatives and friends who joined their criticism of philosophical idealism with an affirmation of Christian faith (like his interlocutors Hans and Rudolf Ehrenberg and Eugen Rosenstock). On the nature of this homecoming, a difference in emphasis remained even between Rosenzweig and Martin Buber, Rosenzweig's closest friend in his last years. In opposition to the Paulinian and Lutheran as well as the Spinozistic and Hegelian identification of Judaism with Law, Rosenzweig stressed that in Judaism it is not the law but only the people that can be compared with the Christian Gospel. But in contrast to Buber, for Rosenzweig the concept of the people of Israel led to the question of the present importance of the law. He also criticized Buber's dialogical principle as being too narrow.[11] Significantly, Buber declined Dilthey's offer to edit Hegel's early writings; Buber obtained his philosophical foundations from authors such as Feuerbach and Simmel. Rosenzweig, however, drew his initial philosophical inspiration from Hegel, and indeed was decisively influenced by his confrontation with him. It is thus instructive to consider Rosenzweig's relation to Hegel.

I

About 1800 Hölderlin asked in a poem "An die Deutschen" whether or not action will spring spiritually ripe from thinking, "like a bolt of lightning from the clouds." These verses are the original motto put by Rosenzweig in 1909 at the head of his book on Hegel. Obviously Rosenzweig was willing to take Bismarck's founding of a nation-state for such an action, or for the first step of an action springing from "the thinking of 1800." Rosenzweig's passionate defense of Chancellor Bethmann-Hollweg during the First World War indicates a reserved acceptance of the dynamics of competing nation-states or federations of states. When Rosenzweig worked on Hegel he wanted to find an understanding of his own time and of those impulses of the past that led to the present. He joined a circle of young men from Heidelberg, Freiburg, and Strasbourg who met at Baden-Baden and tried to revive the discussion of the romanticists and idealists. "What we want is '1900'—a '1900' that knows the contrast to 1800." [12]

On 24 May 1908 Rosenzweig wrote in his diary: "Continuous development from autumn 1900 to autumn 1906; from then to autumn 1907 the negation of this development: until then, I had developed 'within Goethe'; then I ventured further, moving along his boundaries. Finally, starting with autumn 1907, the attempt to renew the contact: the thesis, Goethe, and the antithesis, Kant, have been followed by a synthesis for which as yet I have no name, unless it be, as I hope, my own." [13] The first synthesis at which Rosenzweig arrived bore the name *Hegel* (from whom Rosenzweig drew the concept of a development through negation). At Freiburg Rosenzweig studied Hegel with the famous historian Friedrich Meinecke. To his delight, Meinecke's book *Cosmopolitanism and the National State*—published in 1907, the very year Rosenzweig began his studies in Freiburg—dealt with the truths of 1900 and their sources.[14] At Berlin Rosenzweig explored Hegel's manuscripts and wrote to Hans Ehrenberg (11 November 1910): "I've joined the philologists. I make excerpts, collate, experience commas, make tracings, graphologize, and like Goethe's Wagner am infatuated with the noble parchment. Especially in the beginning it was very exciting and solemn, and from time to time I recapture the experience. This feeling of being an eyewitness, a direct observer of Hegel's various attempts to formulate his ideas, is sublime. Besides I have the pleasant sensation of being at the ultimate source and not, as when one depends on books, of forging ahead with the uncomfortable feeling always that one look at the manuscript might bring my house of cards tumbling down." [15] Rosenzweig remained a pupil of Meinecke's (although in his letters he occasionally appreciated Spengler and Wölfflin more than Meinecke). Meinecke's method is the history of ideas, *Ideengeschichte.* His book explores how the Western European nations and the German nation came to the parting of the ways when German idealism and romanticism rejected the cosmopolitan ideas of the tradition of natural right and of Enlightenment. History of ideas (as pursued by Meinecke) wants not only to see how certain ideas permeate a literary tradition; history of ideas explores how leading ideas were formed in the lives of men and especially at moments of historical change. Meinecke's second famous book on *raison d'état* or Machiavellianism, *Die Idee der Staatsräson* (1924), not only examines the impact of Machiavelli's writings (as Robert von Mohl had done), but attempts to show how the idea of *raison d'état* became a leading factor in European history—with Machiavelli and his followers, with Frederick II of Prussia, and with Hegel.

It was precisely Rosenzweig's Hegelianism that broke up the circle of Baden-Baden: the other members of the circle, all devoted students of Meinecke, could not accept Rosenzweig's Hegelian "perversion" of history.[16] In the retrospective view of 1920, however, Rosenzweig regarded his former Hegelianism as a kind of mere historicism. As a result of his religious crisis during 1913 and then during the First World War, the world of 1800 and the world of 1900 died, and therefore the effort to understand his own time through Hegel became a kind of historicism. On 30 August Rosenzweig wrote to Meinecke about Siegfried Kaehler, his fellow student at Freiburg: "I remember how sinister my insatiable hunger for 'forms'—a hunger without goal or meaning, driven on solely by its own momentum—then appeared to him. The study of history would only have served to feed my hunger for forms, my insatiable receptivity; history to me was a purveyor of forms, no more. No wonder I inspired horror in others as well as in myself!" Rosenzweig continued to describe his religious "conversion and homecoming," explaining it rather academically to his former teacher: "I had turned from a historian (perfectly 'eligible' for a university lectureship) into an (utterly 'ineligible') philosopher."[17] Rosenzweig's second step was a step from philosophy to life itself; but was the first step from history to philosophy not a new kind of Hegelianism? In any case this quarrel about Hegelianism and historicism belongs to the quarrel about value judgments that was fought in connection with the works of Max Weber: Is it the task of the humanities and the social sciences to explore history and society without making value judgments, or is all research, in any case, ultimately determined by value judgments and prejudices? Fifty years later Hans Georg Gadamer put this question in another way: Is the task of the humanities a neutral reproduction of the past (as Schleiermacher claimed) or an integration of the past into the present (according to Hegel's views)?

In Rosenzweig's book, Hegel—according to the method of a history of ideas—is taken as the representative "world philosopher" of his time (as he was regarded by Marx and Kierkegaard). Hegel put into explicit conceptual form what in "pill form" (for instance, in the paragraphs of a code of law or in the slogans of public opinion) determines the historical world.[18] Hegel found his way to an affirmation of the state, but he regarded the world of the European states as a realization of the new liberty of Christian faith; because Rosenzweig understood his own time as founded by Hegel and Hegel's contemporaries, it was only a matter of logical consequence that he contemplated conversion to Christianity. But ironically his Christian interlocutors (Eugen Rosenstock as well as Hans and Rudolf Ehrenberg) had taken a critical distance from German idealism and "cultural Protestantism."

Hegel had given an interpretation of Christ as the historic realization of the unity between idea and history, and therefore of real historic liberty, whereas Schleiermacher had seen in Christ both a holy individual and representative man who became the founder of a parish. The Christian theologians Albrecht Ritschl and Adolf von Harnack had interpreted the religious hopes (with Kant) as postulations of moral consciousness. In the years before the First World War, however, Albert Schweitzer pointed out, on the basis of research on the life of Jesus, how alien to the idealistic dogmatics the historic Jesus with his reference to messianism remained. Schweitzer, who was to have been invited to the circle of Baden-Baden, left Europe. But many impulses (for instance the new impact of Kierkegaard) led to a new Christian theology, and this Christian faith obliged Rosenzweig to reconsider his own Jewish heritage in a more genuine fashion. He studied with Hermann Cohen at Berlin, and already in 1914 he drew the conclusions that he outlined in his essay "Atheistic Theology." Rosenzweig discerned a parallel between developments in modern Christianity and Judaism: enlightenment, idealism, and "cultural Protestantism" made Christ the representative of an idea, but a romantic reversal inspired many to try and find their way back to the historic Jesus; in the Jewish sphere a singularly "atheistic theology" made the historic being of the Jewish people the pivotal point of orientation in life. In opposition to these parallel trends, Rosenzweig contended that religion can truly give life "orientation" only by virtue of a historic revelation (that is, not by an abstract idea or by mere human being).

In a letter to Rudolf Ehrenberg dated 31 October 1913, Rosenzweig explained the different steps of his return to Judaism: "I thought I had Christianized my view of Judaism, but in actual fact I had done the opposite: I had 'Judaized' my view of Christianity. I had considered the year 313 as the beginning of a falling away from true Christianity, since it opened a path for the Christians in the opposite direction to that opened in the year 70 for the Jews. I had begrudged the church its scepter, realizing that the synagogue bears a broken staff. You saw how, on this assumption, I began to reconstruct my world." [19] Rosenzweig wanted to convert to Christianity, because in this reconstructed world there seemed to be no room for Judaism: whereas Judaism was merely an interesting historical phenomenon (as a generous Christian clergyman wrote to Rosenzweig's mother, and as was Hegel's opinion too), original Christianity seemed to be the completion of history. In a second step Rosenzweig accepted the year 313, that is, the Edict of Milan, which made Christianity the soul of the Roman Empire and of the European states—the soul of an uncompleted, open history. Rosenzweig also accepted the year 70, that is, the destruction of the Second Temple, because he believed that the Jews in exile and dispersion anticipated the end of history (the judgment of God, as the Yom Kippur service proclaims it).

In 1915 Rosenzweig wrote a critical review of Cohen's essay "Deutschtum und Judentum." In a later note to a poem by Judah Halevi, he can remember only with irony Cohen's hope that the messianic era might perhaps begin in fifty years—when, through liberal Protestant theology, the Christians would accept the pure monotheism of Judaism (i.e., of Cohen's Kantianism).[20] In his review, however, Rosenzweig affirmed the promise of *galut*, the exile: "A nation always concentrates its strength in those spots where it senses danger; in the next few decades it will be the *galut* (no matter what its outward destiny) that must prove the inner strength of Judaism."[21] In a similar vein he acknowledged the twin status of the Synagogue and the Church that stand at the entrance of many medieval Christian cathedrals; he interpreted their symbolic significance as indicating that the Church and Synagogue together constitute the completion of history and religion, the church as conqueror of the world and the synagogue as a people in exile and dispersion.

After finishing his book on Hegel, in 1919, Rosenzweig rejected both Hegel's connection of idea and history and Meinecke's history of ideas. This rejection was prompted by the insights gained through Cohen's lectures in Berlin and work on the religion of reason: Rosenzweig understood Cohen's posthumous book as a break with the idealistic tradition, but as a break not carried through to its radical conclusion. In 1921 Rosenzweig wrote to Scholem about Cohen's words *idea* and *correlation:* "These words can never come home. They can never become entirely Jewish because they never were entirely German." Rosenzweig found words such as *Heil* and *shalom* better than the Greek word *idea* and its offsprings, such as *moral*.[22] Rosenzweig himself used the concept of revelation (for instance in 1917 in his correspondence with Rosenstock and then in *The Star of Redemption*): Revelation leads creation to redemption, furnishing it with an orientation that vouchsafes both to the individual and to the community a place, an absolute above and below. Despite all his criticism of Buber's dialogical principle, Rosenzweig replaced the I that dialectically disposes of ideas by the dialogue of Thou and I that leads respectively to revelation and redemption.

For Rosenzweig redemption occurs through the dualism of Judaism and Christianity. Accordingly, he criticized Cohen for transferring the Jewish understanding that "We [in dispersion and exile, secluded from the world] reached the goal" to Christianity. The Christian reality Rosenzweig finds in Kierkegaard, who is for him the original dialectical theologian: what the Jewish prophets set as the determination of a people in exile against the victorious Persians was claimed by Kierkegaard for the individual—an individual in misfortune and distress is able to find the meaning of life as an "exception" because God wants to be known in the finiteness of life and time. According to Rosenzweig, Christian history is a finite and unfinished one; it is also the history of Christian *peoples*. In 1917 Rosenzweig wrote to Hans Ehrenberg that the resurrection of the dead belongs to the coming of the Messiah; Rosenzweig did not, however, understand resurrection "animistically" as immortality, but as a transformation of time into "absolute history." Rosenzweig refers to Augustine, who understood the death of Christ as the beginning of his lordship and therefore Christian history as the messianic era.[23] With this interpretation Rosenzweig's protest against Hegel thus remains a kind of Hegelianism. In his philosophy of history Hegel, in the tradition of Daniel, understands history as a sequence of four kingdoms: the four beasts are followed by the appearance and sovereignty of "one like a man coming with the clouds of heaven" (Dan. 2, 7 : 13). For Hegel history in the real sense begins in the Middle East. In fact, it was there that mankind had the never-to-be-forgotten experience—the sudden end of Assyria (in 612 B.C.E.) and of the following kingdoms—out of which grew the apocalyptic schema. When in the twentieth century Mediterranean and European history expanded to include the entire planet, this understanding of history encountered other traditions, each with its own way of understanding history, and was relativized.[24] But Rosenzweig retains the Hegelian view; what *The Star of Redemption* says about China, India and Islam, about the aesthetics of Greece and art in general, about Christianity and Judaism, belongs to a Hegelian philosophy of history.

In the winter semester 1921 Rosenzweig gave a lecture course at the Freies Jüdisches Lehrhaus, which he entitled "An Introduction to Jewish Thinking"; significantly he added the descriptive subtitle "A Summary Statement of the Totality of Philosophy." The course was accompanied by a seminar on the foundations in the history of philosophy, especially German idealism from Kant to Hegel.[25] Rosenzweig presented Kant (like Cohen) in Hegelian fashion. For Rosenzweig, the universal aspect of the categorical imperative becomes situation and *kairos*, "the just-now-present state of the universe"; Kant's critique of practical reason, he asserted, led to Hegel's philosophy of history.[26] Hegel's system is distinguished by the attempt to grasp the genesis of the system and its presupposition in faith or its connection with the faith. Whereas Descartes and Spinoza remained "heretics," Hegel was thus the last philosopher and a new father of the church. Here Rosenzweig is thinking of the church of the so-called age of Saint John, when the fathers of the church will no longer sit on bishop's thrones in the capitals of Europe, but work in frontier stations.[27] Rosenzweig retains Hegel's union of faith and philosophy, but he accentuates the protest against Hegel too: Philosophers such as Kierkegaard, Schopenhauer, and Nietzsche use theological concepts such as reversal, overcoming, and renewal and set the individual against the system. No longer is the totality of substance or subject grasped in an objective method—the dialectics, the union of idea and history, are only a "one-dimensional" procedure, as Rosenzweig says in The Star of Redemption. According to "the philosophical principle of relativity," which has been increasingly asserted since Schopenhauer, the philosopher, that is, the individual, is the ultimate ground of philosophy. Although philosophy cannot abandon the concept of the absolute, the reference to the absolute is now the task of the individual. "Man became master of the matter (i.e., philosophy), therefore he is ready to hear the voice of God (which is never heard as long as the individual works behind the screen of some matter.)[28]

Rosenzweig not only gives a theological solution ("to hear the voice of God"), he also points out that his book on Hegel took the system as an open history of ideas. Rosenzweig uses Victor von Weizsäcker's concept of a flexible and open system; but he stresses against Weizsäcker that in the field of history one has always to ask who (which historic individual) had the idea.[29] Whereas his friend Eugen Rosenstock builds the concept of a whole in a lyric and Pindaric manner and then relates myths as documentary evidence, Rosenzweig seeks to point to the totality of history and to think "with the heads of all involved."[30] According to the philosophy of Bergson and Dilthey (and later existential philosophy), all living beings have only a few moments in which they speak the truth. Rosenzweig regards the dialogue emerging from these monologues as the "whole truth." That the monologues (or the systems with their one-sided perspectives) build a dialogue "is the great mystery of the world, the manifest and revealed mystery, the content of revelation." Here Rosenzweig again uses a Hegelian play on words (*offenbar/ offenbart*); his protest against Hegel relies on Hegelian terms.[31]

## II

Rudolf Haym in his early book on Humboldt tried to describe the promising union between Prussian politics and the German spirit; in his book on Hegel he sought to point out that Hegel, through a series of metaphysical illusions, transfigured the aesthetic view of life espoused by Weimar classicism into a political ideal. In the preface to his book on Hegel, Rosenzweig takes note of Haym's thesis; he himself also wanted to point to "the seeds [planted] in the time about 1800 which shot up about 1900." Here Rosenzweig explicitly differs from Dilthey, who placed Hegel in the company of the romantics, emphasizing his way to a new culture.[32] Rather Rosenzweig follows Meinecke, who saw Hegel as moving toward a nation-state. But Rosenzweig points out that only after Hegel's death did political philosophy develop the idea of a nation-state and integrate it into a Hegelian view of history. Unfortunately, Meinecke did not heed these observations of his former student; therefore, his presentation of Hegel's position in his history of *raison d'état* is misleading.[33]

When in 1913 Rosenzweig was completing his book on Hegel, he had begun to work out his own unique "way" in the wake of his spiritual crisis. His essay on the oldest program for a system of German idealism already belongs to the years of his "homecoming" (1914–17). The book on Hegel also seems to be silently determined by thoughts that later were to become important for Rosenzweig. When in his Frankfurt writings Hegel takes the Jewish people as an example of an unfortunate people, Rosenzweig merely notes this without any discussion; he does not yet think or point out that for him the misfortune of exile is the decisive destiny of the Jewish people. It is perhaps not insignificant that whereas Dilthey considers Hegel's Frankfurt writings as his most interesting (because he is interested in Hegel's new explanation of the genesis of the myth of Christ), Rosenzweig prefers a text of Hegel's years in Bern on the reli-

gion of fantasy, a fragment postulating national mythology or religion as the soul of a state or fatherland and praising the Jews because
they killed a messiah who did not want to be a political messiah.
Whereas Hegel in this document of a life crisis puts the Maccabees,
Massada, and Bar Kochba beside the people of Carthage and Sagunt,
Rosenzweig (not in his book, but in later letters) gives this comparison another meaning (referring to the discussion of Saint Augustine). He distinguishes between "the great and venerable naïveté
of pagan *fides* that lives and dies for itself" and the messianic hope.[34]
After his momentous encounter with Eastern European Jews during
the war, Rosenzweig said about Judaism what Hegel said about
Greece: "The Jews are today the only people (note: *people*) with a
national myth"—with, as it were, a theater, the content of which is
known by everybody (as was the case in the ancient theater).[35]

Rosenzweig understands the development of Hegel's thinking as a
way through a crisis. He adopts Hegel's remark that the decisive life
crisis tends to happen about the twenty-seventh year. Already in
1911, when he was twenty-five, he pointed out that he could speak
about Hegel's crisis only in "anticipation" (as Goethe said); in later
years Rosenzweig notes that the twenty-seventh year was for Hegel
the transition from Bern to Frankfurt and for himself 1913, the year
of his religious crisis.[36] Rosenzweig's book on Hegel unfolds the
leading idea that Hegel had to find his way to an affirmation of the
state through a crisis. Rosenzweig's friend Siegfried Kaehler (1885–
1967) treated Humboldt in a parallel way: only in the time of war
and Prussian reform could Humboldt have found the way from in-
dividualism to a stronger affirmation of the state. Whereas Rosenzweig praised the "respectful hatred" of Kaehler's book,[37] Meinecke
had to reject this iconoclasm. Indeed, Rosenzweig and Kaehler perhaps did dramatize Hegel's and Humboldt's way in an inadequate
manner.[38] Although in the twentieth century the Germans would
lead Europe to a catastrophe through a perversion of the national
idea, it is obvious that the Germans of the nineteenth century (as
distinguished from the French) had to find their way to a nation-
state. But it is not permissible to use this later drama for dramatiz-
ing Hegel's way. Rosenzweig gives misleading interpretations when
he continues the legend of Hegel's misfortune at Frankfurt, when in

Hegel's Jena writings Rosenzweig always reads "state" where Hegel says "people" (the translation of *polis*), when he does not connect destiny with the life of a people but with the relationship of an individual to a people, and so on.

When Rosenzweig joined in criticizing the philosophical idealism of his friends such as Hans Ehrenberg,[39] and when he himself rejected the union of idea and history or the history of ideas for a union of revelation and redemption, he saw in Schelling's later philosophy a way out of idealism. Many of his remarks rate Schelling higher than Hegel. Indeed, *The Star of Redemption* mirrors in its disposition Schelling's *Ages of the World*. Just as Schelling began with the eternal past, that is, the theory of powers or potencies, Rosenzweig in the first part of *The Star* presents a protology, that is, a theory of philosophical elements. (The second and third books of *The Star* then deal with present and future, i.e., with revelation and redemption or eschatology.)[40] But Rosenzweig never actually studied Schelling in detail (as he had Hegel, who influenced him accordingly).[41]

As a translator of Judah Halevi and of the Bible, Rosenzweig gained a distance from philosophy in general; he now appreciated (together with Ludwig Strauss) the late hymns by Hölderlin. He followed romantic tendencies; thus he was interested in the politics of Friedrich Wilhelm IV because this Prussian king was not interested in the emancipation of the individual Jew, but was concerned to secure public rights for the Jewish community qua community (as opposed to creating a new ghetto).[42]

About 1800 Hegel tried to combine the impulses of Enlightenment and romanticism; in the first decades of the twentieth century Rosenzweig believed that only in a protest against Hegel could he find an understanding of the time. Indeed, I concur that if Hegel is also to be the "world philosopher" for the year 2000, or if he is to become the representative philosopher even more than in former times, we have to decide on the appropriate relationship between the elements of Enlightenment and romanticism. As Rosenzweig correctly anticipated, European history led to a catastrophe; yet it is still not clear whether or not this catastrophe was a purifying deluge. The task remains to build an all-encompassing world civilization that grants room for the different historic societies. The scientific and technical endeavor to secure human survival ought not sever the different human communities from their respective traditions in such a way that they cannot see a meaningful future as distinct cultures. Rosenzweig is right when he follows the romantic insistence on the individuality and historicity of all human communities; he is right, too, in attempting to find a concept of history by returning to the great religious traditions. In this point we have to strengthen his criticism of idealism and especially Hegelianism.[43]

The question remains whether Rosenzweig gives the romantic tendencies an inappropriate superiority over the tendencies of the Enlightenment. Every attempt to inquire about the nature of East European Jewry—especially, of course, today after this important facet of human history has been destroyed—is of utmost value. Nonetheless, we must ask whether Rosenzweig's idealization of East European Jewry and his return to the foundations of religious tradition was not a way of evading many of the exigent problems of the contemporary West (and real East) European world. Above all, we must question his dubious assignment of exile and seclusion from the historical world to the Jews as their decisive destiny. In any case, this view combines theological presuppositions and history or, more precisely, philosophy of history in a rather short-circuited fashion. Rosenzweig lost sight not only of the tradition of the Enlightenment and natural right that attributes human rights to the individual as such, but also of the distinction between historic faith and a philosophy that seeks to be universal and binding upon everyone.

# 6

# Franz Rosenzweig on History

## Alexander Altmann

I

From the autumn of 1908 until the summer of 1912, with one year's interruption, Franz Rosenzweig studied history in Freiburg under Friedrich Meinecke, the celebrated teacher and leader of national liberalism in Germany. Rosenzweig was greatly impressed by Meinecke's *Nationalstaat und Weltbürgertum* (*Cosmopolitanism and the Modern State*) which had appeared in 1907 and seems to have formed a topic of discussion in the seminars of the period.[1] The method of *Ideengeschichte* (history of ideas) which it had introduced[2] became one of the formative influences in Rosenzweig's thinking. It taught him to see the force and interplay of ideas at the root of history. The book showed the tremendous impact that philosophical ideas had had on nineteenth-century German politics. It brought Rosenzweig close to the fundamental issues in modern political thought and stimulated all kinds of literary plans in his own mind.[3] These projects finally crystallized in his doctoral thesis, the two-volume work *Hegel und der Staat* (1920), which Meinecke regarded very highly.[4]

Rosenzweig brought to his historical studies a strong philosophical bent, as his teacher was not slow to recognize.[5] This involved the temptation to "construct" history and in the end led him into paths far removed from historical science proper. Yet the training he received in Freiburg served as a salutary check in curbing any flights of pure speculation. He remained conscious of the need to observe philological criteria and to ascertain the empirical facts concerning the ideas assumed to have played a part in individuals and groups.[6] Meinecke's warnings against "speculative constructions"[7] had obviously not failed in their purpose. But while Rosenzweig was determined to avoid false or superficial constructions, he was equally convinced that historical insight was impossible without the right kind of construction.[8]

The focal point of Rosenzweig's historical thinking is the year 1800, around which cluster the dates of the French Revolution, Hegel and Goethe.[9] The historical perspective offered by these dates suggests to Rosenzweig that the Christian world has entered into its last, Johannine, phase. The notion of Johannine Christianity formed one of the leading ideas of the German idealist movement. It occupied Fichte's mind since 1804, as Hans Ehrenberg has shown.[10] Schelling concludes his lectures on the Philosophy of Revelation with the words, "If I had to build a church in our time, I would dedicate it to Saint John."[11] Peter is the apostle of the Father, Paul of the Son, and John of the Holy Spirit.[12] John represents the church of a free, undogmatic Christianity.[13] This concept of a progressive liberalization of Christianity is a modern, secularized version of the revolutionary doctrine of the three churches that was first propounded by Joachim of Fiore, the twelfth-century abbot, and had paved the way for the Reformation.[14] The hopes that the German idealists associated with the Johannine form of Christianity had an eschatological ring and were echoed in Jewish circles during the period of emancipation. The messianic fervor that seized the Jewish Reform movement in the nineteenth century and that is reflected in the philosophical writings of S. Formstecher and S. Hirsch down to Hermann Cohen stems from the idealist concept of Johannine Christianity. Rosenzweig, who took the notion from Schelling,[15] still retains its eschatological flavor but gives it a new interpretation. It arises from a close study of the relationship between Christianity and philosophy, the latter representing the force of paganism, the "wisdom of the Greeks." It also presupposes the acceptance of Hegel's view that having comprehended itself historically, the Mind has reached the full consciousness of itself. Rosenzweig sees in the history of philosophy from Thales to Hegel ("from Jonia to Jena") one sustained pagan effort of idealist thinking that is gradually neutralized by the impact of the Jewish-Christian tradition, that is, revelation, and spends itself in Hegel. The Christian world *post-Hegel mortuum* (after Hegel's death) is identical with the Johannine church.

The theme is one that engages Rosenzweig's mind from an early period and is worked out in his letters and writings in a variety of shades and emphases, yet with a remarkable constancy of construction in fundamentals. Already in his letter to Hans Ehrenberg (dated 11 December 1913) Rosenzweig outlines the view that was to become characteristic of his entire historical thinking: The separation of Church and science from the Reformation onward means that the Church had by then completed the absorption of Greek philosophy. The pagan Aristotle was no longer a power. Descartes, Spinoza and Leibniz cannot be considered pagans outside the Church but heretics within it. In Kant, Fichte, Schelling, Hegel, the heretics return to the fold of the Church. They regard themselves as Christian philosophers. The philosopher has ceased to be synonymous with freethinking. He is no longer *discipulus Graeciae* (disciple of Greece, i.e., of pagan culture), as Tertullian called him, but simply a Christian. Hegel is the last philosopher and the first of the new Church Fathers, that is, of the Johannine church.[16] More outspoken is a letter from March 1916: "The idealist movement is both the end of philosophy (that is of paganism) and the beginning of the Johannine epoch (its patristic age as it were)."[17] The letter also introduces for the first time the recognition of Freemasonry as an expression of the third (Johannine) church. The theme is more fully elaborated in Rosenzweig's letter to Eugen Rosenstock, dated 30 November 1916: Since 1789 the Church has no longer any relationship with the state but only with society, the reason being that the Church has now entered into its last (Johannine, to use Schelling's term) epoch. There exists no more Greek wisdom, no more Roman Empire, only Christianity. This is what the Johannites wanted from the start, but it did not happen earlier because wisdom and empire had not yet fulfilled themselves in time.[18] The emancipation of the Jews is another expression of the Johannine period. Until 1789 the Old Testament was the book in which the Church had found its typology. Hence its opposition to Israel, the denier of its claim. Since 1789 the Church can look to its own history of the past when the hierarchy and the book had an institutional character, and those earlier, substantive periods now move into the position of the Old Testament. What remains of the Jew and for the first time enters into the horizon of Christianity is the "naked Jew," seen without the prism of the Old Testament.[19]

In his *Star of Redemption* Rosenzweig further elaborates Schelling's idea of the three churches. They represent the three fundamental virtues of love, faith and hope respectively. In the love of the missionary who goes out to convert those still dwelling in darkness, the church of Peter created its own empire and at the same time built in its institutions the visible body of the Church. But throughout the Middle Ages it failed to come to grips with the paganism in its own soul. Paganism had been repressed but not truly converted. Hence the dualism of faith and reason in medieval scholasticism. A new power accrues to Christianity after the revival of paganism in the Renaissance when the Pauline church of the Reformation could baptize the Christian's invisible, inward soul. But, again, the work remained incomplete. By subscribing to faith alone (*sola fides*), reality had been split into the pure inwardness of faith and an external secular world that no longer owed allegiance to the Spirit. Christianity had lost control of the world. Body and soul had become separated. German idealist philosophy reflects this Protestant error. The Spirit presumes to produce everything out of itself. With Goethe's pagan assertion of individuality, wholeness, and personal destiny a new period enters. Now man feels completely at home in the world and becomes fully alive. The nations too discover their individual soul and destiny. In the Petrine church they had been subject to the Holy Empire. In the Pauline church they obeyed secular authorities. Now, in the Johannine era they are Christian nations that believe in their own historical destiny. As Rosenzweig put it in one of his let-ters,[20] nationalism is the "complete Christianizing of the concept of peoplehood." The Johannine church is historically connected with the Eastern church but now assumes a universal significance. It can lay claim to no institutional form of its own. It cannot be "built," as Freemasonry mistakenly believes; it can only grow. Its message is one of hope. In this Johannine world, the Christian no longer converts the heathen around him nor the pagan within him. Now the Jew is meant to convert the pagan lurking in the Christian soul. For only in the Jewish blood hope lives eternally, and hope is what the Chris-tian needs today more than anything else. This is why the emanci-pation of the Jew had to happen precisely in this modern age.[21]

Rosenzweig's reading of the history of Christianity is a remark-able blend of *Ideengeschichte à la* Meinecke and theological con-ceptualism. History is seen as the dialectic of pagan myth and reve-lation, as the field in which the kingdom of God grows toward its realization. There is an eschatological urge or *nisus* at work in the history thus constructed. Obviously, Rosenzweig is fascinated by the plenitude of visions that the panorama of the struggles within Christianity evokes in him. From his first excitement in reading Ter-tullian's *Apologeticus* in 1911, which gave him a vivid impression of Christianity in the Roman Empire,[22] down to his no less exciting correspondence with Eugen Rosenstock, he learned to see history proper enacted in the Christian centuries. History became to him tantamount to the history of Christianity against the background of Greece and Rome. His theology of creation, revelation and redemp-tion is but the conceptualized application of this historical vision. Creation, the Alpha of history, expresses the pagan world; revela-tion, though stemming from from Judaism, transforms creation only through Christianity; and redemption is the goal toward which the world is moving.

Judaism itself remains essentially outside history. Not only after the year 70 but long before, it had seceded from active participation in the growth of the surrounding world, a view that comes close to the results of Max Weber's sociological analysis of Judaism.[23] Rosen-zweig himself acknowledged this affinity and regretted the fact that at the time of writing *The Star of Redemption* he had not yet known

Max Weber's work.[24] His discovery of the ahistorical nature of Judaism first produced a serious crisis in his life. The disquieting question it posed was: Was there still any room for Judaism in a world in which Christianity was the motive force? It was this question that lay at the root of his intention to leave Judaism and embrace Christianity. The story of his "conversion" to Judaism need not be retold here.[25] What interests us in this context is the fact that his affirmation of Judaism entailed a revaluation of history as such. History, for all its fascination to the historian, becomes a temporary, provisional affair, and the emphasis is shifted to the eschatological realm, the end and goal of history. The significance of Judaism lies in the fact that it anticipates, represents and ensures that end and goal. True, Judaism lies outside history, but what seemed to constitute its weakness now appears as its unique strength. History itself moves into a relative position. It is not itself the realm of the Kingdom but only the intermediate realm (*Zwischenreich*), and while Rosenzweig the historian can do full justice to Christianity as the decisive power in the intermediate realm, Rosenzweig the Jew is more vitally interested in the final Kingdom of which Judaism is the representative and trustee. "For me God alone is reality; I am a member of the intermediate realm only by the compulsion of nature (i.e., history), not by free will. Jesus belongs to the intermediate realm. Whether he was the Messiah will become clear only when the Messiah comes. Today he is to me as problematical as the whole intermediate realm. I am sure only of God and His Kingdom, not of the *Zwischenreich*."[26]

Rosenzweig holds that it is the task of the Jew to sacrifice life in the world for the purpose of testifying to the messianic goal of history. Judaism, he repeatedly declares, lives and has its being in the *eschaton*: It "is alive only in so far as it is with God. Only when the world too will be with God, will Judaism be alive also in a worldly sense. That, however, will happen only beyond history."[27] The inevitable price Israel has to pay for being the people of the Kingdom is a loss of worldly creativity. "The sacredness which attaches to it as a nation of priests sterilizes its life." It prevents it "from surrendering its soul to the yet unconsecrated world of the nations."[28] War and revolution, the only realities that the state knows and that create the epochs of world history, do not affect the inner life of Israel.[29] The formula Rosenzweig uses to denote the metahistorical existence of Judaism is: The Jew is at the goal of history, the Christian is eternally on his way.[30] This phrase expresses not only a theological belief but a historical truth as Rosenzweig sees it. It means, as the context of its discussion in *The Star of Redemption* clearly shows, that, in contrast to the Christian, the Jew has no inner conflict that history is expected to solve. The Christian soul is divided between nation and Church, between "Siegfried" and Christ, between myth and revelation. For the Jew no such inner discord exists. His sense of national destiny and his allegiance to God find themselves in complete harmony.[31] Whereas the history of Christianity is one of constant growth—represented by the succession of the three churches—Judaism has no history after the first exile and particularly after the year 70. It has left behind the contradictions that lie at the back of the historical life. It has reached the goal.

Yet for all its intrinsic remoteness from the course of history, Judaism fulfills a messianic purpose in the world. Living at the extreme point of history, symbolizing and anticipating it, Israel is the incarnation, we might say, of the Kingdom, the messenger of hope. Moreover, in this world of the dissolution of the hierarchical (Petrine) church and of the (Pauline) church of the Word there is no real substance left in the Christian life. In this epoch of "naked Christianity" the Jew is the only reality that binds Christianity to the Kingdom.[32] It prevents it from disintegrating into a myth or philosophy. It reminds the Christian that salvation comes from the Jews, not from the Greeks.[33] And it urges the Christian to realize that the world is not yet redeemed, that faith is not yet redemption. In Christianity the eschatological orientation is somewhat indistinct and easily merges with either creation or revelation. The Jew who hallows his flesh and blood under the yoke of the Law and continually lives in the reality of the Kingdom serves as a reminder to the Christian that redemption cannot be achieved by the mere inwardness of feeling.[34] He is the "eternal *enfant terrible*," the "mute admonisher,"[35] whose function is always resented yet indispensable.

Rosenzweig's view of the ahistorical character of Judaism accords, in a way, with certain traditional attempts at Jewish self-interpretation. The exclusion of the Jewish people from the realm of history was keenly felt in many epochs and led to the doctrine of God's exile (*Galut Shekhinah*), a theme with wide and profound ramifications in Jewish mystical thought. His concept of Christianity as a missionary of Judaism to the Gentile world, preparing it for the Kingdom, also stands on traditional ground. It is taken from the medieval Jewish philosophers and their modern disciples (S. Formstecher, S. Hirsch, Hermann Cohen). In support of his view Rosenzweig is able to preface and conclude his chapter on Christianity with quotations from Maimonides and Judah Halevi respectively. How far Judaism may be said to have "reached the goal" is another matter. Rosenzweig's idyllic notion of the freedom of the Jewish soul from inner conflict can hardly stand the test of closer scrutiny. The strong antinomian tendencies that reveal themselves in certain kabbalistic writings—notably in the *Sefer ha-Temunah* and in the literature it engendered[36]—and in the Sabbatian movement clearly show the stresses and tensions within Judaism itself.

II

Rosenzweig's view of history is carried a stage further in the very conception of the Kingdom as outlined in *The Star of Redemption*. Revelation from which redemption flows as from its source is the dialogue between God and man. More particularly, it is the experience of the love of God. This experience has not necessarily a historical place, but is a happening between God and man wherever and whenever they meet. Revelation is not an end in itself. The love of God challenges man to love his neighbor. This is the only commandment, and all the others are but its derivatives.[37] In German idealism revelation tends to be regarded as the one and only concern of the soul.[38] Rosenzweig warns against all mystical enjoyment of revelation.[39] He insists that Schleiermacher's and Fichte's "Being immortal in every moment" is "a mere phrase," that *all* the time must be fulfilled in order that the fruit of eternity may ripen.[40] What he means by the ripe fruit of eternity is the ensouling (*Beseelung*) of the world through love, something analogous to the ensoulment of an object of nature by the artist.[41] By loving what comes our way ("our neighbor"; *der Nächste*), we endow it with soul and life. Each individual waits for the loving response of his fellow men by which alone his individual character can be redeemed from the tragic futility of self-enclosure.[42] The notion of individuality lay at the root of German idealism and historicism and engaged in Rosenzweig's interest already in his student days, when he meant to write a book on "the history of tragic individuality in Germany since Lessing."[43] The kingdom of the world, that is, the natural path of world history, has laws of its own expressed in terms of state and legal order. But they are merely the groundwork of creation from which the Kingdom of God has to emerge. Love is the force that brings about redemption. It creates the Kingdom.

The Kingdom, Rosenzweig emphasizes, is not the result of "progress" as the philosophers of *Aufklärung* (the Enlightenment) suggested. As he remarks in one of his letters (dated 30 May 1917), every progress in the direction of the good entails *pari passu* a corresponding growth of evil: Democracy means both responsibility and release of anarchic power; tolerance means conviction and indifference; Goethe is both Faust and Mephisto.[44] The problematical nature of progress could not have been seen more clearly.[45] Hegel's optimism he had discarded long ago. "Why should we be in need of God if history were God-like, if every deed, once it entered history, became *ipso facto* God-like and justifiable?" No, he says, every human deed is liable to become sinful precisely after it has entered history and has become part of it, since through the interrelation of acts in history no act is merely personal but is caught up in an impersonal nexus of cause and effect beyond the control and intention of the doer. For this reason God must redeem man not through history but—there is no alternative—through religion.[46] Rosenzweig rejects the ideology of progress for yet another reason. Revelation, he says in *The Star of Redemption,* is the ground and source of the Kingdom. In revelation eternity breaks into time, and it is this element of eternity that defies any attempt to account for the coming of the Kingdom in terms of a continuous, linear time-process. Eternity in the sense of the Kingdom is the fullness and totality of all the single moments in which revelation is experienced.[47] Eternity, he says in another place, is "not a very long time but a tomorrow which could equally be a today." It is the dimension of the Kingdom. "A being that has once entered into the Kingdom can never drop out of it; it has become eternal."[48] The rapturous words "But we are eternal," which Hermann Cohen uttered at the end of his last lecture,[49] and which Rosenzweig quotes at the end of his chapter on redemption,[50] are understood by him in this sense. Eternity, in Cohen's original meaning, was "an ethical concept," the "eternity of the progress of moral endeavour," "the orientation (*Blickpunkt*) for the restless, infinite striving of the pure will": "eternity means the eternal task, the task of eternity."[51] Rosenzweig himself re-echoes this concept during the period prior to his writing *The Star*, when he describes the ethical deed as determined by the infinite and unconditional, and as acted as if the fate of eternity depended on it.[52] But in *The Star of Redemption* eternity is more than the horizon of the ethical. It is the triumph of redemption over death, man's glorious release from his temporal existence,[53] the reality of the Kingdom.[54]

The eternity of the Kingdom implies a paradox: it is both presentness, the "eternalizing of the moment"[55] and future, being "eternally on its way."[56] Rosenzweig defines it as "a future which without ceasing to be future is nevertheless present."[57] It grows but the time required for its growth is not determined; more precisely, its growth has no relation at all to time.[58] For "eternity consists in this that no time is allowed between the present moment and the end, but the future is already seized today."[59] It is characteristic of the eschatological future that the end must be expected any moment. This constitutes its eternity. "That every moment may be the last makes it eternal."[60] Nothing, Rosenzweig says, is more objectionable to the ideology of progress than this notion that the ideal goal may be reached at the next, nay at the present, moment instead of as the result of an infinite progress in time.[61] Yet this is the very essence of the Kingdom. It would be wrong to assume that Rosenzweig wishes to deny altogether the relevance of time for the growth of the Kingdom. No one is more emphatic than he that time is needed for the growth of the world into the Kingdom. It takes time until man experiences the love of God,[62] and it takes time for the world to come across the fructifying and ensouling love of man. God alone knows the hour. He has given the world the law of its autonomous growth.

His revelation calls forth the response of love. Redemption issues from Him at the hour of grace.[63] In his essay "The New Thinking," Rosenzweig left no doubt that there is in his view an irreversible order of time in every single happening and in reality as a whole.[64] Yet for all this there exists, strictly speaking, no history of the Kingdom, only a prehistory of it. Eternity has no history.[65]

In the light of eternity, eschatology itself takes on a new meaning. It is no longer the end of history but the eternity beyond history. And this eternity is presentness and future at the same time. It is a dimension of existence rather than a fixed point to be reached. The "waiting for the Messiah" is not mere passive expectancy but means entering into eternity, living in the Kingdom, and giving birth to the Kingdom. "Das Warten entbindet das Reich aus der Welt."[66] The future ceases to be a historical category. It no longer denotes a time to come but the Kingdom to come. Future, the Kingdom, and eternity become synonymous terms in Rosenzweig's eschatological thinking. They are existential terms, not concepts denoting objective reality. They do not deny and invalidate history. On the contrary, they seek to give meaning to history. Rosenzweig realizes that the meaning of history cannot be spun out of its temporal substance. Historical time is incapable of yielding meaning unless it is related to the horizon of eternity. It is through revelation that eternity penetrates time, fulfilling and redeeming it. In a sense, the *eschaton* is in the present, and eschatology points to the future only in so far as it is realized in the present. In the concept of *kairos* Paul Tillich expresses a similar eschatology.[67]

It might seem that Rosenzweig's interpretation of history as the *locus* of eternity obliterates the distinction between past, present, and future and altogether destroys the character of history as an order of time. Yet this is certainly not his meaning. On the contrary, he emphasizes that it is precisely revelation that "brings an absolute symbolical order into history."[68] "Revelation is orientation." It establishes not only "a real above and below" but also "a real and firm before and after in time." It means the *Verabsolutierung* of time and creates an "absolute history."[69] What Rosenzweig intends to convey by these metaphysical notions is this: Through the irruption of revelation, history receives a clear and definite articulation.

What lies before revelation is paganism and what flows from it is redemption. Moreover, revelation orientates our historical perspective by offering an absolute standard of what is truly meaningful in history. It "creates the stage and content of world history." Neither Plato nor Aristotle knew anything like this. The terms "the end of days" and "the whole earth" are missing from their vocabulary.[70] "Only for Jews and Christians exists that firm orientation of the world in space and time, exists the real world and the real history."[71] Rosenzweig repudiates Troeltsch's *Historismus,* which equalizes all historical phenomena and speaks of the "nations of the Christian *Kulturkreis* [cultural sphere]," a term that obliterates the distinctiveness of revelation.[72] "Jews, Greeks and Romans will remain the eternal content of history." For they are the figures in which revelation and its counterfoil appear on the stage of history. In them history possesses its eternal, classical theme. "The Sumerians, the Accadians will not neutralize Moriah, Marathon, Brutus."[73] "Immortality in history belongs only to what positively or negatively belongs to revelation."[74] Revelation creates an absolute history.

### III

Rosenzweig traveled a long road from his erstwhile preoccupation with German imperial history to his theology of creation, revelation and redemption. What drew him away from purely secular history was not, as Meinecke suggested, a sense of despair arising out of the German collapse of 1918,[75] but, already prior to the war, a deep yearning for eternity, an eschatological urge in which he discovered his Jewishness. From the very start he is troubled by such metaphysical questions as "the origin of evil, God and history."[76] He also moves away from Meinecke's German orientation and develops an interest in universal history. But again, history tends to become mere "material for rambling"; it is to him "neither Hegel's *Gang* nor Ranke's *Mär,*"[77] neither the process of universal reason nor factual story. Clearly, he moves toward a viewpoint outside history itself, toward religion. His antipathy to Hegel grew stronger with the years. In 1918, after reading Fichte's *Die Grundzüge des gegenwärtigen Zeitalters* (The basic characteristics of the present age), he wrote: "The contrast to myself became so fully clear to me. Fichte, like Hegel, is perfectly transparent to me, free from contradictions in detail, but *en bloc* contrary and to be rejected." [78] In another letter from the same time: "I am an anti-Hegelian and anti-Fichtean." [79] Hegel's contemplative approach to history antagonized him. [80] He felt much more akin to Schelling, [81] whose impact on Rosenzweig's view of history is pronounced. Schelling's descriptions of myth and revelation as presenting a necessary process and free history respectively is reflected in Rosenzweig's concept of the relationship between the pagan world of myth and the truly historical world of revelation. [82] Rosenzweig was particularly impressed with Schelling's great Fragment of "The Ages of the World" (*Die Weltalter*) in which the philosophy of the future is announced as one in the form of narrative (*Die künftige Philosophie wird bloss erzählend sein*). [83] What is implied in this statement Rosenzweig elucidates in his essay "The New Thinking." He feels that the method he himself adopted in the second book of *The Star of Redemption* conforms to Schelling's precept. By tracing creation, revelation, and redemption not as pure concepts but as the stages of world history, he had in fact fulfilled Schelling's promise. [84]

In comparing Rosenzweig's concept of history with Hegel's and Schelling's one is struck by a strange anomaly. For all their idealist tendencies, Hegel and Schelling retain in outline the biblical view of history as a field of divine action and providence. Both echo Schiller's famous sentence in which this view is expressed: *"Die Weltgeschichte ist das Weltgericht"* (history is a world court of judgment). [85] As Ernst Benz has shown in a recent study, [86] German idealism reflects in many ways the theological doctrines concerning history that were current among the Swabian Pietists of the eighteenth century. Its eschatological orientation, which was alien to the spirit of *Aufklärung*, derives from here. Hegel's *List der Vernunft* (cunning of reason), which exploits the private egotism of man in the service of universal Reason, is a secularized form of the biblical idea that the rulers of the world are but the instruments of God's providence. In Rosenzweig this biblical heritage is silent. History ceases to be the manifestations of Divine Providence, of Judgment, the dialectic of freedom and necessity. It becomes instead the realm of dialogue, of eternity, of the growing Kingdom. History does not move along with the urge that Providence alone could instill into it. It somehow hovers between time and eternity, and one fails to see how the final day can be reached with the Jew eternally at the goal and the Christian eternally on the way.

The reason that prevented Rosenzweig from introducing Providence into history is the same that enabled Hegel and Schelling to do so. In idealist philosophy history culminates in the complete self-realization of God, the absolute Spirit. In Schelling's words, "The last period is one of complete realization, i.e., the complete humanization (*Menschwerdung*) of God. . . . Then God will be indeed *all in all*, and pantheism will be true."[87] History is a divine process in the sense that in it God realizes himself. The New Testament phrase describing the final day as one in which God the Father will be "all in all" plays a prominent part in German idealism.[88] It has a pantheistic ring—already in Swabian Pietism (F. C. Oetinger) it is interpreted to mean that in the end God will be "all in all *in us*"—and lent itself admirably to an expression of the final goal of the historical process. Providence was introduced into the idealist concept of history at the price of identifying it with the self-realization of God in and through history. Rosenzweig, who was at home with this idealist conception and its antecedents in Christian theology, refused to pay the price they paid. For him God remains wholly outside history. He need not "become," for He "is." He is not identical with the world but stands in relation to it. Providence, therefore, cannot mean the self-realization of God. It means the love of God as expressed in revelation. The eschatological goal within history is the Kingdom. Eschatology in its absolute sense falls outside history. Neither God nor the eternal have a history.[89] God who is the first will also be the last. He will be the *One above all*, not the *One in all*.[90] The final day beyond history belongs to God alone.

# 7

# Franz Rosenzweig and the Crisis of Historicism

*Paul Mendes-Flohr*

I

In the city of Freiburg, in which Rosenzweig pursued his university studies, there is a great medieval cathedral. On either side of the magnificent edifice's portals is a sculptured figure, the one representing the Synagogue, the other the Church. With her head bowed, her eyes blindfolded and scepter broken, the Synagogue stands defeated, bereft of divine grace. Opposite her the Church stands triumphant, a full scepter in her hand, her head erect, and her face wreathed with a serene expression reflecting God's love. In contrast to the theological doctrine that inspired these figures—a doctrine laicized in the historiosophical teachings of Hegel and Schelling [1]— Rosenzweig viewed the historical reality depicted by these figures positively. To be sure, Rosenzweig conceded, since her ignominious exile in 70 C.E. Israel has withdrawn from history and secluded herself from the Gentiles in an exclusive ethnic community stubbornly rejecting Christ's call for a new humanity. But Rosenzweig contended that this aloofness from the world, rather than signifying her spiritual vacuity and historical irrelevance, uniquely allows Israel to anticipate the Messianic Kingdom and the goal of universal history. For in the Diaspora, Israel has reconstituted itself as an *ecclesia* or Synagogue, grounding her existence solely in the preservation of biological continuity and in the prayer service of her liturgical calendar. As such, in terms of both her spiritual imagination and her objective reality, the Synagogue is free of the dialectical contradictions of history as they are manifest in the institution of the state and the attendant quest for political power and need to wage war. As a prefiguration of the messianic community, the Synagogue serves the Church as a "mute admonisher," [2] reminding the Church that history, in which her mission to the pagans perforce involves her, is but a necessary byway in the journey of humankind to truth and the *eschaton*. Unable to ignore the Synagogue—an eschatological reference in the midst of time—the Church is challenged to retain the pristine clarity of its mission to bring redemption to the world. Hence, precisely because of its ahistoricity and exclusivity, the Synagogue assures that both the Church *and* history will have a goal and supreme purpose. [3]

This ecclesiological presentation of Judaism as "a nation of priests" living proleptically within messianic time is generally understood as an inspired apologia for "the a-historical nature of Judaism." [4] Accordingly, Rosenzweig's conception of history "as a provisional, temporary affair," [5] is believed prompted by his need to overcome the embarrassment engendered in him by the image of the defeated Synagogue before the triumphant Church. I should like to suggest that Rosenzweig's conception of history—and Israel's role within history—has a broader context, namely, the so-called crisis of historicism that occurred in the first decades of this century. Specifically, I argue that Rosenzweig's conception of a necessary dialectic between metahistory and history emerged from a protracted struggle—which considerably preceded his affirmation of Judaism—with the question of meaning in history and the dilemma of historical relativism.

## II

As Rosenzweig tells us in his diaries, he turned to the study of history in order to overcome his incorrigible, debilitating skepticism. History, the nineteen-year-old Rosenzweig wrote, would render his skepticism productive, for the historian requires a scrutinizing, critical disposition. Moreover, the study of history would oblige him to distinguish his self from the world. History, he writes, "means to become 'more pluralistic,' for the subject is singular, the object plural." [6]

The study of history, however, did not rescue Rosenzweig from his skepticism. About a year after his decision to become a historian he summarized epigrammatically his initial impressions of the discipline: "People of the past did not live consciously as we do; they did not know whether they were living in the 5th or 4th century B.C." [7] History gives one consciousness of one's position in time and, if we may extrapolate, consciousness of one's position to truth. History relativizes.

Not insignificantly, Rosenzweig began his historical studies as the "crisis of historicism" was beginning to take shape. In the winter semester of 1908 he went to the University of Freiburg to study with two of the leading protagonists in the debate over the meaningfulness of history, Heinrich Rickert and Friedrich Meinecke. The former has been frequently referred to, albeit somewhat erroneously, as "the father of historical relativism." [8] Although he heatedly rejected what he deemed to be a dubious honor, this philosopher of historical method undeniably fostered relativism with his concept of *Wertbezogenheit*—values as they are manifest in history are not timeless, but are culturally bound. It is the task of the historian, Rickert taught, to ascertain the values of a particular society and to determine the relation of these values to its cultural history. Rickert held that methodologically such an approach was justified, but he readily admitted—as early as 1904—that should it be elevated to a *Weltanschauung* it would be "a monstrous thing [*Unding*], a form of relativism and scepticism" that carried to its logical conclusions can lead only to complete nihilism. [9] In the diaries from his student years Rosenzweig often debated with Rickert; in one instance, he declared, "values should be rescued from history as well as from the natural sciences: space and time are coffins." [10]

When Rosenzweig came to Freiburg, Meinecke had just published his monumental *Weltbürgertum und Nationalstaat* (*Cosmopolitanism and the Nation State*).[11] Rosenzweig was thoroughly enamored of Meinecke the teacher and of his book. He shared his enthusiasm with his mother, to whom he wrote: "Meinecke more than pleases me"; "I would give ten years of my life to write such a book [as *Weltbürgertum und Nationalstaat*]." [12] Rosenzweig's doctoral dissertation (later published as *Hegel und der Staat*, with the assistance of Rickert), was inspired by a chapter in Meinecke's magnum opus.[13] Appropriately, Rosenzweig dedicated his study to Meinecke. Methodologically, Meinecke's work had a twofold significance. In it he introduced the new concept of *Ideengeschichte*—the treatment of ideas as inseparable from the lives in which they take shape and the institutions that they affect—and the use of this method to strengthen the view of history known as ethical historicism.[14] Starting with Herder, the predominant tendency in German thought was to attribute a positive ethical significance to the unfolding of history. The emergence and retrenchment of the particularistic nation-state, however, seemed to contradict the cosmopolitan ethical vision expressed by so many of Germany's leading spirits. In *Weltbürgertum und Nationalstaat*, Meinecke sought to demonstrate that the existence of the nation-state was consistent with this vision and, indeed, may be regarded as the most effective setting for the realization of universal human values.[15]

In the midst of the horror, death and myopic nationalism wrought by the First World War, Meinecke's ethical historicism weakened considerably, although he continued to resist relativistic conclusions.[16] Even before the war, Rosenzweig began to doubt his teacher's faith. In a long letter of 4 August 1909 to his cousin Hans Ehrenberg (1893–1958), Rosenzweig contends that a genuine intellectual history of the German Reich should also consider what he cumbersomely called the *Allzeitmehrerdesreich-Politik*—the compulsively expansionist policy of the Reich. He is certain such an inquiry will indicate that although "not at all apparent [at its founding] the German *Reich* was already more than merely one nation beside other nations, more than a body that sought *suum esse conservare* and nothing else, even if the *Imperium* was [viewed] only in cultural terms. *Von der 'Kultur' zur 'Kanone' ist ein kleiner Schritt.*" Indeed, at the very outset of his studies at Freiburg he was puzzled by his teacher's indifference to the brutal, violent aspects of political history. Writing to Ehrenberg several weeks into the first semester of study with Meinecke, Rosenzweig ironically observed that he takes down every word of the celebrated historian's lectures because they are "madly beautiful. He treats history as though it were a Platonic dialogue and not murder and killing, [as though it were only] oil-colors, rhyme, dissonance, book-prefaces and obeissance."[17]

Rosenzweig concluded that contemporary German academic culture, girded by a superficial self-confidence and narrow professionalism, was the desiccated legacy of the nineteenth century.[18] He shared these sentiments with other young historians and philosophers who met at Baden-Baden in January 1910 to found a society "to realize 1900 as distinctly different from 1800."[19] They were determined, as Alexander Altmann has noted, to retrieve the ripe achievements of the previous century (social progress, the historical view of the world, nationalism, the scientific attitude) for the twentieth century, "so as to possess them no longer as mere objects of a struggle but as elements of a new civilization."[20] This new civilization would be prompted by an approach best described as neo-Hegelian: "Contemporary culture would be made the subject of contemplation."[21] From the historical perspective and objectivity obtained thereby, the proposed society hoped to forge a new subjectivity, not a mere consciousness of one's own subjectivity (as the nineteenth century sought), but rather a consciousness of the self qua subject of the *Zeitgeist*.[22] Furthermore, historical consciousness of the present will provide men with a new unity, not the false unity of Bismarck's Reich or of Wagner's Bayreuth festivals. In the unity that Rosenzweig and his friends wished to foster one will cease to worship one's "private God," for he "will find himself more or less objectively conscious of the time, and herein one will revere something greater, the God who reveals Himself in measure in the here and now."[23]

The society envisioned by the Baden-Baden conference failed to materialize. In Rosenzweig's case at least, this failure was accompanied (if not prompted) by a disaffectation with Hegel's religious "intellectualism." In a letter of 26 September 1910 to Hans Ehrenberg, Rosenzweig declares that Hegel had erred in ascribing to history an ontological status. History is not the unfolding of Being, rather it is but the discrete act of men (*Tat der Täter*). "We see God in every ethical event, but not in one complete Whole, not in history." Indeed, history that takes shape in the phenomenal world cannot serve as a vessel for divinity. "Every human act becomes sinful as it enters history"; although the actors intended otherwise, the morality of an act is neutralized by the material world of necessity.[24] We are hence left with only one possible conclusion: God redeems man not through history but—"es bleibt nichts anders übrig"— through religion.[25]

This is not a statement of faith, but a philosophical proposition, a logical deduction. Rosenzweig would adopt a living religious faith only after his later encounter with the testimony of faith given by a coparticipant in the Baden-Baden conference, Eugen Rosenstock. The two friends, both historians with broad philosophical concerns, for several months engaged in an intense, nigh-daily dialogue that culminated in Rosenzweig's acceptance of Rosenstock's *Offenbarungsglaube*—faith based on revelation, revelation as a historical fact and as ever-renewed possibility.[26] Recalling the momentous summer evening in 1913, Rosenzweig wrote: "In that night's conversation Rosenstock pushed me step by step out of the last relativistic position that I still occupied, and forced me to take an absolute standpoint. I was inferior to him from the outset, since I had to recognize the justice of his attack. . . . Any form of relativism is now impossible to me."[27] Rosenzweig became a man of faith.

The themes of Rosenzweig and Rosenstock's extensive dialogue of 1913 undoubtedly varied, but they seemed to have focused on the sterility of the scholarship of their own generation and the untenability of maintaining an "irresponsible, neutral academic attitude which precludes personal involvement, feelings of shame, embarrassment and hope."[28] Their deliberations on these issues were accompanied by a profound awareness that what one holds to be "objectively true at the moment is conditioned by time and history, and that perfect objectivity is simply not possible."[29] Thus not only are "the Academic shibboleths of their day" futile, but when dealing with ultimate ontological questions, one is doomed to perplexity and frustration.[30]

*Offenbarungsglaube* was presented by Rosenstock as the way beyond the impasse. How Rosenstock at that time understood revelation may be surmised from letters written by Rosenzweig several months after his "conversion" to religious faith. In these letters Rosenzweig explains that revelation is not a mere postulate of reason but a historical fact, and therefore we may understand that what happens in history is not merely a struggle between man's faith and man's reason, but a struggle between God and man. Revelation breaks into the world and transforms creation, which is the Alpha of history, into redemption, which is the Omega.[31] Revelation, as Rosenzweig was to write a bit later, is a "historical-cum-meta-historical concept";[32] revelation impinges upon history and gives it direction. This conception of revelation was elaborated in his famous epistolary debate with Rosenstock during the World War.[33] In that debate Rosenstock defined revelation as orientation. "After revelation there exists a real Above and Below in the world, and a real Before and Hereafter in time. In the 'natural' world and in 'natural' time the point where I happen to be is the center of the universe; in the space-time world of revelation the center is fixed, and my movements and changes do not alter it."[34] This formulation particularly appealed to Rosenzweig, who soon related it to the problem of historicism: historical relativism and the question of meaning in history. For the "pagan"—or the individual who seeks to grasp reality on the basis of natural understanding alone—there is, according to Rosenzweig, a confounding multiplicity of worlds and possibilities, innumerable contingencies, goals and values. For the Jew and the Christian, on the other hand, reality is anchored "in the exemplary fact"—"revelation, which establishes an Above and Below, a Europe and Asia, an earlier and a later, past and future. . . . [Through revelation] the world is ordered. It is no longer everywhere and nowhere, but it has calculus; one knows the goal." The Word resounds through time and the Name penetrates "the chaos of the unnamed [that is, unordered] world," thereby creating "the stage and content of world history."[35]

The very first essay Rosenzweig wrote after his affirmation of faith and Judaism relates the concept of revelation to history. In "Atheistic Theology," written in 1914 just prior to the outbreak of the World War, Rosenzweig freely uses terms characteristic of the crisis of historicism. He refers to "the critical science of history" as "an illness"; he speaks of "the killing force of history," "the temporality of the historical process," "the phenomena of the past . . . [regarded as] dead matter," "the curse of historicity."[36] In the essay, which was actually only published posthumously, Rosenzweig incisively criticizes modern historical theology for having capitulated to the canons and assumptions of critical scholarship, and having, accordingly, reduced religious teachings and principles to human, historical terms. Behind this exercise to render theology amenable to modern historical sensibility, Rosenzweig discerns a contempt for the concept of revelation. But the elimination of revelation from theology is tantamount to endorsing atheism. To be sure, Rosenzweig observes, if man were self-sufficient and free of self-contradiction he could then "dispense with God." But, alas, "Man now finds himself under the curse of historicity"—he knows himself to be living in unfulfilled time and despairs of history's inner capacity to fulfill itself: "Man is thus unable to eliminate the God to whom by His historic deed [i.e., revelation] the historicity of history is subject."[37]

### III

As it was for other world views, the World War was a veritable purgatory for historicism, deepening its votaries' sense of crisis. Rosenzweig emerged from the war greatly confirmed in his conviction that history cannot generate its own meaning. In the first years of war, however, he actually maintained a restrained optimism that the war would quicken *historical* forces that would in fact render history meaningful.

In a frequently quoted letter of October 1916 to his cousin Hans Ehrenberg, Rosenzweig claims to be utterly indifferent to the war:

The War itself has not caused any break in my inner life. In 1913 I had experienced so much that the year 1914 would have had to produce nothing short of the world's final collapse to make an impression on me. . . . Thus I have experienced the War, I have nothing to do with it. . . . I carry my life through the War like Cervantes his poem.[38]

Notwithstanding this protestation, Rosenzweig remained acutely involved in the war, as is witnessed by his correspondence during these years, several pseudonymous articles on *Kriegspolitik,* and an unpublished monograph on the significance of the war for universal history.

Implicit in these writings on the war is a historical perspective known as Johannine eschatology. Reaching back to Lessing, Fichte, Hegel and Schelling, this perspective was recurrent in German idealism. Schelling concludes his lectures on the *Philosophy of Revelation* with the words, "If I had to build a church in our time, I would dedicate it to Saint John."[39] Peter is the apostle of the Father, Paul of the Son, and John of the Holy Spirit. "John represents the Church of a free, undogmatic Christianity. This concept of a progressive spiritualism of Christianity is a modern, secularized version of the revolutionary doctrine of the three Churches which was first propounded by Joachim of Fiore, the twelfth-century abbot."[40] The eschatological hopes that German idealists associated with the Johannine form of Christianity were resonated anew by Rosenzweig and several other participants in the Baden-Baden conference of 1910—Rosenstock, Hans and Rudolf Ehrenberg—who together with others had founded in 1915 an informal group known as the Patmos circle.[41] Having presentiments of an imminent collapse of Western civilization, they shared, according to the testimony of Rosenstock, the sense of loneliness and vision of another age, felt by John when he wrote the Book of Revelation on the island of Patmos.[42] Rosenzweig apparently endorsed the view that humankind is approaching the conclusion of the second age—conceived as the unification of space, both geographically and technologically—and that we are on the threshold of the third, the Johannine Age—the Age of the Spirit, which is dedicated to the creation and preservation of *the* truly human society. Although this theme is only implicit in the writings we shall consider, it is important that we keep it in mind, lest we construe these writings as mere metaphysical adornment for Rosenzweig's German patriotism. His one explicit reference to the war in Johannine terms may serve as a summary introduction to these writings. In an entry to his diary on 14 January 1916, Rosenzweig observed that "the Johannine transformation of the Church brought about by the Enligtenment, has only become apparent in *this* war which embraces all of the Christian world and which is leading to supra-Christian politics."[43]

In 1917 Rosenzweig published two essays, one following the other, in the *Archiv für exakte Wissenschaft,* a journal edited by his uncle, Richard Ehrenberg, a professor of law at the University of Leipzig. The first essay, "Realpolitik," appeared under the name "Dr. Adam Bund (*im Felde*)"; the second, "Nordwest und Sudost," was signed "Macedonicus (*im Felde*)."[44] Rosenzweig undoubtedly intended that these essays be read together, the themes echoing each other in a sort of counterpoint. Writing from the Macedonian front, where he served in an antiaircraft unit, Rosenzweig argues that the war has engendered geopolitical tendencies that, if properly seized by Germany's leadership, should inspire the nation to transcend its narrow, self-centered interests and join its destiny to that of the world. The war has confronted Germany with a "world-historical mission,"[45] but to realize it the regnant political policy will have to be summarily discarded. *Realpolitik,* which served Bismarck so well in creating a united Germany, is no longer appropriate. Bismarck's policy, Rosenzweig emphasized, was adapted to the historical exigencies posed by his appointed task; but his epigones have celebrated *Realpolitik* as an absolute, sacrosanct value. This has left German politics in disarray, void of clarity and purpose, and ill prepared for the historical challenge borne by the war.

In pursuit of its world-historical mission, Germany must, Rosenzweig pleaded, reject both "the calculating cunning" of *Realpolitik* and the temptation to a spiteful jingoism.[46] This mission has become manifest with the emergence of a north-west–south-east axis of geopolitical configurations now governing Germany's history. This axis, which runs from Antwerp to Suez, has replaced the former north-east–south-west axis that determined the formation of Bismarck's Reich. The new axis confronts Germany's leadership with the dilemma of turning north-west and pursuing an imperialistic policy of annexation or turning south-east, to central Europe and beyond, in the spirit of political and cultural cooperation. The latter prospect, in Rosenzweig's opinion, has world-historical implications, for it promises a significant German contribution to the creation of an authentic cosmopolitan culture, the integration of Germany into the common historical destiny of the world.

In a long, until recently unpublished monograph entitled "Globus: Studien zur weltgeschichtlichen Raumlehre,"[47] Rosenzweig sought to place these thoughts in the perspective of a comprehensive analysis of world history and the development of political community through its various stages, from the *imperium Romanum* to the formation of the principal nation-states engaged in the current war. After apparently long and arduous gestation, the first and longest part of the monograph was completed in January 1917. In this part, entitled "Ökumene: Weltstaat und Staatenwelt," Rosenzweig provides a systematic analysis of Meinecke's thesis about the historical nature of the modern nation-state, albeit he does not explicitly refer to Meinecke. Employing his teacher's method of examining the interplay between ideas and political reality, but using a broader world-historical canvas than was Meinecke's wont, Rosenzweig seeks to delineate the salient dialectical tensions in Western political history. These tensions, according to Rosenzweig, first took shape in the Holy Roman Empire where there was a dialectical affiliation, but not identity, between the mundane (national) and the spiritual (universal) concerns of the Christian *Ökumene*. This dialectic was weakened by the rise of the absolute state in the sixteenth century. Henceforth, throughout Europe the decisions of government became more strictly national and secular. The regnant concept of corpus Christianum was eclipsed as a guiding principle of government. Machiavelli's focus on the dynamics of *Realpolitik* captured the new mood. By 1800, Rosenzweig observes, every state of Europe was solely interested in securing its own well-being and power. The old imperial-cum-religious notion of a world government was tacitly renounced. Inevitably, the ascendancy of the principle of *Realpolitik* increased the political antagonism between states. The first war to involve the new system, the Seven Years' War, also witnessed the emergence of the future political antagonists of Europe, Russia, Austria, England, France and Prussia. The emergence of Prussia as a major power was almost totally unanticipated. More significantly, Prussia introduced a new concept of the state, which restored the spiritual element to government. This is expressed in Fichte's ideal of the nation-state in the service of world history. The articulation of this concept was occasioned by the struggle against Napoleon; hence the Prussian ideal of the nation-state may be viewed as the true, dialectical significance of the French Revolution. Moreover, being coterminous with an ethnic community, the nation-state as conceived by the philosophers of Prussia represents a deepening of the democratic principles of the French Revolution. For the nation-state understands itself as primarily representing its constituent *Volk*—a primordial *demos* with its own historic needs and destiny. Thus, by seeking to resonate with the deepest aspirations of the *Volk,* the nation-state is governed by the profoundly democratic and ethical principle of the *volonté generale* (general will). The state has ceased to be guided by the overriding imperatives of political power. Rosenzweig refers to this view of national politics, which was soon adopted by most European states, as the ensouling (*Beseelung*) of the state concept.

Rosenzweig's discussion of the Prussian conception of the nation-state is largely a restatement of Meinecke's thesis. But now he proceeds to note two basic contradictions in the nation-state that dialectically negate its ethical, universal character. In practice the nation-state, he observes, is superimposed upon the "scaffold" of multiethnic societies, obliging the government of the nation-state to heed the capricious, pragmatic, and superficially democratic *volonté de tous* (will of all). Second, the nation-state, especially as it evolved in Germany, understands its role as the protector and provider of its constituent or rather dominant *Volk*. This is in contradistinction to "the [Western] democratic concept of citizenship which makes the citizen a responsible co-worker in the mechanism of government." Ideally, the nation-state with its exclusive focus on the deeper needs of its people was not to be as aggressive as the old *Machtstaat* with its singular concern for power and borders. But in actuality, animated by the desire to extend its protection to its ethnic diaspora and irredenta, Germany, for one, pursued an imperialistic *Realpolitik*. Especially after the Congress of Berlin in 1878, Germany, together with the other major powers of Europe, engaged in secret diplomacy and imperialistic intrigues, a policy that ineluctably led to the World War.

How is one to ascertain the significance of the war? Rosenzweig queries. As a criterion he introduces the Hegelian concept of the world historical: Will the war—and indirectly, the institutions, namely, the nation-state, and the processes that contributed to it—further the realization of the goal of world history? Rosenzweig established this goal to be the creation of a unified world, a *Weltstaat* and not a *Staatenwelt*. "Die Grenzlosigkeit [ist] der Erde letztes Ziel" (the absence of boundaries is the world's ultimate goal). Clearly the present war does not seem to be leading to the realization of this goal. None of the imperialistic antagonists has a genuine understanding of the ecumenical imperium that world history calls for. At the most the war will beget the establishment of a world organization—apparently he was thinking of the League of Nations—but this will not constitute a real unity or genuine *Ökumene*. Yet Rosenzweig concludes the essay on a hopeful note, elliptically suggesting that there may yet be a favorable turn in events: "One speaks of the eternally separate spheres of culture. I do not believe this. For God, of whom it is written that he is a warrior, created only one heaven and one earth."

Upon completion of this, the first part of his monograph, Rosenzweig sent a copy to Rosenstock.[48] His friend responded critically, decrying the essay on methodological grounds: it was too scholarly, too erudite, and, worse, historistic. Rosenstock accused Rosenzweig of writing history as a nineteenth-century historian, recording the past "wie es eigentlich gewesen" (as it really was). Rosenzweig profusely apologized to Rosenstock, admitting to these violations of their pact against the academic nihilism of their generation.[49] He also agreed that his scholarly approach obscured the essay's real questions and answers. He thus sought to reformulate for Rosenstock and the presuppositions of the essay in a clearer, more direct manner: There are developments that are presently unfolding in "our and God's earth" which must find expression in the writings of the war and in the "border treaties" that will mark its conclusion. It must then be asked what is the relationship between imperialism and the establishment of a genuine imperium. To be sure, imperialism as a political phenomenon seems to vitiate any hope of new world order, but surely we must acknowledge that the war has manifestly indicated that the "soul" of the imperium has acquired new life: "This soul exists today as pure soul, an *Ökumene* neither of the pope nor of the emperor, nor of some constitutional organization, but as an Idea. Here is the beginning of eternal life. . . . This pure spirit is clothed anew in flesh . . . and resurrected in the [new] ecumenical politics: 1914." Despite contradictory evidence, we are—Rosenzweig affirms—"experiencing the beginning," indeed if we properly understand the extensive implications of current political events, we may say "even a full beginning."[50]

In December 1917 Rosenzweig wrote a supplement to "Ökumene," hoping to render his thesis more lucid and credible.[51] This supplement—entitled "Thalatta: Seeherrschaft und Meeresfreiheit" (Thalatta: Domination and freedom of the seas)—will, as Rosenzweig wrote to Hans Ehrenberg, clearly indicate how he has parted from the methods of nineteenth-century historiography. In contradistinction to Ranke, for instance, Rosenzweig does not regard history as "a curve between the coordinates of time and the *soul*"; that is, unlike Ranke he does not seek to lead his subject back to its psychological underpinnings. Rosenzweig prefers to regard history as "a curve between the coordinates of time and *space*." "The curve between time and the soul," he writes, "yields but the *Geist*, my curve yields the *movement* of history." Rosenzweig concludes his letter to his cousin by elliptically noting that Ranke's approach amounts to "a glorification of history, whereas for me history is a naked fact which frees beliefs [*Glauben*] from their dependence on history."[52] Presumably Rosenzweig wishes to say that by grounding history ultimately in immanent psychic factors, Ranke implies that history is its own justification. On the other hand, Rosenzweig's emphasis on the movement or the dialectical tendencies of history points to its open-ended possibilities, and thus nothing in history is inevitably so—that is to asy, if we understand Rosenzweig correctly, a belief in history as bearing inherent justice and meaning is naïve, if not dangerous: history may or may not be the *Weltgericht.* For it is up to us to direct the dialectic of history: history presents us with opportunities and challenges, *c'est tout.* This statement of the theoretical presuppositions of his writings on the world-historical significance of the war allows us a clearer understanding of his restrained optimism during the first three years of that great conflagration. The war has given rise to new dialectical possibilities, confronting Germany—and not her alone—with a world-historical challenge and mission. This is the explicit theme of his essay "Thalatta," the supplement to the essay "Ökumene." [53]

"Thalatta," "the sea" was the inebriated cry of Xenophon's troops who after years of wandering reached the Aegean waters leading homeward to Hellas. This cry served the essay as its seminal metaphor. From time immemorial the sea has either intimidated man because of its "yawning chaos" or has beckoned man to conquer it. World history has been determined by the latter movement, for the seas of the world ultimately flow one into another, endowing the world with a continuity and unity. That unity is our home. *Thalatta*—the sea, homeward.

The transformation of the world into an *Ökumene* can thus be traced through the evolving history of the conquests of the sea and the concomitant evolution of man's conception of the world, his *Weltbild.* Accordingly, Rosenzweig delineated as highpoints of history's thrust toward an *Ökumene,* inter alia the Greek conquest of the Aegean Sea, the Roman conquest of the Mediterranean and the coastal waters of Spain, and England and Islam's conquest of the Indian Ocean. The great breakthrough, however, came with Christopher Columbus and his determination "to sail *around* the world." Columbus thus commenced a decisive chapter in world history—a chapter that perhaps may reach its glorious culmination in the current World War. For surely, the present struggle between the contending powers for domination of the world's seas transcends the small-minded imperialistic aims prompting the conflict.

The battle of the seas is a struggle of world-historical significance, for it potentially implicates all of humankind; dialectically, such a worldwide struggle might affect a consciousness of a shared universal destiny and the creation of a genuine *Ökumene.* From this perspective, the World War is strategically a war over Africa because that great continent constitutes the crucial link of all "the world-historical seas and thereby the world." The imperialistic-colonial motives are irrelevant because history is determined by "unforeseen results": "Letztes Kriegsziel und letzter Kriegsgrund sind stets eins." The ultimate fruition of the war's dialectical possibilities, however, is contingent, in the first instance, on the eventual entrance into the fray of Japan and the United States. (We recall that this essay was written in December 1917.) But Rosenzweig despairs of this eventuality. Neither of these powers seems to have any inclination to appreciate the challenge of world history. The United States, a young and immature power, is too self-centered; Japan, an ancient and sapient power, is too circumspect. And without Japan's and the United States's participation, the war cannot be said to be truly a *world* war. The decision of these two powers to isolate themselves from the conflict proves that the earth—although it is universally recognized to be geographically a "globe"—"is still not actually a sphere (*Kugel*)"—that is, an uninterrupted circuit in which all particulars cohere into one continuous unity. The work of the great seafaring explorers da Gama, Columbus and Magellan has still to reach completion. "To be sure," Rosenzweig says in the peroration to his essay, "the waters around Africa's three coasts flow one into the other forming one sea. But the dry land of the earth has yet to be unified. Humankind has still to reach home, and Europe is not yet the soul of the world."

These last lines betray an incipient loss of faith in the war and its world-historical significance. It is important to recall that Rosenzweig began to write the essay "Thalatta" in the latter part of December 1917, completing it perhaps in January 1918. By this date the historical situation had begun to change rapidly. First was the dismissal in July 1917 of Bethmann-Hollweg, the moderate and cautious but nonetheless patriotic Reichskanzler whom Rosenzweig had extolled as the one German leader who grasped the world-historical significance of the war.[54] Upon Bethmann's departure from office and his replacement by a civilian puppet of the German Military High Command, Rosenzweig wrote to his parents that he was stunned: "Ich bein trostlos"—"I am inconsolable." Whatever reservations one may have had about Bethmann's weak leadership, his dismissal, Rosenzweig contends, signals Germany's "renunciation of its future."[55] In another letter to Rosenstock, he bewailed the turn of events, for he was convinced that it would lead to "the rule of the Hindenbergs and Ludendorffs."[56] Less than a year later, in May 1918, he notes that his worst premonitions were confirmed.[57] The clique that replaced Bethmann had for all intents and purposes transferred power to the kaiser and the German High Command, and *Realpolitik* reigned unchecked. As a result, Germany was rendered a technologically all-powerful but politically impotent nation. Further, the war "over Africa" was taking an unfavorable direction. And to compound matters, by the spring of 1918 the military position of Germany and its central European allies took a decided turn for the worse. By the time the United States entered the war in earnest, in the late spring and summer of 1918, Rosenzweig seems to have relinquished his faith in war as a unique and promising dialectic moment in history. The world-historical hour had been lost. In April 1918 Rosenzweig wrote to Hans Ehrenberg that he, Rosenzweig, a Jew has firm knowledge only of the Synagogue's proleptic residence in the Kingdom, whereas the *Zwischenreich*—the realm of time, placed in the charge of the Church, through which the peoples of the world must march before reaching the Kingdom—remains for him problematic. This realm, of course, is coterminous with world history. He tellingly adds: "for me God alone is reality; I am a member of the intermediate realm by the compulsion of nature (= history), not by free will."[58]

This shift in his mood is reflected in the preface Rosenzweig appended to the proposed booklet "Globus," which would couple the two essays "Ökumene" and "Thalatta."[59] In the preface, probably written in early 1918, Rosenzweig asked whether history alone has the power to realize its goal of obtaining a unified world polity (*Weltstaat*). The question and its answer are presented in the form of an allegory. That allegory plays with the images—"ökumene" and "thalatta"—of the essays it introduces. Here in the allegory Rosenzweig establishes a tension between the two, with *thalatta* serving *ökumene* as a regulative principle. In the essays themselves this theme is only vaguely expressed, and perhaps only with the perspective of the preface. But more significant, in the essays the image of *thalatta* is emphatically a historical principle, namely, an image denoting the historical conquest of the seas that circumscribe and potentially unite the world, whereas in the preface *thalatta* and *ökumene* are both purely regulative, metahistorical principles.

World history, Rosenzweig tells us in his allegorical preface, is the process of defining space, of drawing boundaries, "demarcating a parcel of land and the definition of mine, yours and his." The rest of world history is but the extension of that first border, "with an ever renewed interweaving of mine, yours and his; and, dialectically, the ever more inclusive shaping of I and Thou relations out of the undifferentiated chaos of the It." Just as the first bounded I of history leads to the first bounded We of history, the unbounded We at the end of history will correspond to the unbounded deepening of the I, which will mark the last moment of history. But the earth (*die Erde*), Rosenzweig continues, by its very nature knows but borders and boundaries. That which inspires the earth to eliminate borders and boundaries between men necessarily lies beyond the earth, namely, the sea. "In the sea nature presents to man the image of unity which should inspire him in his daily work to create unity upon the shore." As long as the image of the sea remains in view, shore-bound man will be ever dissatisfied with his existence on the divisive, boundaried earth. But should we lose sight of the sea and myopically regard the existent earth as the ultimate reality, we will be gripped by a cynical despair, estranging us from our historical task. Only the call of "thalatta, thalatta"—the sea, the sea—which to the ancient Greeks meant home, destiny—can inspire man to redeem history.[60] Thus concludes the allegory. Its message rings clear: History must have an extrahistorical reference to realize its eschatological destiny.

IV

In *The Star of Redemption* the call of *thalatta* will be assigned to the Synagogue—the embodiment of eternity and the promise of redemption. It is striking to observe that here in the allegorical preface to "Globus," no reference is made to Judaism. It may be argued, however, that behind the image of *thalatta* Rosenzweig may have had in mind the image of the Synagogue. For already in several lectures from 1913, and later in his 1916 correspondence with Rosenstock, Rosenzweig refers to the image of the Defeated Synagogue as being beyond history, yet serving it.[61] There, however, the Synagogue serves history in a purely theological capacity; as a reminder to the Church, which has entered history in order to transform and elevate pagan sensibility, most refinely expressed in philosophical culture, by infusing it with the Word of God. Without the Synagogue, however, the Church faces the danger of debasing the Word so as to accommodate pagan sensibility and philosophy. The Synagogue reminds the Church of its mission to teach the pagan world that Truth ultimately comes from God and not from the natural mind. But in *The Star of Redemption,* the Synagogue's metahistorical posture will be construed as "messianic politics."[62]

Before turning our attention to *The Star,* we should conclude our consideration of Rosenzweig's struggle with historicism in the crucible of the war by examining the preface of his dissertation, *Hegel und der Staat,* which he prepared for publication during the first years of the war, but did not publish until 1920. In the preface he declares that the book was written with the hope of checking, in a modest way, the parochial tendencies then regnant in the state created by Bismarck. The Hegelian concept of the state,

which became the dominant concept in the foregoing century and which "like a bolt of lightning from the clouds" appeared on 18 January 1871 [i.e., with the founding of the Second Reich] as a world-historical fact— this idea as it unfolds in the life [of Hegel] was to place before the eyes of the reader the internal and external propsects of Germany's auspicious future [*eine nach innen wie aussen geräumigere deutsche Zukunft*].[63]

These prospects, Rosenzweig laconically notes in his preface of 1920, were, alas, not realized. "A field of ruins marks the place where formerly the *Reich* stood."[64]

To a circle of friends, Rosenzweig is reported to have said: "We believed we were on the threshold of a new beginning, and we experienced an *ancien régime*" ("Wir glaubten an einem Anfang zu stehen and haben in einem Ancien Régime gelebt").[65] This surely was a profound disappointment for Rosenzweig. The critical question, of course, is whether his conviction that a world-historical hour had been missed effected his view of history. It may be held that the glorification in *The Star of Redemption* of Israel's separation from the wiles and hazards of politics and world history is indicative of Rosenzweig's rejection of history. In support of this thesis it may be noted that with the conclusion of the war and the completion of *The Star,* Rosenzweig devoted himself to deepening his relationship to the Synagogue as a student of its sacred texts, as a man of prayer, and as a teacher of his fellow Jews. The intensity and nigh exclusivity of his involvement with Judaism is witnessed by his declining the prestigious position as a university lecturer that Meinecke had arranged for him. To a baffled Meinecke he explained that "the man who wrote *The Star of Redemption* . . . is of a very different caliber from the author of *Hegel und der Staat.*"[66] Rosenzweig continued that he was not interested, indeed not capable, of cognition for its own sake. "Not every question seems to me worth asking. Scientific curiosity and omnivorous aesthetic appetite mean equally little to me today, though I was once under the spell of both."[67] It would, however, be erroneous to interpret Rosenzweig's moving letter to Meinecke as a rejection of history per se: rather he is passionately rejecting the then-prevailing modes of historical scholarship. As he himself tells Meinecke: "The one thing I wish to make clear is that scholarship no longer holds the center of my attention."[68] Rosenzweig's disaffection with scholarship, of course, was already expressed in the Baden-Baden conference of 1910, and, indeed, it was one of the convictions he shared with Rosenstock and the entire Patmos circle. In fact, their rejection of academic scholarship was inspired by the sublime task of saving history from the trammels of historicism. In the midst of the war, Rosenstock—in part at the suggestion of Rosenzweig[69]—embarked on a revaluation of history that would take him nearly fifteen years to complete. The book, *Die Europäischen Revolutionen: Volkscharaktere und Staatenbildung* (Jena, 1931; *Out of Revolution: Autobiography of*

*Western Man,* 1938), held that "scholars cannot demobilize until the World War has reformed their method and their purpose in writing history."[70] Rosenstock observed:

The incoherence of modern knowledge in history and nature . . . became so frightening even before the World War that nothing but a breakdown of civilization could be expected from a kingdom so terribly divided against itself. The World War seemed more a test than a surprise to those who had suffered from the atmosphere of an occidental university and the absurdities of its specialists.[71]

Rosenstock's book, in which he introduced his unique method of "calendrical thinking" as a way of appropriating the "hidden" meaning of history as autobiography—as the existential and spiritual ground of one's personal history—was a protest against the pervasive sense that history was "dark and confused."[72] Interestingly, when Rosenstock's faith in scholarship began to falter it was Rosenzweig who endeavored to renew his faith by providing a refreshing messianic perspective on the value of historical scholarship. "I underline emphatically," Rosenzweig wrote to Rosenstock in the winter of 1916, "all that you say about [the faults] of scholarship."[73] Yet it is precisely because we wish to combat nihilism that we must affirm scholarship.

For "the turning of the hearts of the fathers to the children" is, according to the final verse of the Prophet Maleachi, a final preparation for the last day. Without scholarship each generation would run away from the preceding one, and history would seem to be a discontinuous series (as in fact it really is) and not (as it ought to appear) the parable of a single point, a *nunc stans* (as history really is in the final moment, but thanks to scholarship . . . appears to be already in advance, here and now).[74]

Implicit in the historian's endeavor to endow history with coherence and structure is an anticipation of the meaning of history that will become manifest with the redemption.

Rosenzweig succinctly amplified this thesis with two aphorisms. While working on the essay "Thalatta," apparently in the exhilaration of "writing" history, he observed in a letter to his parents that Aristotle, by denigrating history as having as little philosophical value as art, proved himself a "real pagan"—"for he did not know how history appeared *vue par le temperament de Jesajas.*"[75] One of the last items Rosenzweig was able to write in his own hand was a diary entry from 30 March 1922. There he queries: "How is the science of history possible?" The answer: "Through Redemption." [76]

To be sure, Rosenzweig rejected academic scholarship—or what is called historicism [77]—but this rejection did not imply his estrangement either from scholarship or from history as a meaningful process. In *The Star of Redemption*, the Synagogue as a metahistorical fact within the midst of time serves to make history as a coherent and redemptive process possible.

## V

*The Star of Redemption* may be said to be animated by a passion to master time—temporal finitude, death, history. And time, we learn in this book, is overcome by eternity. [78] From different perspectives and with varying nuances, Rosenzweig presents eternity as the future anticipated in the present. "Eternity," he writes, "is just this: that time no longer has a right to a place between the present moment and consummation and that the whole future is to be grasped today"; eternity is "a future which without ceasing to be future is nevertheless present." It is a prolepsis of the Kingdom, and as such it "eternalizes the moment." [79] The future—that is, the future of messianic promise—has thus in a sense ceased, as Alexander Altmann has pointed out, "to be an historical category. . . . Future, the Kingdom and eternity become synonymous terms in Rosenzweig's eschatological thinking. They are existential terms, not concepts denoting objective reality." [80]

Israel, Rosenzweig declares, is the Eternal People, for she embodies eternity in time. Both objectively and spiritually, the exiled Israel has anticipated the end of history, eternity; objectively, the Jewish nation reconstituted as the Synagogue in the Exile is free of the parochial and invidious claims of geography and politics; spiritually, the liturgy, cult and Law of the Synagogue all serve to propel the Jewish people beyond mundane time and into the bosom of eternity. "God withdrew the Jews from [historical time]," Rosenzweig writes with respect to the Law, "by arching the bridge of His Law high above the current of time which henceforth and to all eternity rushes powerlessly along under its arches."[81] Elsewhere he remarks, "a kiss from Helen made Faustus immortal; the Law, the Jew."[82] Rosenzweig's focus on eternity by no means constitutes a repudiation of the historical world. Theologically, this would be repugnant to Rosenzweig. Hence his scathing criticism of mysticism in which he declares the mystic's quest for God by withdrawal and detachment to be "a thoroughly immoral" position.[83] The experience God, Rosenzweig rapsodically affirms, must enter to "the orbit of the world."[84] In the first instance, God is brought into the world through acts of agapic love; through love of "the nighest." But even more emphatically, through Judaism and Christianity qua configurations (*Gestalten*) that not only bear witness to eternity ("eternally reflecting a reality eternally renewed"),[85] but actually implant the seeds of eternity within the world *and* history. In establishing this relationship between eternity and history, the Church and Synagogue are complementary: The Synagogue rests within the lap of eternity; the Church, gripping, as it were, the skirt of the Synagogue, enters the world and history. Here Rosenzweig notes a paradox: the Church, which is charged with entering history, tends to foster an experience of the eternal that is totally divorced from the temporal. Christian piety

depicts an eternity wholly beyond time. It was not and could not be a bridge on which emotion might move to and from between one shore and the other. [In Christian piety] the two shores were structurally too diverse for this, the one too exclusively temporal, the other too exclusively eternal. True, it was an idea that the Son of Man would one day turn over his dominion, but this does not alter the fact, that within time, he was defied. True, it was an idea that God would one day be all-in-all, but this does not alter the fact that he was granted precious little influence on the Aught-in-Aught of this temporality where his *locum tenens* was lord.[86]

There is no such ambiguity, however, with regard to the metahistorical significance of the Synagogue: its detachment from history constitutes a vicarious suffering, as depicted in Isaiah 53, for "the nations of the world who walk in the bright light of history."[87]

As configurations (*Gestalten*), the Synagogue and Church are concrete embodiments of eternity in the midst of time: through them "a piece of redemption is already, really placed into the world, the

visible world."[88] The significance of this thesis is perhaps best expli-
cated by Rosenzweig himself in a letter to Gertrude Oppenheim
during the period of *The Star*'s composition:

What I call goal is not at all essentially different from that which Kant,
Fichte and Hegel so designated. But they claimed such without foundation. . . . But from a fact I require *facticity*, not reasons. The reality of the
goal in the world is what I require. "The Spirit which I saw could be a
devil," as Hamlet doubted . . . ; but a reality which is seen by all the world
and which is acknowledged by all the world's *real*-reaction to it cannot be
doubted. One can distance oneself from this reality, but one then knows
what one does.[89]

In a word, Rosenzweig wishes to assign an ontological status to the
future. As he states in *The Star,* "the world is created in the beginning not, it is true, perfect, but destined to be perfected. . . . Its future perfection is created, as future, simultaneous with the world."[90]
Hence, while Rosenzweig vigorously rejects the idea of historical
progress, he passionately affirms growth, indeed perfection in time.[91]
It is the proleptic reality of the future that ultimately allows for genuine growth in time. "For without such anticipation [of the future, of
the Kingdom], the moment is not eternal"—and with oblique reference to Hermann Cohen, who celebrated historical progress as an
asymptotic or eternal task, Rosenzweig critically adds that without
such anticipation, the moment "is something that drags everlast-
ingly along the long, long trail of time."[92] But the eternalization of
time, he emphasized, is not the *only* source of the world's growth.
Morality, secular activity, indeed even politics are necessary. (He
once commented that within the Western world socialism, even in
its atheist form, contributes more to the establishment of the Kingdom of God than institutional religion.)[93] Thus, we understand the
cryptic remark in *The Star:* "From two sides there is . . . a knocking
on the locked door of the future."

# 8

# Franz Rosenzweig and the Kabbalah

*Moshe Idel*

A major stumbling block stands in the way of any attempt to establish the existence of possible connections between the philosophy of Franz Rosenzweig and the Kabbalah. Rosenzweig's extensive knowledge of Schelling's doctrine and its profound influence on his thinking should be appreciated in light of the affinity between some of Schelling's views and kabbalistic literature. The views discussed in this chapter will therefore reflect only on some of the points in which there is a clear influence of kabbalistic ideas—or rather ideas that Rosenzweig considered to be kabbalistic and that at times he himself contrasted to those of Schelling. The evaluation of indirect influences of the Kabbalah, transmitted through Schelling, Jacobi, and others, are not within the scope of this chapter, but are manifestly worthy of a separate study.

With reference to the nineteenth-century theologian David F. Strauss's work on the life of Jesus, Rosenzweig writes in his now famous essay "Atheistic Theology" that the liberal, or rather "atheistic," theology represented by Strauss "clearly borrows its theory concerning God's birth from man from ancient mysticism."[1] Rosenzweig himself, of course, does not accept the "atheistic" premises of this theology, for it endeavors to reduce the transcendent God to the expression of "the divine" born out of human experience;[2] in this way atheistic theology seeks to eliminate the human-divine dichotomy, which, in Rosenzweig's opinion, is indispensable for a genuine religious life.

However, Rosenzweig's observation about the sources of atheistic theology is important for understanding his own approach to theology. Indeed, one may ask whether we cannot regard Rosenzweig's theology, which establishes an intimate relation between God and man, as also influenced by ancient mysticism? In "Atheistic Theology" Rosenzweig writes: "It is not by chance that the famous maxim of one of the masters of the Kabbalah—'God speaks: "if you do not bear witness to me, then I am not"'—is spoken as the word of God, the written word of God [viz., Isa. 43: 12] read into the maxim by an exegetical device. God makes himself dependent upon the testimony of man."[3] Here Rosenzweig proposes an alternative to atheistic theology: the close relation or even dependency of the divine on the human is expressed or rather revealed by God himself. Rosenzweig hereby offers a theistic perspective that assumes the existence of a transcendent, revealing God. Not insignificantly Rosenzweig claims that the maxim illustrating this theological presupposition is that of a kabbalist. In fact, the maxim is that of no other than Rabbi Simeon bar Yochai to whom Jewish tradition has attributed the Zohar, the most important document of Kabbalah. The maxim, however, is found in midrashic sources and has no connection with Kabbalah whatsoever.[4] Nonetheless, the opinion expressed by Rosenzweig is important: One may contrast the ancient mysticism from which atheistic theology draws its inspiration,[5] with another form of ancient mysticism—namely Kabbalah—from which insight may be obtained for the understanding of the theology Rosenzweig sought to construct. Indeed, in *The Star of Redemption* Rosenzweig interprets the aforementioned maxim of Rabbi Simeon bar Yochai, whom he once again refers to as a "kabbalist," in the following manner: "the love of God for man becomes eternal only when it is acknowledged by human love."[6] In Rosenzweig's opinion the divine is not born in the soul, it is only renewed in the soul. Here, when he traces to ancient mysticism the source of this idea, we see the clear contrast between Rosenzweig's theology and atheistic theology. The author of *The Star of Redemption* uses the early midrashic saying to build his own theory, which has developed since his writing of "Atheistic Theology."

A similar phenomenon, this time in connection with an authentic kabbalistic theory, is apparent upon comparing two other subjects dealt with in the aforementioned works of Rosenzweig. In "Atheistic Theology,"[7] Rosenzweig takes a positive attitude toward what he terms "the theology of the Jewish people," viewing it as a link and ingredient that can serve the further development of a fuller, more genuine Jewish theology. The theology of the Jewish people, in Rosenzweig's description, deals with the dichotomy between a meta-historical, ideal Judaism and its historical expressions. The tension between these is, in Rosenzweig's opinion, of vital importance; he believes that it expresses the polarity between God and the Jewish people. Rosenzweig regards the denial of this dichotomy by recent Jewish theologians—whom he does not mention by name—as contradicting the vocation of the Jewish people to reflect in its everyday life the transcendent unity of God.[8]

In Rosenzweig's opinion the idea of unity is transferred from the realm of dogma—where it describes God—into the realm of morality, where it serves as a guide for proper conduct. *Duties of the Heart* by Bachya ben Joseph ibn Paquda, in Rosenzweig's view, pivots around this theme;[9] only in recent times has it become clear how thoroughly the book was studied by the kabbalists in the time of its composition and in later times. Even the blessing before the Shema in the morning prayer, which dates from before medieval scholasticism and mysticism and is still used, is built on the reciprocal relationship between the unification of God by man and of man by God. The emphasis lies, however, on the reciprocal nature of this relationship; our forefathers would not have understood the separation of human morality from God's truth. Here Rosenzweig points out that unification as "love" is a reciprocal act, basing this on the blessing before the Shema: "Thou has chosen us from all peoples, and nations, and hast forever brought us near to thy truly great name, that we may eagerly praise thee and acclaim thy Oneness." In his explanation, Rosenzweig claims that the concept of "unity," which lies behind these words, dates from before the Kabbalah, but was translated into action, that is, the rite of unification, first in the book of Bachya ibn Paquda and later by the mystics,[10] who studied the book extensively.[11]

In "Atheistic Theology" Rosenzweig does not hint at the nature of this act of unification. In *The Star of Redemption,* on the other hand, the kabbalistic idea of unification occupies a very important place: the Jew fulfills endless precepts and commandments "for the sake of uniting the holy God and his Shekhina."[12] This unification is constituted by the constant gathering of the holy sparks, which are dispersed all over the world, and their reunification with God. The Jew thus serves to effect the process of God's unification, which will be complete at the end of days; it is not a dogmatic statement about the unity of God but an effort to reach this unity through living a certain type of life.[13] What we have here is clearly a version of Lurianic Kabbalah, which places the idea of tikkun at the center of Jewish religious experience and makes the keeping of the commandments the key to achieving the unity of God. Significantly, with Rosenzweig as in Lurianic Kabbalah, the attainment of the aim of tikkun is clearly eschatological in character. The Shekhina and the sparks are redeemed by returning them to their original place in the Divinity. This action is "nothing less than the process of redemption embracing God, world and man."[14] By fulfilling the commandments, the Jew redeems the sparks exiled in the world and returns them to their source; by doing this he redeems God Himself. These two redemptions effect the redemption of man himself. The above is a clear example of the influence of Lurianic Kabbalah on the definition of one of the three pillars of Rosenzweig's theology, namely redemption. The expression "Star of Redemption," which appears after the above quotation,[15] is an expression of the unique way of the Jew, the kabbalistic way, leading to God and the world: the Jew in his own unique way intends to redeem God, himself and the world.[16]

Another central concept in Rosenzweig's theory is stated clearly in kabbalistic terms. In speaking about revelation, Rosenzweig writes:

Mysticism bridges the gap between the "God of our Fathers" and the "Remnant of Israel" by the doctrine of the Shekhina. The Shekhina, God's descent upon man in His sojourn among men, is pictured as a dichotomy taking place in God Himself. God Himself separates Himself from Himself, He gives Himself away to his people. . . . The idea of the wanderings of the Shekhina, of the sparks of the original divine light being scattered about the world, this casts all of revelation between the Jewish God and Jewish Man, and thereby anchors both, God as well as the remnant, in all the depth of revelation.[17]

Here the kabbalistic ideas of the wandering Shekhina pave the way to revelation; the scattering of the divine sparks in the world is the way God chooses to reveal Himself to His people; exile is a way to revelation. God who gives Himself over to suffering makes it possible for the Jewish people to redeem Him through a process of tikkun, just as the loving God is rebuilt, as we have seen above, through man's love.

In describing the concept of divine redemption as tikkun and the exile of the Shekhina as the scattered divine sparks, Rosenzweig uses the terms of Lurianic Kabbalah. This use is intentional. As early as 1917, Rosenzweig suggested in a letter to Hermann Cohen that toward the end of their studies, future teachers of Judaica should be able to elect courses in the *Zohar* or in the Lurianic Kabbalah.[18] This suggestion shows that Rosenzweig was familiar, at least superficially, with the main principles of this system. An additional and more important testimony appears in his letter to Rudolf Ehrenberg, the so-called germ cell of *The Star of Redemption*.[19] In Rosenzweig's opinion, "God exists before all relation, both between Him and the world and Him and Himself, and only this existence of God which is completely non-hypothetical is the origin of the reality of God—what Schelling . . . calls 'somber basis.'[20] This inner nature of God precedes not only His revealed essence (*Selbstentäußerung*) but His essence (*Selbst*) itself (as taught, to the best of my knowledge, by Lurianic mysticism, as I once told you)."[21] Here we have clear testimony of a conversation Rosenzweig had before 1917 which shows his familiarity with Lurianic Kabbalah. Further study of this passage shows that Rosenzweig believes in the existence of an Absolute Divine beyond what Schelling calls the "somber basis." Schelling describes God in negative terms, whereas Rosenzweig tries to extract the divine from every relative system, including the relation of God to Himself. Lurianic mysticism provided him with a suitable thought: the divine before contraction (*tsimtsum*), the divine to which the relation of God even to Himself does not apply. This relationship appears only in the process of contraction, and the relationship of God to the world is expressed in the process of emanation after the contraction. The term *emanation* used in Lurianic mysticism is, it seems, parallel to the "revelation of His essence" mentioned by Rosenzweig in the above quotation. In *The Star of Redemption* we find a clear parallel to the argument used in the "germ cell." Rosenzweig describes the infinite divine nature as located "before the Yea and the Nay. . . . It is not a 'somber basis' that can be named with Eckhart's terms, or Boehme's, or Schelling's." [22]

A comparison of the two arguments shows beyond a doubt that the theory mentioned by Rosenzweig in the germ cell as the doctrine of Lurianic mysticism concerning the Divine is the theory he places opposite the negative theory of Eckhart, Boehme and Schelling,[23] though in *The Star of Redemption* Rosenzweig makes no mention of the kabbalistic source of his doctrine. It seems to me, however, that the very definition of God quoted above from *The Star of Redemption* is taken from the kabbalists. In a number of kabbalistic treatises available to Rosenzweig, the *Ein Sof*, the Infinite, is described in terms taken from Ismailiya theology; for example, "It is equally incapable of being affirmed or negated." [24] Here we see how Rosenzweig translated the saying "not a Yea" and "not a Nay" into ontological terms. God is above the category called "Being" and above the category called "Not-Being." In Kabbalah, the Infinite is above the "Nought," that is above the Sefirah *Keter* and above "Being," or the Sefirah *Hokhmah* (wisdom). In Rosenzweig's theology, the concealed God is above the Nay found in German mysticism.

Furthermore, the words *Yea* and *Nay* are, in Rosenzweig's terms, archetypal words denoting the initial states within God Himself; they sumbolize a process of becoming. In Kabbalah the words *Being* and *Not-Being* are used to symbolize this process. "The self-negating nought was the self-negating nought of God. . . . the Yea in God was His infinite essence." In Rosenzweig's view it is only the Yea that is the source of creation. "This first 'Yea' in God establishes for ever and ever the divine essence."[25] This first Yea is the beginning, in accordance with a well-known kabbalist theory in which the Yea or the *Hokhmah* is the beginning of the process of creation; the Sefirah *Hokhmah* is therefore called by the name *Bereshit* (in the beginning) or *Reshit* (beginning). In his attempt to understand from language the basic conditions within the Divine, Rosenzweig also chooses the way of the kabbalists. The latter, as already shown by Gershom Scholem,[26] find in language an "inner logic" of a higher order than philosophical logic.

We find that the formulation of the third part of Rosenzweig's theory, namely creation, was also inspired to a certain extent by the Kabbalah. In another part of *The Star of Redemption,* Rosenzweig admits that Jewish mysticism replaces the general concept of creation with that of the "mysterious or hidden creations," the "tale of the chariot" as it is called in an allusion to the vision of Ezekiel.[27] The concept of "mysterious creation" fits the above discussed processes of the Yea and the Nay.[28]

We can sum up the matter as follows: We may discern a kabbalistic influence in the way Rosenzweig builds and expresses the particular nature of the three basic principles of his theology, namely, creation, revelation and redemption. In attempting to construct an alternative to what he calls atheistic theology, Rosenzweig uses Jewish mysticism, which provides him with important terms and concepts. The new or atheistic theology built a myth around the life of Jesus or the life of the Jewish people and made that myth its centerpiece. Rosenzweig does not, however, divorce himself completely from myth, but instead of anchoring the myth in the changing flow of life he anchors it, following the kabbalistic mythology, in the life of God Himself, giving it an absolute speculative character. Just as he uses the words of Rabbi Simeon b. Yochai to reject a mysticism that views God as born out of the human experience, so Rosenzweig uses the kabbalistic myth about the contraction (*tsimtsum*) to reject Boehme's and Schelling's conceptions of the infinite divine nature. Aided by a speculative interpretation of Jewish mysticism and myth, Rosenzweig is able to offer an alternative to atheistic theology.

In this connection it is proper to mention a possible influence of Christian mysticism. In *The Star of Redemption,* Rosenzweig describes the relationship between revelation and creation as follows:

The created world itself is full of mysterious relations to the law, and the law is not alienated from this world but is the key to the enigma of the world. The plain wording of the law conceals a hidden meaning which expresses the essence of the world. For the Jew, the book of the law can thus, as it were, replace the book of nature or even the starry heavens from which the men of yore once thought they could interpret terrestrial matters by intelligent omens.[29]

This comparison between an astrologer's reading of the book of heaven and a kabbalist's reading of the book of the law reminds us of the words of Pico della Mirandola in his last thesis: "Sicut vera Astrologia docet nos legere in libro dei, ita Cabala docet nos legere in libro legis" (Just as the true astrology teaches to read in the book of God, so the Kabbalah teaches to read in the book of the law).[30]

As seen earlier, Rosenzweig stresses the fact that Rabbi Simeon b. Yochai's words about the testimony of Israel, which changes the infinite Divine into God, was put into the mouth of God Himself. The aim of this emphasis is to create the concept of an objective divine Being, which is the only Being able to become a goal toward which man can direct his life. In describing the relation between God and man, Rosenzweig uses a terminology derived from Jewish mysticism. Against those who call some descriptions of God in the Bible "anthropomorphisms," Rosenzweig claims that we can never speak of God in terms of "personification" and that quite the opposite is true:

It is not that we imagine that God sees, hears, speaks, is angry and loves because *we* see, speak, are angry and love, but rather the opposite: *we* are able to see, to hear, to speak, to be angry, to love because *God* sees, hears, speaks, is angry and loves. When one analyzes this idea and its implications, however, one comes to the conclusion that this dogmatic theory which starts with God is not less worthy of rejection than the dubious theory which starts with man.[31]

The taking of God as a standard reminds us much of the kabbalist's theories that see in man and his actions a reflection of the *Sefiroth* system and the processes taking place there. One clear example comes from Rabbi Emmanuel Hai Rikki:

The *Parzufim* [configurations] of the divine system consist of the spirituality of the letters of the Torah, and therefore all the names of the members of
the human body mentioned therein are their true names . . . but in us these
names are derived because, according to the powers we receive from them,
we give names to the physical members of our body which carry out actions
with the help of this power in the name of the divine source through which
the energy runs.[32]

It is true that in Rosenzweig's statement, the emphasis is on those
divine actions that are reflected in human action, an emphasis not
found in kabbalist literature. But Rosenzweig does not negate anthropomorphism altogether. In his opinion, anthropomorphic descriptions have validity if viewed as descriptions of encounter, as a
theological attempt to describe an event taking place between man
and God, but not as a final description of God's essence. This distinction between the revealed side of God, which can be described
in anthropomorphic terms, and the hidden side, which transcends
all description, has a certain parallel in Kabbalah, where the anthropomorphic descriptions of the revealed God are seen in the
form of the *Ten Sefiroth* or of the *Adam Kadmon*. Rosenzweig describes the development of Jewish theology in terms of the tension
between the various concepts concerning God:[33] God and the spiritual logos of Philo,[34] on the one hand, and the complete humanization of God found in Christianity on the other hand, are phenomena on the borders between Jewish thought and that of the other
nations. In contrast, Jewish thought preserved, especially, in its Ag-
gadic literature, examples of moderate anthropomorphic descriptions that are the result of "the Jews' certainty that our experience
of God, comes from God himself." However, with the emergence
within Judaism of a theory describing God in terms of physical dimensions—and here Rosenzweig clearly alludes to the book *Shiur
Koma*[35]—Jewish theology had to fight against this development, as
seen in the philosophies of Sa'adya Gaon and Maimonides; the abstract conception of God in medieval Jewish philosophy induced a
reaction in the writings of the kabbalists who combined the theory
of God without attributes—the *Ein Sof* (Infinite)—and the anthropomorphic theory of the revealed God.[36]

This doctrine, which Rosenzweig describes as the doctrine of "the Kabbalah at the height of its development and of the late Kab-balah," is very close to his own presupposition of the two layers within the Divine. The further development of the aforementioned tension is, however, extremely important. In Rosenzweig's opinion:

Judaism enters its third stage of the battle against anthropomorphism at the start of the Emancipation. This time the battle is fought against the exag-gerations which appeared in the realm of Kabbalah. Since this period is still present time, it is difficult to give a clear historic answer, but judging from my own personal experience I would say that the great converts to Christi-anity of the 19th and to my regret also of the 20th century are the answer.[37]

From this statement we learn two things: First, Kabbalah—which Rosenzweig calls "the Kabbalah at the height of its development and the late Kabbalah"—contains anthropomorphic exaggera-tions, and from here is implid his positive attitude toward the Kab-balah of the time of the *Zohar* and the Lurianic Kabbalah. Second, for our purpose, however, it is more important to notice his negative view of the reaction to these exaggerations. The conception of Juda-ism in the time of the Emancipation emptied its theology of per-sonal and anthropomorphic content, and the void resulted in a search for other theological doctrines, a search that led a number of Jews to Christian "anthropomorphism." This explanation is impor-tant for the understanding of Rosenzweig's view of Jewish theology since the Emancipation.

If the lack of anthropomorphism (and thus personalism) in Juda-ism led some Jews to Christianity, the Kabbalah can, through its an-thropomorphic symbols, perhaps satisfy the religious needs of those Jews.[38] The early appearance of kabbalistic influences in the Jewish theological writings of Rosenzweig himself therefore bear testi-mony to his own search for a religious thought system that could provide him, at least partially, with what he had formerly sought in Christianity.

# 9

# The Concept of Language in the Thought of Franz Rosenzweig

*Nahum N. Glatzer*

I

For many centuries thinkers tried to understand the importance of human languages—the role of the word and the name—or to deny the validity of speech. In Plato's *Cratylus* he asks whether through an understanding of names we may reach an understanding of things. Hermogenes denies any relationship between name and reality; Socrates maintains the connection. Plato abandoned the position of this dialogue in his *Seventh Epistle*. There the realm of language is taken to be only the first step to knowledge. Ultimately, instead of expressing reality, the word becomes a barrier between the speaker and the one spoken to. The thinker is left alone to meditate in silence on the paradox of name, word, and language.

The two positions of speech continued through the Middle Ages. The "realism" (supported by Aristotelian logic) cultivated the word; "nominalism" perpetuated by the skepticism of the word. The reality of language appeared at least as a problem to most modern philosophers. Wilhelm von Humboldt perceived the interdependence of speech and cognition, and recognized that the word was not only an expression of reality but also a means by which to explore it. Hegel also believed that language possessed the power to express reality. But in the case of Hegel it becomes clear that language is primarily conceptual terminology and the word but an element of definition. The French traditionalist V. G. A. de Bonald questioned the value of autonomous reason and argued that the root of both reason and intellectual life was grounded in language. The word, he maintained, comes to man as a divine revelation. Man's thought participates in it, but does not create it. Theological dogmatism led de Bonald astray; from beneath his religious theory shines Hegel's "Objective Spirit."

The more recent trends in philosophy move toward even greater distrust of language. Bertrand Russell sees in language a collection of abstract nouns expressing an atomized universe of sense data (*The Scientific Outlook*). It is a language that can no longer serve as a means of communication between men. In the words of W. M. Urban, we may speak of "a progressive paralysis of speech." Henri Bergson finds language to be "static" and unable to express the dynamic continuity of reality. Reality can be fathomed only by immediate intuition, which is both nonlogical and wordless (*Creative Evolution*). That language does violence to immediate experience is the conviction of A. N. Whitehead. He, therefore, wishes to create a new system of categories of speech. Our universe, being a realm of "events" and "activity," calls for a language of verbs (*Process and Reality*).

Man and world seem radically isolated, one from the other. Nietzsche alluded to the root of this isolation. "That world is well hidden from man! . . . that heavenly nothingness. The bosom of Being does not speak to man, except in the guise of man. Truly, all being is difficult to prove; it is difficult to make it speak." A tragic silence seems to prevail between man and man, man and world. In Sartre's words, "there is no sign in the world." [1]

The contemporary literary historian George Steiner speaks of a "breakdown of language." "The syntheses of understanding which made common speech possible, no longer work." "Language today deals only with surfaces of experience; the rest is silence." But, to

Steiner, "the word should be seen as the very essence of humanity"; language is "the defining mystery of man; it is language that should sever man from the silence that inhabits the greater part of being" (*Language and Silence*). This brings us to a consideration of the role of language in the work of Franz Rosenzweig.


## II

The central position of language, of speech, of the word in Rosenzweig's thought is well known. However, what is needed is a clarification of these terms and a knowledge of the contexts in which they appear. He seems to anticipate a later insight when he writes to Eugen Rosenstock (19 October 1917): "My 'I' originates in 'you.' By saying 'you' I realize that the other person is not a thing but 'as myself.'"[2] Thus language is at the base of thought and ethics; they would become distorted by the application of logical terms. "A bas la terminologie, vive la *Sprache*," he exclaims.[3]

In the "Urzelle" of *The Star of Redemption*,[4] Rosenzweig outlines some of the major themes of his magnum opus. He lets man discover himself as an existing individual bearing a name, an I, a free agent, a being that loves God and as a lover may, or better must, demand—against Spinoza and Goethe—that God respond to his, man's, love. Or perhaps man must expect that God expresses his love first, and man who has waited for the redeeming word to come from God's mouth is the one who responds and thus opens the divine-human dialogue.

Equally significant is the road Rosenzweig saw leading from the I-conscious person to his fellow man. The latter is recognized as an equally endowed I. He is not a he-she-it, but an I, a brother. This view of man, world and God becomes possible once revelation is recognized as the center of a world system whose beginning is creation and whose endpoint is redemption.

Creation-revelation-redemption are the tenses of reality that help Rosenzweig's "sound common sense" to understand our world and that underlie his anti-Hegelian, anti-idealist *Star of Redemption*. This vast scheme allows the author to include an interpretation of

Eastern religions and Islam, as well as of Judaism and Christianity, Greek tragedy, and the role of speech, the word, language, and silence. The tragic hero of Greek antiquity has the use of only one language: silence. (The world before revelation is the world of paganism, and its symbol is creation.) "By keeping silent, the hero breaks down the bridges which connect him with God and the world, . . . delimiting himself . . . into the icy solitude of self. The self, after all, knows nothing outside itself: it is inherently solitary" (77).[5]

The language of logic is not yet real language, belonging as it does to the realm of creation, that is, the realm before revelation. This language is but a prognostication of the real language of grammar; it is not more than a promise of the real word (109) and of speech. "Speech is truly mankind's morning gift from the Creator, and yet at the same time it is the common property of all children of men." When did man become man? "When he first spoke." For "language makes human" (110). Language is the instrument of revelation. "Created from the beginning, [language] nevertheless awakes to real vitality only in revelation." "The human word is a symbol; with every moment it is newly created in the mouth of the speaker . . . but the divine word is more than symbol: it is revelation only because it is at the same time the word of creation" (111).

We note that so far Rosenzweig has dealt with language and word as such, without touching upon dialogue and interhuman communication. Let us see whether the three books of part 2 and the part 3 will enlighten us on that issue. In introducing book 1 of part 2 (on creation) the author emphasizes that "God created" (112). Gradually silence gives way to speech, though it is only a speech within the speechless protocosmos. In this realm, mathematics is the objective language. Ultimately, "A science of living sounds must take the place of a science of speechless signs; mathematical science must be replaced by the morphology of words, by grammar" (125). Moreover, it must ultimately be recognized that the sentence, not words, constitutes, language (cf. 126). In Rosenzweig's thinking, creation points to revelation ("Creation is the prophecy which is confirmed only in the miraculous sign of revelation" [134]) and creation's silence is overcome by the voice of revelation. But Rosenzweig does not underestimate the opposing view, especially the view of German idealism. "Idealism seeks to elevate itself over language with a logic of its own." The world of idealism did not originate in the word but in thought and in "pure" logic foreign to language and beyond man (141). No wonder it "lacked straightforward confidence in language" (145). "It was incapable of acknowleding the word of man as answer to the word of God" (147).

In contradistinction to this critical denial of the role of language, Rosenzweig affirms "the word" as the only visible witness to man's soul, "the one which he cannot lack without ceasing to be man" (147). The author goes as far as saying that though "the ways of God are different from the ways of man, the word of God and the word of man are the same." His own human speech is the very word that issues from God (151).

The second book of part 2 deals with the central concern in Rosenzweig's system: revelation. It starts, significantly, with the biblical quotation "Love is strong as death." From this point on, the love motif accompanies the motif of revelation. Can we attribute love to God? asks Rosenzweig. "Should the revealer reveal himself . . . from love?" (163). Yes. "It is over man that divine love is poured out" (167), a love that is "present, pure and simple" (164). The soul receives the love of God; God never ceases to love, nor the soul to be loved. "Previously man had been a senseless [*fühllos*] and speechless introvert; only now is he—beloved soul" (169). The "first audible word" (of revelation, its root word is *I* (173). "To the I there responds in God's interior a Thou." But the Thou, remaining in God's interior, is no authentic Thou, neither is the I an authentic I "for no Thou has yet confronted it." Only when the I relates itself to the Thou as to something external to itself, that is, only when it makes the transition from monologue to authentic dialogue, "only then does it become an actual I" (174). The "Where art Thou?" addressed to Adam, Rosenzweig reads as "the quest for the Thou." In the very act of asking for the Thou, in asserting the existence of the Thou, the I discovers itself. It discovers itself, not the Thou. Man (Adam) hides; he does not respond; his answers are evasive. Only when called by his proper name does man (Abraham) answer, "all unlocked, . . . all ready, all-soul: 'Here I am'" (175f.).

This ready, receptive, individual human I, addressed by his name, is given the commandment, "the sum and substance of all commandments: 'Thou shalt love the Lord thy God,' etc." (176). God's I, "the root-word of the entire dialogue of revelation . . . marks the individual commandment as a command of love." This I remains the key word, traversing revelation like a single sustained organ note" (178).

The dialogue between God and man is commencing. The soul's reply to the commandment of love is the admission that there was a period of lovelessness; in biblical terms the soul says: "I have sinned" (178f.). In reply, God "reaches back into the past and identifies himself as the one who . . . initiated the whole dialogue between himself and the soul: 'I have called thee by name: thou art mine [Isa. 43: 11]" (183).

The last thing that can be achieved in revelation is prayer. Prayer is "the greatest gift presented to the soul in revelation." Its essence is: "Let not my prayer and your love depart from me [Ps. 66: 20]" (184). Gazing into the future, the soul prays for the coming of the kingdom. "Here ends the dialogue of love" (185).

"With the summons by the proper name, the word of revelation enters the real dialogue." The breakdown of the rigid wall of objectness (Dinglichkeit) was due to the use of the proper name. "That which has a name of its own, can no longer be a thing" (186). The importance of the name is evident not only in the realm of man but also in the animal kingdom. Adam's first deed is to give names to creatures of the world [Gen. 2: 19] (187). However, the ground of revelation is "the revelation of the divine name." With considerable excitement Rosenzweig exclaimed: "For name is in truth word and fire, and not sound and fury. It is incumbent to name the name and to confess: I believe it" (188). In a letter from 1922 Rosenzweig called the last sentence the central insight in The Star.[6] And word, name, speech language—all originated in revelation and its manifestation of divine love, when the mute, silent self was transformed into a speaking soul (198).

Rosenzweig concludes book 2 of part 2 with an analysis and interpretation of the Song of Songs, which he considers to be "the great historical testament of revelation" (198) and its "focal book" (202). For his exegesis Rosenzweig makes use, naturally, of insights gained so far on the themes of soul, love, and speech.

So we hear that "man loves because God loves and as God loves; his human soul is the soul awakened and loved by God" (199). And, "Love simply cannot be 'purely human'"; by speaking (and it must use speech), love "already becomes superhuman, for the sensuality of the word is brimful with its divine supersense. Like speech itself, love is sensual—supersensual." It is "only apparently transitory" and, quoting Goethe, "may be 'but simile'; in truth, it is eternal" (201). "Love is—speech, wholly active, wholly personal, wholly living, wholly—speaking," and "the speech of love is all present" (202).

From the miracle of divine love the path leads into the earthly world, the world of the neighbor whom you shall love as God loves you (204).[7]

The concluding book of part 2 is devoted to love of neighbor, action in the world, the kingdom of God and redemption. "The love for God is to express itself in love for one's neighbor" (214). But who can receive the commandment to love his neighbor? "Only the soul beloved by God" (215). The neighbor is not loved for his own sake but as a representative of man at large and the world (218). "And the Kingdom's growth in the world, hopefully anticipating the end already at the next moment—what is it waiting for at this next moment if not for the act of love?" (228). This is what happens in redemption.

The root sentence of redemption, "the roof over the house of language," is: he is good. This sentence becomes "the content of the communal chant" (231), for now community has been founded (232) in the place where—in creation—the lonely, silent Adam stood and where the soul received the revelation of divine love. The communal chant of redemption concludes "in a mighty unison of a 'we'" (236). All individual voices and their melodies "adapt themselves to the same rhythm and unite in a single harmony." As a chant, *we* would be something final; as a word, *we*, like any word, is not "final, never merely spoken; it is always speaking as well." This is "the actual mystery of language: the word speaks" (237). The ultimate word is spoken by God himself, "and it may no longer be a word." Our words "sink back into one single blinding light" and "each and every name vanishes," and "all merges into this totality" (238).

Going back to the commandment of love of one's neighbor, Rosenzweig, pointing to the text that reads "like yourself," explains that in this commandment, man's "self is definitely confirmed in its place" The world is not "thrown in his face as an endless melee," but "out of the endless chaos of the world, one nighest thing, his neighbor, is placed before his soul and concerning this one he is told: he is like you. You remain You . . . but he is not to remain He for you and thus a mere 'It' for your 'You.' Rather he is like You, an 'I,' a soul" (239f.).

The distinctive form in which redemption can be the theme of revelation is the congregational hymn. "The congregation is not, or not yet, all; its 'We' is still limited." (250) The best testimony for this is the Book of Psalms (250), especially Psalms 111 to 118, the group of pure We-psalms (251).

As an example, Rosenzweig offers a ("grammatical") analysis of Psalm 115 ("Not to us, oh Lord, not to us, but to thy name give glory"). It is a prayer for the advent of the kingdom (251). "It begins and ends with a mighty and emphatic We." Yes, the dead will not join in the hymn of redemption. "But we, we will praise God from this time forth and to eternity." "The We are eternal"; "life becomes immortal in redemption's eternal hymn" (253).

We notice how a close reading of a psalm (it could be any text) helped Rosenzweig clarify to himself (and to others) the method of what he called "grammatical thinking." Though he was too deeply steeped in conceptual thought and constructs to undergo a radical change, he succeeded in fighting off the temptation of abstract thought in favor of a guidance by the word, by language, by speech in its various forms, and by a sincere dialogue.

Before embarking on part 3, Rosenzweig, in a chapter named

"Recapitulation" (254–61), stresses the outcome of his argument so far. First: Man's love of his neighbor is deeply motivated by his, man's, being loved by God. "Being loved comes to man from God, loving turns toward the world." The neighbor, representing the world, "is God's creature"; "his [man's] love of neighbor is love of the creatures" (259). Second: "The miraculous gift of speech was created for man and upon man at his creation." He did not make speech for himself; in becoming man, he started to speak; speech made man a human being in the deeper meaning of the term (260).

The introduction to part 3 is devoted to an intricate analysis of prayer in the variety of its forms and themes: the prayer for the advent of the divine kingdom, the sinner's prayer, prayer as a temptation of divine patience, the prayer of unbelief, the prayer of the fanatic, the prayer of the believer. For liturgy (and liturgic gesture) are the instruments of the realm that Rosenzweig depicted in part 3. The miracle of love is speech-endowed. In the realm of "silent enlightenment" speech is not needed (only "where there is world, there speech is also" [295]). *The Star* calls this realm "the silent anticipation of a world gleaming in the silence of the future." "Here is no longer any need of the word; it is the silence of consummate understanding" (295). The supreme component of liturgy, on the other side, is not the common word but the common gesture. Liturgy "makes gesture something more than speech," and disbelief and belief unite their prayer in the silence of the liturgical gesture (296).

The three books of part 3 deal with Judaism, Christianity, the Truth, respectively. Judaism is presented as the fire in the center of the Star, Christianity as the rays issuing from the fire; Judaism represents "eternal life" ("planted in our midst"), Christianity the "eternal way" (in spreading the Gospel), and the concluding book "the eternal truth"—God.

From among the characteristis of (classical) Judaism, Rosenzweig points out that this people has lost its own language and speaks the language of a given host country or the language of the people from whose country it emigrated. The Jewish people "never quite grows one with the language it speaks." And, "the most fundamental spontaneity is denied the Jew because he addresses God in a language different from the one he uses to speak to his brother." The

Jew maintains a profound distrust of the power of the word and a fervent belief in the power of silence (302).

Word-liturgy-silence: these are the key terms that guide Rosenzweig's presentation of the sacred calendar of Israel: the Sabbath and the sequence of holy days. "The spoken word fades away into the silence of perfect togetherness—for union occurs in silence only; the word unites, but those who are united fall silent. Liturgy . . . must introduce man to this silence." But before this goal is reached "the word still dominates the theme. The word itself must take man to the point of learning how to share silence" (308f.).

The liturgy of the Sabbath is a memorial of creation, though it contains the entire content of the festivals of revelation and the motif of redemption (311). On that day, man obeys the command of the prophet (Isa. 58: 13): he "lets his tongue rest from the talk of everyday" and learns to be silent, to listen in silence (314). Here silent listening institutes community (315).

The three pilgrimage festivals "give an image of the people as the carrier of revelation" (316); the third is also the festival of ultimate hope, a festival of redemption (321). The Days of Awe place the eternity of redemption within time; judgment is here placed in the immediate present (324). The liturgy of the Day of Atonement, the last of the Days of Awe, ends with an exultant profession: "'The Lord is God': this God of love, he alone is God" (327).

Christianity, too, being eternally "on the way," celebrates a sacred year (353) in which communal silence is central. Here unification is being established in the hearing of the common word. "The word truly takes the individual by the hand and guides him on the way which leads to the community" (358).

The community celebrates Sunday as the festival of the week's beginning; "the Christian is the eternal beginner" (359). Christmas, Easter, Pentecost are the festivals of revelation. "Ultimate redemption is not celebrated yet . . . only its prelude in revelation; accordingly there is no reference to that supreme communion of humanity in silent devotion" (365). This union can only be a subject of exhortation, and withal in universally understood language. "This understanding cannot be attained in silence; it requires the intervention of speech. Through the miracle of language (and translation) speech overcomes all resistance." But "God speaks everywhere with the words of men" (366).

Book 3 of part 3, the conclusion of *The Star,* deals with that of which both Judaism and Christianity are mere participants: Truth. "God is truth." Now the author is able to overlook the entire universe of life and discourse. "The mute darkness of the proto-cosmos has found speech in death. And something stronger, love, had overpowered death. Now life rallies in the silence of the hyper-cosmos." "God loves . . . The revelation of divine love is the heart of the All" (380f.). We men "catch sight of the Creator and Redeemer only from the vantage point of the God of love" (381). Redemption "redeems God by releasing him from his revealed name." The end is nameless; it is above any name. "Beyond the word . . . there shines silence" (383). "The name itself falls silent on our lips . . . as it will fall silent one day—when he is One." "It is the ultimate silence with which he keeps silent in us . . . God himself is there redeemed from his own word. He is silent" (384).

Of the revealed world it is said: "You have seen no figure only heard speech [Deut. 4: 12]" (418). But in the redeemed world . . . there the word falls silent. Of this world . . . it is said: 'May he make his countenance to shine upon you' [Num. 6: 26]" (418). "To walk in the light of the divine countenance is granted only to him who follows the words of the divine mouth For—"he has told thee, oh man, what is good . . . but to do justice and to love mercy [Mic. 6: 8]" (424).

Thus ends *The Star of Redemption.*

### III

Soon after the publication of *The Star,* Rosenzweig realized that the book (which appeared without a preface or introduction) was being grossly misunderstood; in particular, the new approach to thought itself, "the grammatical thinking," the philosophy of the healthy common sense, failed to find appreciation. Therefore Rosenzweig, already paralyzed, decided to offer an explanation of his "non-philosophical" speech-thinking in contradistinction to the abstract thinking of academic philosophy. This explanation was contained in "The New Thinking" (1925).[8]

Rosenzweig characterizes abstract thinking as a thinking for no one that speaks to no one; speaking, on the other hand, means speaking to someone and thinking for someone. "In the new thinking, the method of speech replaces the method of thinking maintained in all earlier philosophies." "I do not know in advance what the other person will say to me . . . I do not even know whether I am going to say anything at all. . . . The thinker knows his thoughts in advance and his expounding them is merely a concession to what he regards as the defectiveness of our means of communication." However "we cannot anticipate, we must wait for everything, and what is ours depends on what is another's. All this is quite beyond the comprehension of the thinking thinker, while it is valid for the 'speaking thinker.'"[9]

From Rosenzweig's explanation one gains the impression that *The Star,* which uses the new method of speech-thinking, is indeed concerned with the word exchanged between human beings, with human speech that awakens the I in a fellow human; that in its view dialogue is an interhuman dialogue and love more than a simile and metaphor. But when we go back to the text of *The Star,* we are confronted with the fact that word, speech and language take place in the sphere between God and man; that it is God who awakens the I in the human person; that language in most instances is the language of prayer and hymn addressed to the Godhead; and that love is a sacred state communicated to man in revelation and answered by man in sacred devotion.

Thus the most telling examples for speech-thinking Rosenzweig could offer came from the realm of man's relationship with the divine. To be sure, he does say that theological concerns of the new thinking do not mean that it is theological or that it "centers on the so-called 'religious problems' which it treats side by side with problems of logic" and so forth. He concludes his argument by stating that "theological problems must be translated into human terms, and human problems brought into the pale of theology."[10] Rosenzweig thus demands a serious approach to religion and theology. In

*The Star* he does more than that. Rather than "translating theological problems into human terms" (except by implication), he "brings human problems into the pale of theology."

We may ask whether the change—from the religious meaning of language to the role of speech in interhuman relations—is due to a conscious development: Is it not more than an attempt to make explicit in "The New Thinking" what lay dormant between the lines of *The Star?* This question I am unable to answer.

# IO

# Franz Rosenzweig in Perspective: Reflections on His Last Diaries

*Stéphane Mosès*

## I

In the complete edition of Franz Rosenzweig's writings, which is now being published at The Hague, there is in the second volume of the *Letters and Diaries* an unedited text of extreme importance. It is a diary by Franz Rosenzweig, his last, written between 23 March and 13 September 1922.

Rosenzweig had kept a diary between 1905 and 1918. His decision to resume it in 1922 was possibly prompted by the discovery, six weeks previously, that he was afflicted with an incurable disease.[1] According to the testimony of his physician, Dr. Richard Koch (1882–1949), Rosenzweig expected a "quick and almost solemn" death.[2] The notes jotted down between March and September 1922, this sequence of feverish, breathless reflections, of flashing and paradoxical intuitions, are those of a man who feels that his time is running out and who is desperately trying, before it is too late, to review his thoughts, to reassess their essential themes, and to pursue to their ultimate conclusions the ideas that had always obsessed him.

These reflections are also connected with a course of lectures Rosenzweig had planned to give during the third trimester of that same year of 1922 at the Freies Jüdisches Lehrhaus he had founded in 1920 at Frankfurt.[3] In this course, which was to be entitled "The Science of the World" ("Die Wissenschaft von der Welt"), he wanted to apply the theological categories of *The Star of Redemption*, in particular the category of creation, to the analysis of the problems posed by the modern world. Chief among them, for Rosenzweig, was the question of power in the modern world—political power, ideological power, and technological power.

These last reflections gain their particular inflection precisely from this wish of Rosenzweig's to confront the principal categories of *The Star* with the reality of the modern world. In them he expressed something of his need to reinterpret his own thoughts in the light of experience—to confirm them, give them different nuances, or even refute them. In contrast to the systematic structure of *The Star*, in which the philosophical discourse is carried on by a dialectic of extreme rigor, here his thought bursts forth in discrete unlinked fragments; it proceeds by way of intuitions, aphorisms, and paradoxes to reveal the tensions at work in it.

The critical review of the system of *The Star*, confronting it with the questions posed to it by the modern world, gives these last diary pages both a retrospective and anticipatory cast. To the extent that Rosenzweig submits his thought to the scrutiny of new questions, these reflections can be considered an attempt to place his thought in historical perspective. Thought not identical with our perspective here in Jerusalem, fifty years after the catastrophic collapse of the cultural world to which Rosenzweig wanted to bear witness—that of the "Jewish-German symbiosis"—the viewpoint emerging from these last diary notes, the avenues they open up, the problems they illuminate, are nevertheless so close to us that we can use them as a point of departure for a retrospective glance at Rosenzweig's thought. To assess the possible relevance of these notes and reflections for today's reader, I shall consider three themes of great importance for Rosenzweig: first, the conception of revelation as antireligion and, in this context, the reference to Freud's theses on the origin of religion; second, Rosenzweig's temptation by "quietism" and, in the same context, his hesitations about history, messianism and Zionism; and finally, the meaning in the modern world of the concept of creation.

## II

The notes on the dialectic nature of revelation, which culminates in the definition of revelation as antireligion,[4] were put down in the short period from 26 March to 4 April 1922. They frame a long letter to Rudolf Hallo (1896–1933), whose last paragraphs are devoted to this very topic. It seems that these reflections may have been inspired by a passage in a letter from Rudolf Hallo, received in January 1922, in which the latter wrote: "Behind Judaism, for me, a millenium, many millenia of pre-Jewish culture are burning more and more brightly. How the aspect changes!"[5]

The problem Rudolf Hallo raises here is that of the *method* to be used for understanding Judaism. He opposes Rosenzweig's religious approach in *The Star* with the historical method that sees in monotheism a stage in the evolution of the cultures of the Near East. Confronted with this methodological problem with which *The Star,* being a work of purely philosophical and theological inspiration, does not deal at all, Rosenzweig reacts, in his reply to Hallo and in his diary notes, not by denying the validity of scientific methods for the study of cultures and religions, but by proclaiming that Judaism is neither a culture nor a religion; he adds: "Revelation has only this function: to make the world unreligious again."[6] Seemingly paradoxical, this statement in fact relates to the classical thesis of Jewish theology, according to which the biblical revelation is distinguished from all pagan religions not by any of its specific features but by its very essence, just as the unique God who created the world and who revealed himself on Mount Sinai is of a radically different nature from the false gods of paganism. According to Rosenzweig, all human experiences are necessarily profane, not divine; what is derived from experience is, by definition, immanent in the world and cannot pretend to any divine status. The cultures and the religions that are the products of the human mind are radically opposed to the biblical revelation, which teaches the absolute transcendence of God the creator. Paradoxically, the world of creation would then have to be understood as a purely profane reality, and creation be identified with nature. On 26 March Rosenzweig writes: "Revelation renews the creation, that is to say, it reestablishes the norm, the natural."[7] In the dialectic of culture and nature, culture (i.e., religion) denies nature, and revelation denies religion, thus reestablishing the world to its original state: "Wherever the created nature has been turned into culture, revelation has again made nature manifest [*offenbar*]."[8]

This schema is totally different from that proposed in *The Star,* which is as follows: originally, the pagan world was an enchanted world; then science came and disenchanted the world; finally, man, by spreading revelation among the world, undertakes to make it sacred again.[9] The three stages of this dialectical schema (which, by the way, is very near to that of Schiller, Hölderlin and the German romantics) appear now to be moved forward by one notch: the holy pagan is no longer the original stage of human history; the norm, the primal stage, is that of the world created as pure nature, prior to any religious culture; then comes religion, which obscures and overshadows this immediate connection with nature; the role of revelation would thus not be to sacralize the world, but on the contrary to de-sacralize it again.

It is this schema that Rosenzweig develops in a diary entry dated 4 April 1922:

As long as man does *not* know *anything at all* of God, as long as he simply accepts each of his revelations as they occur to him, he is not a pagan. Only with *theology* does paganism actually start, namely, when man begins to make his experiences. Now he prays *to* the angels which God has sent him. Adventavit religio! Only one thing can help now: that God reveals *himself* (not *something* to man). Thereby giving man an aim for all projections and substantations, thus making all "religion" impossible for him.[10]

The primitive state, that which "religion" overshadowed, was that of an immediately significant world. This immediate significance is indeed of a divine nature, but precisely to the extent that it precedes every culture, every religion, every human institution. That is the old mystic idea of a natural revelation, of an original stage in which mankind, before it had been corrupted by the fall in reflection and in culture, would have directly perceived nature as a manifestation of God. Then the biblical revelation would have the function of delivering the world of the religions, which, like an opaque screen, come between God and nature, and of restoring nature in its original significance. This schema, which Rosenzweig counterposes to the reductionist approach suggested by Rudolf Hallo, is intended to distinguish the monotheistic revelation from all other religious cultures, while nevertheless placing it in the context of the religious history of mankind. Rosenzweig had used this same method in *The Star* to define the nonhistorical vocation of the Jewish people in opposition to the essentially political reality of the Gentiles. As in *The Star*, where Hegel's political philosophy served him as a frame of reference against which he expounded his theory of the nontemporal destination of the Jewish people, here he sketches his thesis of the irreligious character of the biblical revelation in contrast to the concept developed by Freud in *Totem and Taboo*. After noticing that it would be fascinating to try a Freudian interpretation of Isaac's sacrifice, Rosenzweig goes on and writes:

The experience of fatherhood would be an authentic revelation of God, precisely because God is not "contained" in it. (A father can be the representative of God as long as man does not call him "God.") Only the "father substitute," the totem, is idol-worship. Only in retrospect from Revelation does the idol appear as a *God*-substitute. In itself, in its *origin*, it is a *reality*-substitute. It distorts reality to such an extent that God no longer can send his messengers; now, God has to reveal himself; he has to establish his own religion (which is merely *anti-religion*) against the *religionitis* of man. (The second commandment is as unpagan as the first.)[11]

*Totem and Taboo* was published in 1913. Yet Rosenzweig's first reference to the concept of the totem was only in this diary entry of 1922. Before then he had never mentioned Freud's name, neither in *The Star* not even in his correspondence. Moreover, he never reverted to this theme again, except by brief allusions.[12] This note of 4 April 1922 is thus unique testimony to Rosenzweig's attitude on Freud's theses about religion. Let us briefly summarize those theses, as developed by Freud in *Totem and Taboo*. According to Freud, totemism is the primitive stage of religion. In totemist religion the tribe is placed under the protection of a sacred animal, the totem, to whom divine qualities are attributed. Freud's central thesis is that the totem is a father substitute. In a primordial stage in the history of mankind, that of the ancestral horde, in which a tyrannical father appropriated all available females, the sons one day staged a revolt in order to take his wives. The totemic religion preserved the subconscious memory of this original murder; the relation of the tribe to the totem expresed the ambivalence of the son's relation toward the father. The prohibition against killing the totem symbolizes the remorse for having killed the beloved and admired father, while the annual sacrificial rite of eating the totem is the necessary symbolic reenactment of this murder so as to be able to lead an independent existence. For Freud this structure explains the nature of all religions, even the most elaborate ones. God is always the father substitute; rites, precepts, and religious morals are always the symbolic expression of mankind's feeling of guilt for the original murder.

What interests Rosenzweig here is less the psychoanalytical interpretations as such than the fundamental ideal according to which the totem, that is, in biblical language the idol, is a *substitute*. Of the Freudian view all he retains is that in religion symbolism interposes itself like a screen between God and the world. Against this understanding of the role of religious symbols Rosenzweig posits a natural relation to the real world, which, in its living immediacy, has the character of an authentic revelation. The aim of biblical monotheism is to eliminate the "projective" symbolism, in order to re-endow the natural experiences with a spontaneously divine character.

This definition of revelation as antireligion stands in contrast to one of the most fundamental conceptions of *The Star of Redemption,* where Judaism and Christianity are described through their rites and religious symbolism, and where the system of ritual and liturgical signs is presented as the very organon of the knowledge of Redemption.[13] Here Rosenzweig's thought seems to have followed the fundamental ambiguity of symbolism itself. The symbol both reveals and screens the reality it reflects; it makes its object manifest by hiding it as well. Religious symbols have the function of representing spiritual realities, but in representing them they obscure them. In *The Star* Rosenzweig considered the religious symbols in their transparency, as manifestations of the truth. In his diary of 1922 he places the emphasis on their opacity. For Rosenzweig, what makes Jewish revelation antireligion is perhaps precisely the awareness of this ambiguity, the fact that, for Jewish monotheism, God is always beyond the signs that manifest him.

### III

The second theme, Rosenzweig's "quietism," is directly related to the previous one. As early as 1931, in an article that appeared on the occasion of the publication of the second edition of *The Star*, Gershom Scholem emphasized the quietestic aspect of Rosenzweig's thought, especially in respect to his conception of Judaism. In one of his diary entries of 1922 Rosenzweig seems to confirm this interpretation:

Redemption delivers God, man, world from the shapes and morphisms that had been forced upon them by Creation. Before and afterwards is "beyond." But the middle, Revelation, though it is entirely here on our side— for I am I and God is God and world is world—nevertheless is quite beyond, for I am with God. God is with me, and where is the world? It overcomes the creaturely death and establishes the rights of the redeeming death. He who loves *no longer* believes in death and *only* believes in death.[14]

These words give evidence to the ambiguity of the notion of revelation, which lies at the heart of *The Star of Redemption* and is the point of departure for Rosenzweig's entire system. In *The Star* this ambiguity already betrays itself through the semantic ambivalence of the very term *revelation*, which refers now to the totality of the world of personal experience as it was described in the second part of the work, now to the specific experience of the direct relationship between God and man. In its widest sense, revelation describes reality itself, with its three elements—God, the world and man—and the three relations among them. In its narrowest sense, revelation is the quasi-mystical experience of man's encounter with God. In the first case, the philosophical intention of *The Star* would be essentially *realistic:* it would be a matter of demonstrating in what respect the concrete experience specifically of the religious man most spontaneously unveils the immediate reality of things. In the second case, *The Star* ought to be understood as a *mystic* work, since the whole system would lead back to the original experience of the meeting between man and God.

In *The Star* Rosenzweig seems to waver between these two interpretations. At the end, however, he appears to be carried away by realism, since the mystic experience of revelation, even though it is the central moment of the system, is presented as a dialectic moment that must be passed through, as a point of departure destined to lead to life.[15] The problem posed by those last words of *The Star* is the point of departure of Rosenzweig's reflections in his diary note of May 1922.

The term *life* seems to contain an ambiguity even more fundamental than that of the word *revelation*. *The Star* presents itself as a dialectic of life and death, as an attempt not to deny death in the manner of the philosophy "from Ionia to Jena," but to assume it and to go beyond it. *The Star* traces a road "from death to life." The central stage along that road is revelation, which, as the manifestation of God's love for man, is the victory over death; for love, as it is written in the Song of Songs, "is strong as death." In that diary entry of May 1922 Rosenzweig realizes that this victory is nothing but a metaphor, that the kind of life to which revelation gives access is spiritual life, that the road "from death to life" is nothing other than the "mystical road" of religion.

Rosenzweig had conceived *The Star* as a history of the Absolute through the three great phases of its development. The first stage was to correspond to the original unity of all things in the bosom of the Absolute; the second, starting with creation and terminating with redemption, was to cover the entire history of mankind; and the third was to be that of the final reintegration of all reality into the reconstituted divine unity. Only the intermediate stage is that of life; the first and the last are "beyond" (*Jenseits*). Yet to the extent that life is the result of a separation from the original divine unity, it is of necessity bound to limitation, to finitude, that is to say, to death.

In the second part of *The Star*, creation, which is God's relation to the world, separates God the creator from man, conceived here as part of the world, as a thing among things, and consequently doomed to finitude and to death. Revelation in the narrow sense of the term—which is God's relation to man—would thus have a double function: on the one hand it distinguishes man from the world, it removes him from his condition of being a thing among other things, and in the middle of life invests him with the fullness of his humanity; on the other hand, by taking him out of the world and installing him outside it in a privileged relation with God, it also removes him from life itself. Such is the paradox of revelation: it liberates man from death but at the same time from life. In other words, through revelation man gains access to a timeless life, preserved from the attrition and degradation that characterize natural life. Death does not disappear in revelation, it changes its significance. It is no longer perceived in opposition to natural life, for man himself has renounced the latter in favor of a spiritual life that already appears as some sort of symbolic death. In revelation, man is beyond life and death: "I am near God, God is near me, and where is the world?" There is nothing more authentically mystical than this formulation by Rosenzweig, where the spiritual life is already perceived as a symbolic anticipation of death: "He who loves *no longer* believes in death, and *only* believes in death." Here Rosenzweig no longer hesitates to interpret his own philosophy as quietism, as an aspiration to the internal peace, to the timelessness of the spiritual life, at the price of renouncing the reality of the world.

That this quietism was one of the deepest foundations of his world view, and that he did not cease to question it, is attested to by the notes in this diary devoted to Zionism and messianism. Zionism is not explicitly mentioned in *The Star*. The Jewish aspiration for redemption is deprived there of all its historical impetus by the concept of a quasi-timeless Jewish people that realizes its religious vocation far from the hazards of history, in the ever-renewed eternity of its liturgical time. The idea that the Jew does not have to pursue redemption and even less provoke it since he lives it in anticipation through the symbolism of rites, the refusal to let the Jewish people compromise itself in the impurity of history; the severe criticism of politics; the view of Christianity as the agent of the historical advent of redemption—all imply the absolute rejection of any attempt on the part of the Jewish people to hasten the advent of the kingdom of God by historical means. Yet Rosenzweig emphasizes that the symbolic anticipation of redemption through rite—in particular the Yom Kippur rite—is not the same as the real redemption that would put an end to history and that, consequently, cannot be anything but a historic event. At the very center of the Jewish experience of eternity there would thus be an aspiration toward the future, an expectation—certainly purely passive and disconnected from historic reality—of a redemption that can occur unexpectedly at any moment. This abstract messianism, conceived as a purely religious category without any relation to profane time, became the germ of an intellectual evolution that led Rosenzweig to an almost complete reversal of his position. The diary notes of 1922 are an important milestone in this development.

In letters he wrote in 1917 and 1918, Rosenzweig accused Zionism of being an exclusively political ideology aimed at reducing Judaism to a simple nationalism; as such, it would deprive Judaism of its religious vocation, which is the sole guarantee of its eternity. In a note dated 12 April 1922, he seems to reaffirm this attitude: "If Zionism brings the Messiah, then *The Star* will become superfluous. But all other books, too." [16] Here the opposition between *The Star* and Zionism appears complete. The former is placed on a level with "all other books," that is, with the whole of universal culture symbolizing a "spiritual" conception of redemption, while Zionism represents an attempt at bringing the Messiah, forcing his coming, by purely historic means. But what is important is that the possibility of such an attempt is here alluded to for the first time. Messianism is no longer defined as a purely timeless category; although it does not necessarily imply a relation to history, neither does it exclude it. A political and national movement like Zionism is not necessarily messianic, yet it is not a priori excluded from being such. Further on in the same note, Rosenzweig throws light on the fundamental ambiguity of all messianic movements in the history of Judaism. This ambiguity does not detract from them or call into question their messianic character. Such ambiguity is part of the very essence of the messianic event, which is always susceptible to two ways of interpretation—a natural and supranatural one—that are not mutually exclusive; neither is the one more "true" than the other. In the chiaroscuro of history all the great messianic movements *are and are not* what they pretend to be: "Can I dissociate myself from it, because it is only *possibly* messianic? Which movement would *not* be only 'possibly'?"[17]

Another diary entry strongly underlines the presence of this historic dimension at the heart of the Jewish faith. The Jewish prayer, says Rosenzweig, contains in its very essence the hope for a return to the Land of Israel. If Western Judaism of the nineteenth century lost the sense of this national dimension, that is due not so much to the process of social emancipation as to religious alienation: "After 1800 we ceased to pray for the Return, because we ceased to *pray*. If we had continued praying, we would have prayed for the Return."[18] Rosenzweig now recognizes the central importance of the national dimension of Judaism. For him, however, the national dimension is not a factor of Israel's religious faith, nor vice versa; rather the fundamental ground of Judaism remains one's faith. He thus contends that for the modern Judaism of the Diaspora, the expression of religious faith could, indeed must, survive the loss of the longing for national redemption: "It was the error of liberalism that we stopped praying, [simply] because we no longer wanted to pray for the return." But three months later this diary entry of Rosenzweig refers to one of the central ideas of Judah Halevi and of the historiosophical tradition inspired by him, that of the quasi-organic bond of Jewish prophecy with the Land of Israel, and connects it with a classic thesis of Zionism—that of the historic (Rosenzweig says: Jewish and religious) sterility of the part of the Jewish people that has decided to strike roots in the Diaspora:

The connection of prophetism with the land (instead of, as is the case with the Christians, with time) is something which arouses much thought. It is simply true that the Jew who strikes roots in the Diaspora loses his Jewish-religious strength. Without a bit of alienation from the Germans, even Hermann Cohen would not have been such a Jew.[19]

IV

The last theme in Rosenzweig's diaries on which I want to comment is the meaning of creation in the modern world. In the third trimester of the academic year 1921–22, Rosenzweig gave his last course of lectures at the Freies Jüdisches Lehrhaus. In the trimester program of the Lehrhaus, prepared by Rosenzweig himself, this course, entitled "The Science of the World," was outlined as follows:

> The question:  The world as representation
> The world as change: Nature
> The world as form: Art
> The world as order: Law
> The world as conflict: Power
> The world as a work: Spirit
> The world as home: Technique
> The answer:  The world as creation

A great many of Rosenzweig's diary entries between mid-April and early June 1922 are devoted to reflections on this subject. The complex turns around one of Rosenzweig's central problems in *The Star of Redemption:* the reality of the outside world. This was surely the fundamental question he had to confront in his polemic against idealism. "The phenomenon had been the stumbling block of idealism,"[20] writes Rosenzweig in *The Star.* Since we perceive the world only through the representation we make of it, how can we be sure that there exists an objective reality beyond that representation? In Rosenzweig's view this question, by its very nature, is unsolvable. All the originality of his "new thinking" lies in his refusal to pose the question of representation and to base the reality of the world on our own intuitive evidence of it. However, in the second part of *The Star,* when Rosenzweig has to explicate the manner in which this intuition presents itself to us, he is forced to admit that our experience of the world is incomplete; we perceive it as an appearance whose essence escapes us: "The world is mysterious because it reveals itself before its essence exists."[21]

The world is certainly evident, but its evidence is that of an appearance; it has the ambiguous reality of the phenomenon, of the entire external apparition. The being, the substantiality the world lacks, man must give to it. In the experience of revelation, which raises him above the world of things, man becomes conscious that, as a spiritual being, he has within himself a part of indestructible reality. To to the extent that he turns toward the world in order to humanize it, he confers upon it this reality and gives it that solid substance, that ontological foundation that it lacked. This projection of revelation onto the world is what defines redemption. But the concrete modalities of achieving redemption are not clearly defined. From *The Star* we only know that there are two modes of reaching redemption: one consists in transforming the world from inside, the other consists in leaving the world behind in order to take refuge in the eternity of sacred, that is, liturgical, time. There are thus two different modes of man's relation to the world: the first is historical, the second symbolical. In the religious typology of *The Star*, the historical relation to the world defines the collective vocation of Christianity, and the symbolic relation defines the collective vocation of and defines Judaism (although for the individual this schema is quite the opposite: through his faith the Christian is detached from the world; through his destiny the Jew is obliged to take part in it). The third part of *The Star*, comparing the ritual structures of Judaism and Christianity, considers the religious dimension of redemption or the symbolic relation of man to the world. It does not concern itself with deciphering the modalities of man's practical engagement in historic reality. It is precisely this question, left open in *The Star*, that Rosenzweig takes up again in his lecture course in the spring of 1922.

Three years after having completed *The Star*, Rosenzweig realized that in his great systematic work he had unwittingly used an idealistic method. For the idea that man endows the world with reality only by projecting his own experience on it would seem to render the very foundations of man's thought questionable. Is it still possible thus to guarantee the external world's objective reality? What is left of the experience of creation, which according to *The Star* unveils itself precisely in the fact that the world is always there before us? Such were the questions Rosenzweig was asking himself at the time he gave his course "The Science of the World."

In his notes of 1922, Rosenzweig first distinguishes three aspects of man's perception of reality—nature, law and art. These three facets were already present in *The Star,* though in a diffuse and unsystematic form, as the profane version of three fundamental religious categories: creation, Judaism and Christianity. Nature is the form in which creation appears to us when we abstract its negativity, its finitude, when we are insensitive to the horizon of the absolute on which it is reflected. Law, that is, the political organization of society, represents the attempt at controlling historic time from the inside, in contrast with Judaism which, according to Rosenzweig, creates a parallel, nonhistorical time, thus escaping the hazards of history. Art plays the same role toward Christianity as law toward Judaism: it is for the individual a quest for salvation, but a profane salvation, that is, a solitary one that does not care for communion with other humans.

But these three experiences do not give us access to the immediate reality of the world. On the contrary, they themselves are constructions of the human spirit. Nature, law and art are "representations," productions of an original theoretical activity. In his diary notes, Rosenzweig outlines the epistemology of this theoretical activity in its three forms: the scientific, the juridical and the aesthetical. Each of these three theoretical attitudes has its own axiomatics, by which it constructs its specific field of activity. Science creates its own object, which is nature, through a process of relativization: it relates the image we have of the world to the point of view of the observer. The view of the world art gives us also has no objective reality. Each artist deciphers the world in his own fashion; every viewer interprets the work of art as he understands it: this is a twofold process of appropriation in which everything ultimately leads to the pleasure of the viewer, listener or reader. Law constructs a specific type of reality for its own use, which is purely abstract, based on the principle of distinguishing and isolating specific cases. As far as law presents itself as general and pretends to apply mechanically to everyone and always in the same manner, it no longer begets justice but injustice.[22]

Thus science, law and art are abstract spheres that, to be sure, are necessary insofar as they satisfy our needs to understand, yet are unreal insofar as they can in no way guarantee to us that an outside world actually exists beyond them. Opposite these three abstract spheres Rosenzweig places the three most concrete realities of all: those of technology, ideology and politics. These are translations into praxis of the three categories of man's theoretical activities. Technique, politics and ideology (Rosenzweig uses the term *Weltanschauung*)[23] are the practical applications of science, law and art— this time not in order to *interpret* the world, but to *dominate* it. Praxis, too, is a projection of human activity onto the world; just like theory, it does not encounter its object but creates it. Yet in contrast to theory, praxis creates the very matter of the world. In this sense it is even more idealistic than theory, but at the same time infinitely more realistic, since knowledge creates only abstract representations, while man's power over the world shapes reality as such.[24]

Thus, precisely to the extent that they impose an external order on the world, technology, politics and ideology violate its natural structure. While knowledge misses the world through its lack of realism (or through an excess of theory), power misses it through an excess of realism (or through a lack of theory). Here Rosenzweig contrasts the *irreality* of knowledge with the *super-reality* of human praxis.[25] The brutality of man's power creates an oversimplified, schematic, but dangerously *real* world. "The super-reality of the spirit," writes Rosenzweig (*spirit*, to him, signifies "ideology"), "consists in that the world has day and night. But the spirit is always *awake*."[26] This vigilance of the spirit is not that of reason, which incessantly transforms the world through knowledge, but that pitiless vigilance of ideology, which never rests, which watches over the world and supervises it, effacing the difference between the rational and the imaginary, the diurnal and the nocturnal, depriving the world of its sleep and the night of its mystery, throwing a crude and uniform light on all reality. The same applies to technology: the surface of the globe, says Rosenzweig, is made of lands and seas, or, as it is told in Genesis, of the dry and the wet; not all of it is habitable. Nature's subjection by man has its own natural limits; when man oversteps them, he destroys the world he pretended to tame. But technology is not concerned with natural equilibria; it wants to conquer nature as a whole. As for political power, it ignores the duality of earth and heaven, of the temporal and the spiritual. Political power is totalitarian by nature; its ambition knows no limits. Far from submitting itself to transcendental exigencies, it pretends, on the contrary, to determine by itself its own scale of values. "Power," writes Rosenzweig, "is prepared to fight for mastery over heaven itself." Wishing to impose order on the world by force, praxis ends up turning against itself. Technology, politics and ideology appear in reality less as products of human activity than as autonomous forces that enclose man and reduce him to the status of an object. Technological power, ideological power, political power—these are in the final analysis the true dangers that threaten modern man. "The scholar, the artist, the jurist are only stammering," writes Rosenzweig, "they do not attain reality. Whereas the man of power, the ideologist, the technician are really frightening." [27]

The dualities of day and night, of dry and wet, of heaven and earth—these three pairs of opposites define creation in the Bible. For Rosenzweig, the biblical narrative presents us with the most faithful image of reality: a complex network of contrasts, of tensions, of more or less tenuous balances. This complexity, which technology, politics and ideology try to deny, is inscribed in the heart of creation. Between the brute *super-reality* of praxis and the *irreality* of theory, creation—as the biblical text describes it, but also as we feel it intuitively by our immediate experience—reveals to us the world in its very reality, as something that is at the same time eminently complex and absolutely concrete. This concrete complexity manifests itself in three aspects, which are the true intuitive sources of the three theoretical activities of man: creation in itself is *arranged in an order;* each being, each thing occupies its proper place; it is this natural order that makes law possible. From another aspect, the existence of the world is spontaneously perceived as something good; "And God saw that it was good" says the biblical text after each day of the creation. In the simple fact that the world is, lies something fundamentally good. This feeling, says Rosenzweig, is the origin of art. Finally, the Bible does not present the creation as one single moment in which Being bursts forth from nothingness, but as a complicated process, spread out over time, in which every day produces its own order of reality: it is this original complexity that accords to science its objectivity. [28] This conception of creation as an intermediary instance between idealism and realism, between theory and praxis, exemplifies Rosenzweig's philosophical position as it emerges from the study of his last diaries: beyond the systematic, almost dogmatic construction of *The Star of Redemption*, we have here a living tension between opposite poles: contemplation and experience, eternity and history, mysticism and life.

# II

# Rosenzweig: Recollections of a Disciple

*Ernst Akiva Simon*

Was Buber right to regard Rosenzweig as a latter-day Job? Surely Rosenzweig suffered no less, but unlike Job he never sought redress on high for his grievances. Some hold that Job never existed at all but is merely a paradigm; Rosenzweig did exist, yet he is also paradigmatic, personifying the faith expressed by Job: "I know that my Redeemer lives" (19:25). For whom does Rosenzweig serve as a model and in what ways?

This chapter is structured around the three groups that Rosenzweig influenced, which can be seen as three concentric circles. The first, the outermost circle, is made up of scholars of philosophy, both Jews and non-Jews. Closer to the center is a second circle made up of those seeking a path in Judaism who have found Rosenzweig's life and teachings helpful in their quest. This group, which is far larger than the first, is made up almost entirely of Jews but includes a few Christians as well. The third and innermost circle is made up of those few surviving individuals who were close to Rosenzweig personally—his colleagues and disciples. These people can testify directly, if subjectively, to his influence upon them.

### The Philosophical Circle

Gershom Scholem said of Rosenzweig that he had the fortitude to construct a philosophical system. A system has two advantages: it makes it hard for its author to overlook things that make him uncomfortable, and it forces him to organize his thoughts in a manner that is not merely random. Indeed, the opening phrase of *The Star of Redemption* is, "All cognition of the All originates in death, in the fear of death," while the closing sentence is, "Whither, then, do the wings of the gate [of the oracle, of the Sanctuary] open? Thou knowest not? *Into life*."[1] Rosenzweig saw the All, that is, the totality of things, as the hallmark of philosophical systems. In his *Critique of Pure Reason* Kant writes,

By architectonic I understand the art of constructing systems. A systematic unity is what first raises ordinary knowledge to the rank of science, that is, it makes a system out of a mere aggregate of knowledge. . . . In accordance with reason's legislative prescriptions, our diverse modes of knowledge must not be permitted to be a mere *rhapsody*, but must form a system.[2]

The term in the original edition is *Rhapsodie*,[3] which in Greek means an oral declamation or utterance accompanied by renditions of selected Homeric songs. Rosenzweig uses the word *rhapsodisch* in a long letter he wrote in 1917 while serving in the German army in Macedonia. This letter, written to his friend and relative Rudolf Ehrenberg, was first published in 1937 in the posthumous volume *Kleinere Schriften*, edited by his widow Edith. Rosenzweig himself supplied a title for the letter in an oral reference to it: "The Germ Cell of *The Star of Redemption*."[4] In the letter he writes, "The following picture thus emerges: the various relations with which I dealt above, one by one and side by side, have now been fitted together."[5] In the German the "side-by-side" form of argument is called *rhapsodisch nebeneinander*. The reference is to those matters that Rosenzweig takes up at greater length in part 1 of *The Star*, the part he calls "The Elements, or the Ever-Enduring Protocosmos" and that deals with the philosophy of Greek paganism. Furthermore, in his article "The New Thinking: Some Notes on *The Star of Redemption*" (1925),[6] Rosenzweig minimizes the systematic character of that part of the book.[7] Its three subheadings are arranged arbitrarily and could have been arranged differently without detracting from their import. It is only with the second part, where the discussion turns to creation, revelation, and redemption, that the order becomes deliberate and unchangeable: creation in the past, revelation ever present, and redemption in the time to come. In other words (words not used by Rosenzweig in this context), a choppy, even anarchic, rhapsody will do when speaking of the Greek world, which preceded the revelation of the Divine Presence. But with the establishment of the three facts of God, man, and the world, facts not deduced from each another but linked by creation, revelation, and redemption, the architectonics of the system become decisive. Toward the end of the earlier-mentioned article Rosenzweig uses a philosophical catchphrase, "absolute empiricism," to describe his method of relating to these three facts. By this he means that man can *experience* God, himself, and the world. The empiricism is absolute because it can also be applied to that which is absolute; but in himself man finds only the human, in the world only the mundane, and in God only the divine.

Several questions arise in this connection. The first turns on the matter of architectonics. Rosenzweig insists that the latter be all-encompassing, ignoring the danger of its becoming a bit tyrannical once granted methodological omnipotence. Rosenzweig's original and highly successful educational undertaking, the Freies Jüdisches Lehrhaus in Frankfurt, provides an illustration. The academic year was divided into three trimesters, in each of which the students were offered three course groupings. During the trimester of mid-January to mid-March 1922, which saw the onset of Rosenzweig's eight-year illness, the courses were grouped around God, the world, and man. Reading today the course titles offered under these headings, one is struck by certain incongruities, courses that seem not to fit. Rosenzweig was aware of this; he had give the program a kind of "rhapsodic" appendix, a "dessert," as it were, intended to provide "amplification and stimulation of interest" (*zur Klärung und Anregung*). Far more significant is the fact that the invalid insisted on continuing his own teaching, albeit at home, right up to the end of the third semester of that year, that is, until the end of June.

It seems likely that his illness prompted him to make time in the curriculum for some of the ideas in *The Star,* especially since this difficult book had been slow to find a readership. I am not ashamed to admit that I myself did not give the book a thorough reading before the author's death in 1929, and I know that I was not the only one among his friends. Even today, having gone back over the book more than once, I am not sure I understand it all.

The second critical question is whether the philosophical approach is in fact the only legitimate one to problems of faith. There is, as we know, another kind of religious thinker, exemplified by Pascal, Johann H. Pestalozzi (1746–1827), Abraham Isaac Kook, and Buber. A consistent philosophical system in a sense gives rise to a new entity. And precisely because these others agree with Rosenzweig that man *encounters* the world, they approach the problem of understanding it from a variety of angles. They too espouse "absolute empiricism," but only in regard to man and the world; the knowledge of God they approach differently. As an example of the latter I suggest a verse from the Song of Praise (Ps. 100: 3): "It is He who made us and not we ourselves [or, after slight emendation, "and we are His"], His people and His flock." The two readings are equally plausible, but the emended text may be preferable, for in Genesis Rabbah the verse is explained a a fitting answer to Pharaoh's boast, "My river is mine, and I made myself" (Ezek. 29: 3)—meaning, man created his own world and thus "made himself a god."

Else Freund takes up this issue in her important *Franz Rosenzweig's Philosophy of Existence: An Analysis of The Star of Redemption,* in the final chapter, entitled "The System and Its Relativization by Revelation." [8] She maintains that in place of the rigorous superficiality called into question by the preeminence of faith over solipsistic thought comes dialogical thought. The latter is made possible by a view of language as divine revelation, not a human invention but a gift of God.

I myself have called *The Star of Redemption* "the first comprehensive philosophical system to grow out of the spirit of Judaism." [9] It should be stressed that Rosenzweig himself did not see it as an exclusively Jewish book. In a 1921 letter to his relative Hans Ehrenberg (who converted in 1911 as a matter of deep conviction to Christianity), Rosenzweig wrote that if Schelling had finished *The*

*Ages of the World* (*Die Weltalter*), in which he first developed the notion of "the new thinking" that characterizes the first part of *The Star,* "[the latter] would not have been worthy of anyone's attention except the Jews'."[10]

We may conclude our discussion of the first circle by saying that the significance of Rosenzweig's *general* philosophy for us lies in the fact that he liberates us from what he calls the "one-dimensional thinking of German idealism." (Herbert Marcuse uses the same phrase in an altogether different sense in a polemically Marxist context!) Rosenzweig was referring to the great Self—the "transcendent" Self, as Kant called it—which is the author of the laws of nature and which according to Fichte is the creator of the nonself. Thus did Rosenzweig grasp the role of the Creator of the World.

## The Second Circle: Seekers Returning to Judaism

Rosenzweig greeted with reserve the misleading praise given *The Star* by "that part of Jewish youth seeking in various ways to return to traditional Judaism." This reserve is a reflection of the self-limitation required in a comprehensive "philosophical system." But later on Rosenzweig wrote an extremely important article that was in fact addressed to "that part of the youth" seeking a way back to Judaism. The article is called "The Builders,"[11] and it was written as an open letter to Martin Buber. In fact it is not addressed to him alone. True, Rosenzweig begins with Buber's silence on the subject of the Commandments, his refusal in his anthropology to answer Kant's fourth question: What ought we to do? But then he also attacks the idea of predicating the obligation—or privilege—of religious observance upon a dogma of "literal inspiration," an idea Buber seemed to share with the Orthodox. Rosenzweig thus reveals another difficulty with the application of "absolute empiricism" to revelation, for he does not adhere to the Orthodox view and strenuously opposes the slogan of all or nothing. In another exchange of letters he concedes to Buber that the God who reveals Himself is not a lawgiver, and in "The Builders" he goes a long way toward emptying the revelation at Sinai of all specific content other than the first two of the Ten Commandments: "I am the LORD" and "You shall have no other gods beside Me." To grasp this paradox one must read the following two passages from "The Builders" in juxtaposition with one another:

Earlier centuries had already reduced the teachings to genteel poverty, to a few fundamental concepts; it remained for the nineteenth to pursue this as a consistent method, with the utmost seriousness. You have liberated the teaching from this circumscribed sphere and, in so doing, removed us from the imminent danger of making our spiritual Judaism depend on whether or not it was possible for us to be followers of Kant.

And so it is all the more curious that after liberating us and pointing the way to a new teaching, your answer to the other side of the question, the question concerning the Law: "What are we to do?"—that your answer should leave this Law in the shackles put upon it—as well as upon the teachings—by the nineteenth century. For is it really Jewish law with which you try to come to terms and, not succeeding, on which you turn your back, only to tell yourself and us who look to you for answers that our sole task must be to take cognizance of the Law with reverence—a reverence which can effect no practical difference in our lives or to our persons? Is that really Jewish law, the law of millennia, studied and lived, analyzed and rhapsodized, the law of everyday and of the day of death, petty and yet sublime, sober and yet woven in legend; a law which knows both the fire of the Sabbath candle and that of the martyr's stake? The law Akiba planted and fenced in, and Aher trampled under, the cradle Spinoza hailed from, the ladder on which the Baal Shem ascended, the law that always rises beyond itself, that can never be reached—and yet has always the possibility of becoming Jewish life, of being expressed in Jewish faces? Is the Law you speak of not rather the Law of the Western orthodoxy of the past century?

Here too, to be sure, the limiting process of reducing to formulas was not initiated in the nineteenth century. Just as the formulas into which the liberalism of the reformers wanted to crowd the Jewish spirit can be traced back to a long line of antecedents, so too can one trace back the reasons that S. R. Hirsch gives to his *Yisroel-Mensch* for keeping the Law. But no one before Hirsch and his followers ever seriously attempted to construct Jewish life on the narrow base of these reasons. For did any Jew prior to this really think—without having the question put to him—that he was keeping the Law, and the Law him, only because God imposed it upon Israel at Sinai? Actually faced by the question, he might have thought of such an answer; and the philosophers to whom the question has been put because they were supposedly "professional" thinkers have always been fond of giving this very reply.

From Mendelssohn on, our entire people has subjected itself to the torture of this embarrassing questioning; the Jewishness of every individual has squirmed on the needle point of a "why." Certainly, it was high time for an architect to come and convert this foundation into a wall behind which the people, pressed with questions, could seek shelter. But for those living without questions, this reason for keeping the Law was only one among others and probably not the most cogent. No doubt the Torah, both written and oral, was given Moses on Sinai, but was it not created before the creation of the world? Written against a background of shining fire in letters of somber flame? And was not the world created for its sake? And did not Adam's son Seth found the first House of Study for the teaching of the Torah? And did not the patriarchs keep the Law for half a millennium before Sinai? And—when it was finally given on Sinai—was it not given in all the seventy languages spoken in the world? It has 613 commandments, a number which, to begin with, mocks all endeavor to count what is countless, but a number which in itself (plus the two commandments heard directly from the lips of the Almighty) represents the numerical value of the word Torah and the sum of the days of the year and the joints in the body of man. Did not these 613 commandments of the Torah include everything that the scrutiny and penetration of later scholars, who "put to shame" our teacher Moses himself, discovered in the crownlets and tips of the letters? And everything that the industrious student could ever hope to discover there, in all future time? The Torah, which God himself learns day after day!

And can we really fancy that Israel kept this law, this Torah, only because of the one "fact which excluded the possibility of delusions," that the six hundred thousand heard the voice of God on Sinai? This "fact" certainly does play a part, but no greater part than all we have mentioned before, and all that our ancestors perceived in every "today" of the Torah: that the souls of all generations to come stood on Sinai along with those six hundred thousand and heard what they heard. For a Jewish consciousness that does not question and is not questioned, all this is as important as the "fact," and that "fact" no whit more important than these other considerations.[12]

We stand dumbfounded: is this not the language of rhapsody? And rightly so! For this text does not fit into his philosophical system. What is more, it includes a bit of law and more than a bit of lore. At the same time, the Commandments are spoken of here in the sense of the maxim that there is greater virtue in carrying them out if one is commanded to do so. Rosenzweig suggests fulfilling the law not as something juridically binding but as an internalized imperative, where the ability to carry out a certain precept automatically becomes an obligation to do so. And suffering from his terrible affliction while writing this, he speaks of "cruel grace."

The younger generation would face a new and different question, one that would be deeply personal. But for the older, it was a choice between two realms: that of separation and that of return.

## The Third Circle: Colleagues and Disciples

Rosenzweig kept in close contact with Professor Eugen Rosenstock-Huessy (1888–1973). In 1912 he went to hear Rosenstock's lectures on law at the University of Leipzig. After this they met frequently for profound discussions about science and religion as well as Judaism and Christianity, and they became close friends. Their friendship even endured Rosenstock-Huessy's conversion to Christianity—and a decidedly Calvinist version of it at that. Rosenzweig did not take him to task for this, for he trusted Rosenstock-Huessy's spiritual integrity. He himself, after all, had considered making the same move, but in his own case Judaism had won out. Needless to say, neither interlocutor ever got the upper hand in the debate; rather, each emerged from it strengthened in his own faith, having achieved it through so conscious a process of personal decision making. In 1916 the two men were separated by the war, but they continued their debate in an intense exchange of letters.[13]

Later, Rosenzweig sent his friend the essay "The Builders" as a postscript to one of his letters. In reply, Rosenstock-Huessy asked Rosenzweig what influence he expected his (Rosenzweig's) ideas to have in the future: would they stand the test of time? (This is implied in Rosenzweig's reply of 25 August 1924).[14] Rosenzweig's view was that it would take several generations—a century or so—for history to bring in its verdict. While the question confronting his own generation was To return or to leave? he expected his children and grandchildren to face once again a process of "natural selection": To observe or to transgress? In this he was proved correct, though for reasons quite different from what he anticipated. It was not his personal example or his Lehrhaus that would restore large numbers of Jews to normalcy but the establishment of the State of Israel. This Rosenzweig neither foresaw nor hoped for, although he supported the upbuilding of the land of Israel. The very existence of the state created a situation—still with us—in which most of the country's Jewish citizens, religious and nonreligious alike, have had to make a choice between observance and nonobservance, a choice Rosenzweig saw as "biographical," as opposed to the "moral" choice he himself confronted. In his view, the very existence of Diaspora Jewry was predicated on religious observance, particularly on the precept of the study of Torah. In this too he proved right, though his own religious return was not prompted by such pragmatic considerations, which are the result of historical hindsight. It seems likely that the growing interest in his thought among American Jews has been sparked, at last in part, by a concern for group survival. W. H. Hallo's translation of *The Star of Redemption* (New York, 1970) has also been a contributing factor. The latter is the son of Rudolph Hallo (1896–1933), like Rosenzweig a native of Cassel and for a year the director of the Lehrhaus.

The elder of the circle, in the sense of both age and wisdom, was Josef Prager, who recently (1982) died in Haifa at the venerable age of ninety-two. Until his death his mind remained as lively and his spirit as enthusiastic as ever, as his letters to me, written in a firm hand and in flawless Hebrew, attest. Prager's father was the rabbi of Kassel and its environs, and the son absorbed the traditional atmosphere of his parents' home. He also had other teachers. He was a year older than Rosenzweig, whom he first met in "religious studies" classes at primary school. The two were not especially enthusiastic about these classes, but at least they got to hear names such as Sa'adya Gaon, Judah Halevi, and Maimonides. Later they would look together for ways of exploring these matters more deeply and acquiring real knowledge about them.

When Rosenzweig decided to accept the late Rabbi Dr. George Salzburger's invitation to go to Frankfurt to help him and his associates with their Jewish adult-education program, Prager gave him a letter of recommendation to Rabbi Nehemiah Nobel (1871–1922). Rosenzweig went to see him, got to know him personally, and became a devotee of his sermons, which Rosenzweig enjoyed as long as they did not refer to Goethe. He also took part in the weekly Talmud class, which opened up a whole new world to him. I too attended this class, and it was in this way that we became acquainted.

When his only son was born in 1922, Rosenzweig was already ill and feared he would not live to see the circumcision. He asked Prager to come from Breslau to perform the ceremony. It was just at that time that Prager was about to move his family to Breslau so that he could enroll as a regular student in the rabbinical seminary there, founded in the previous century by Zechariah Frankel (1801–1875). (He did not intend to serve in the rabbinate but rather to place his considerable Jewish knowledge on a more systematic footing.) Rosenzweig encouraged him in this undertaking, telling him that a person who was already knowledgeable when he entered such an institution was the real student. And who could be better qualified than this friend to serve as his son's circumciser?

He asked me to be the godfather. At the time I was in Heidelberg, and in his letter of invitation he explained that his intention was not so much to honor me personally—older, more learned candidates were available—but to stand in for Rabbi Nobel, who meanwhile had died, shortly after his fiftieth birthday. Rosenzweig's letters after this misfortune attest to the weightiness of this loss to him and to the community as a whole. Prager kept notes of his meetings with Rosenzweig, part of which were included in Rosenzweig's recently published *Letters and Diaries* (*Briefe und Tagebücher*). After the circumcision, which for Rosenzweig was a real religious celebration in spite of everything, Prager stayed behind to talk with Rosenzweig at length. At the end of the conversation Rosenzweig, who by now could only speak with tremendous difficulty and whose speech was intelligible only to the doctor accustomed to hearing it, told Prager his thoughts about "suffering, death, and the continuation of life in the next generation."

Prager was a psychiatrist who had written, among other things, about Freud and about the pathological factors behind Mendelssohn's long silence in the wake of Lavater's attack upon him. But Prager did not treat Rosenzweig, not so much because of the distance between Breslau and Frankfurt but because Rosenzweig himself rejected any psychological explanation of his illness. Three other physicians who were close to Rosenzweig—Richard Koch (1882–1949), Richard Tuteur (d. 1971), and Martin Goldner (d. 1987)—did write about his illness, but their articles were very much the observations of disciples. None of them found Rosenzweig to be a particularly stoical patient. He did try to make matters easier for his wife, who bore the brunt of his treatment, but he always found a way of suppressing his irritability. Nonetheless, his principal physician Richard Koch summed up his impressions of him in this way: "I must admit that this patient would very likely have succumbed to his illness much sooner had it not been for the fact that he struggled against it with all his might, year in year out, month in month out, and finally from week to week and hour to hour." [15]

One person was so close to Rosenzweig that he undertook to compile an index to *The Star of Redemption*—Nahum Glatzer. The latter's book in English, *Franz Rosenzweig: His Life and Thought* (1959) was assembled largely from Rosenzweig's own writings, [16] and there is no source that compares with it. Nevertheless, I should like to add my own testimony to that of my friend. During the course of a long lifetime I have known many great men, but I have never met anyone like Rosenzweig.

In the first place, he did not know any better than others what would befall the Jews of Germany and later those of central and eastern Europe. He did, however, sense an impending earthquake. One is reminded of the sort of seismograph that registers tremors even before they have arrived. While still serving as a soldier in the First World War, he wrote a little book, "Zeit Ist's" (*"It is Time"*), which sought to rouse German Jewry. [17] What it was time for was education: without intensive Jewish education there could be no future for the community of which he and his disciples felt themselves to be a part. He thus made all of us human seismographs.

Second, he was not content with fine talk; he also acted. A non-Zionist, though by no means an anti-Zionist, he put his beliefs into practice, which is more than most German Zionists were prepared to do. In his own sphere of concern, that of a faith that hearkens to the pulse of history, he was the greatest *baal teshuvah* (returnee to religion) of his generation. With his own life he proved that the path of assimilation was not a one-way street, but that one could—and was therefore commanded to—reverse its direction.

Third, this tremendous strength of will enabled him to withstand a severe illness for eight years and to remain active until the day before he died. He saw this illness not as a punishment for sin, but as the occasion for a struggle that would require every ounce of whatever energy remained to him, to the bitter end.

Concerning Zionism, the two of us debated one another but never quarreled. When, just before Passover in 1928, I told him that my wife and I would soon be emigrating to Palestine, I broke the news to him as gently as I could, for it was clear that we would never see one another again. The prayer quorum it was my privilege to organize in his home when he was no longer able to go out was to continue, but the Talmud lessons I ventured to give him during my last year (1928) in Germany had to stop. He took the news in his wonderfully good-humored way. His lifelong friend Martin Buber (1878–1965) rightly described the mixture of faith and humor as one of Rosenzweig's most characteristic qualities. By this point Rosenzweig could no longer speak, let alone write, but his wife Edith (née Hahn; 1895–1979) understood what he meant, and he was able, on a special typewriter, to indicate letters which she then combined into words and sentences. It was thus that he communicated at our last meeting. At great length the following sentence emerged: "Just as sociology has but one justification—knowledge of many facts—there is but one justification for Zionism—immigration to Palestine." I breathed easy.

It was from Buber that I heard the most apt characterization of him. Rosenzweig did not believe in doctors, but he was finally persuaded to call upon two specialists in the peculiar form of paralysis from which he suffered: Ottfried Foerster (1873–1941) of Breslau, Lenin's physician under duress, and his friend Viktor von Weizsäcker (1886–1957) of Heidelberg, one of the founders of psychomatic medicine. Foerster was an atheist or agnostic, while Weizsäcker was a devout Christian. After examining him, the two came to the same conclusion. Buber, who was waiting in the next room, heard their reaction. Foerster said, "This man is a hero." But Weizsäcker said, "This man is a Jew."

# Notes

## Introduction
(pp. *1–19*)

1. For a biography of Rosenzweig, based on a narrative weave of his diaries and letters, see Nahum N. Glatzer, *Franz Rosenzweig: His Life and Thought*, 2d rev. ed. (New York: Schocken, 1972).

2. Cited in ibid., p. 96.

3. Ibid., pp. 31, 364. The manuscript, a single-folio sheet written on both sides (recto-verso), was among Hegel's papers left in the charge of his student and editor of his collected writings, Friedrich Foerster. Cf. Dieter Henrich, "Aufklärung der Herkunft des Manuskripts 'Das älteste Systemprogramm des deutschen Idealismus,'" in Christoph Jamme and Helmut Schneider, eds., *Mythologie der Vernunft: Hegels "ältestes Systemprogramm des deutschen Idealismus"* (Frankfurt: Suhrkamp, 1984), pp. 144–48.

4. For a translation of the manuscript, together with the original German, see David Farrell Krell, "The Oldest Program towards a System in German Idealism," *The Owl of Minerva* 17(1): 5–13. All our citations from the manuscript will be from this translation.

5. Franz Rosenzweig, "Das älteste Systemprogramm des deutschen Idealismus: Ein handschriftlicher Fund," in *Sitzungsberichte der Heidelberger Akademie der Wissenschaften: Philosophisch-historische Klasse* (1917), 5th sec., reprinted in Rosenzweig, *Kleinere Schriften* (Berlin: Schocken Verlag, 1937), pp. 230–77; also reprinted in Jamme and Schneider, *Mythologie der Vernunft*, pp. 79–125.

6. Cited in Krell, "Oldest Program," p. 7.

7. In his lifetime, Rosenzweig's thesis was disputed, the essay's authorship being variously attributed to Schelling's friends Hegel or Hölderlin. There are also scholars who conjecture that the essay is actually that of a

fourth unknown author. For a history of the philological dispute, see Krell, "Oldest Program," pp. 5–8; and Jamme and Schneider, "Der Streit um die Verfasserschaft," in *Mythologie der Vernunft*, pp. 63–69.

8. Franz Rosenzweig, *Hegel und der Staat*, 2 vols. (Munich and Berlin: R. Oldenbourg, 1920). Published with the support of the Heidelberg Academy of Sciences. Reprinted in 1962 by Scienta Verlag of Aalen, Germany.

9. Rosenzweig to Hans Ehrenberg, dated 26 September 1910, in *Franz Rosenzweig: Der Mensch und sein Werk. Gesammelte Schriften*, ed. Rachel Rosenzweig and Edith Rosenzweig-Scheidmann, with the assistance of Bernhard Casper (The Hague: Martinus Nijhoff, 1979), vol. 1: *Briefe und Tagebücher*, pt. 1, p. 112. On the Baden-Baden conference, see ibid., p. 96f., note. (Henceforth this edition of Rosenzweig's collected works will be referred to simply as *Gesammelte Schriften*.)

10. Glatzer, *Life and Thought*, p. 20.

11. For Rosenstock's recollection of their conversations, see his "Prologue/Epilogue to the Letters: Fifty Years Later," in *Judaism Despite Christianity: The "Letters on Christianity and Judaism" between Eugen Rosenstock-Huessy and Franz Rosenzweig*, ed. Eugen Rosenstock-Huessy (New York: Schocken, 1971), pp. 71–74.

12. See Rosenstock's note in Franz Rosenzweig, *Briefe* (Berlin: Schocken Verlag, 1935), p. 639.

13. In a letter to Rudolf Ehrenberg, 31 October 1913, Rosenzweig reviews the fateful discussion he had with Rosenstock the previous July (at which Ehrenberg was also present) and his decision to convert to Christianity with, however, the reservation that he do so as a Jew. "I considered the decision," he wrote, "purely personal, and you approved of it, remembering early Christianity." Cited in Glatzer, *Life and Thought*, p. 24f. In his recollection of his July dialogue with Rosenzweig, however, Rosenstock vigorously maintains that he was utterly unaware of Rosenzweig's decision to enter the church. Cf. his "Prologue/Epilogue," p. 74. It is, of course, conceivable that Rosenzweig confided his decision only in his cousin Rudolf Ehrenberg (who, incidentally, was actually only Jewish on his father's side).

14. Rosenzweig to Rudolph Ehrenberg, 31 October 1913, cited in Glatzer, *Life and Thought*, p. 28.

15. Cf. the chapters by Gershom Scholem and Moshe Idel in this volume.

16. Cf. Franz Rosenzweig to Eugen Rosenstock, 7 November 1916, in *Judaism Despite Christianity*, p. 133.

17. Cf. Buber's exchange with Rosenzweig on "the law," in Franz Rosenzweig, *On Jewish Learning*, (New York: Schocken, 1955), pp. 72–92, 109–18.

18. Cf. Rosenzweig's posthumously published essay, "Atheistische Theologie," in *Gesammelte Schriften*, vol. 3: *Zweistromland*, pp. 687–98. This essay has been translated and annotated by Robert Goldy and H. Frederick

Holch, "Atheistic Theology: From the Old to the New Way of Thinking," *Canadian Journal of Theology* 14(2): 79–91.

19. Cf. Frederick de Wolfe Bolman, Jr.'s, introduction to his trans. of Friedrich Schelling, *The Ages of the World* (New York: AMS Press, 1967), p. 47. Schelling, *Sämmtliche Werke,* ed. K. F. A. Schelling (Stuttgart: J. G. Cotta, 1856), pt. 1, 2:587.

20. On Schelling's positive philosophy, see Bolman's introduction to Schelling, *Ages of the World,* pp. 3–82, esp. 31–65.

21. Friedrich Schelling, "Ueber die Quelle der ewigen Wahrheiten," in *Gesammelte Werke,* pt. 2 (1856), 1:590. Schelling delivered this lecture at the Academy of Sciences in Berlin on 17 January 1850. The passage we have cited is rendered into English in Samuel Hugo Bergman, *Schelling on the Source of Eternal Truths, Proceedings of the Israel Academy of Sciences and Humanities,* pt. 2 (Jerusalem: Magnes Press, 1964), 2:28.

22. *Schelling's philosophisches System* (Leipzig, 1897), p. 221. Cited in Bergman, *Schelling on the Source of Eternal Truths,* p. 28.

23. Cf. Paul Tillich's autobiographical account of the importance of Schelling for him: "Another prelude of things to come occurred in the period between my student years and the beginning of the First World War. It was the encounter with Schelling's second period, especially with his so-called 'Positive Philosophy.' Here lies the philosophically decisive break with Hegel and the beginning of that movement which today is called existentialism. I was ready for it when it appeared in full strength after the First World War, and I saw in light of that general revolt against Hegel's system of reconciliation which occurred in the decades after Hegel's death and which, through Kierkegaard, Marx, and Nietzsche, has become decisive for the destiny of the twentieth century." Tillich, *My Search for Absolutes* (New York: Simon and Schuster, 1967), p. 37.

24. Schelling, *Sämmtliche Werke,* pt. 10, 1:141. Cited in translator's introduction to *The Ages of the World,* p. 36.

25. On Schelling as a precursor of existentialism, see n. 23, above; also cf. Paul Tillich, "Schelling und die Anfaenge des existentialistischen Protestes," in *Gesammelte Werke* (Stuttgart: Evangelisches Verlagswerk, 1961), 4:133–44.

26. Cf. Paul Tillich, *The Construction of the History of Religion in Schelling's Positive Philosophy,* trans. Victor Nuovo (Lewisburg: Bucknell University Press, 1974).

27. Franz Rosenzweig, *The Star of Redemption,* trans. William Hallo (New York: Holt, Rinehart and Winston, 1970), pp. 104, 106. On Rosenzweig's indebtedness to Schelling, see Else Rahel Freund, *Franz Rosenzweig's Philosophy of Existence,* trans. Stephen L. Weinstein and Robert Israel (The Hague: Martinus Nijhoff, 1979), passim; Stéphane Mosès, *Système et révélation: La philosophie de Franz Rosenzweig* (Paris: Editions du

Seuil, 1982), pp. 35–41; Moshe Schwarcz, *From Myth to Revelation* (Tel Aviv: Hakibbutz Hameuchad, 1978), passim (Hebrew). Cf. Rosenzweig's comment: Schelling's *Ages of the World* "is a great book from beginning to end. Had it not remained a fragment, the *Star* would deserve no attention, aside for [its special interest] to the Jews." Rosenzweig to Hans Ehrenberg, 18 March 1921, *Gesammelte Schriften*, 1:701.

28. Ibid., 1:12.

29. Cf. "The main influence [on my thought] was Eugen Rosenstock; a full year and a half before I began to write [*The Star of Redemption*] I had seen a rough draft of his now published *Angewandte Seelenkunde* [Applied psychology]." Franz Rosenzweig, "The New Thinking" ("Das neue Denken"), cited in Glatzer, *Life and Thought*, p. 200.

30. Ibid., p. 196.

31. Franz Rosenzweig, "Ein Gedenkblatt," in *Gesammelte Schriften, (Zweistormland)*, 3:239f. For Rosenzweig's writings on Cohen, see ibid., 3:163–240.

32. Cf. Hermann Cohen, *Religion of Reason out of the Sources of Judaism*, trans. Simon Kpalan (New York: F. Ungar, 1972).

33. Rosenzweig to Friedrich Meinecke, 30 August 1920, cited in Glatzer, *Life and Thought*, p. 96f.

34. Cf. Glatzer, *Life and Thought*, p. 98; and F. Meinecke's remembrance of his student Rosenzweig, in *Strassburg, Freiburg, Berlin: 1901–1919. Erinnerungen von Friederich Meinecke* (Stuttgart: K. F. Koehler, 1949), p. 97.

35. Rosenzweig, "Das neue Denken," p. 140.

36. Rosenzweig to Hans Ehrenberg, 11 March 1925, cited in Glatzer, *Life and Thought*, p. 145f.

37. Ibid., p. 146.

38. "Das neue Denken" was initially published in the German Jewish journal *Der Morgen* (February 1925). Reprinted in Rosenzweig, *Gesammelte Schriften*, 3:139–61. Judicious excerpts are translated in Glatzer, *Life and Thought*, pp. 190–208. *Von gesunden und kranken Menschenverstand* was first published in English translation in a limited edition under the title *Understanding the Sick and the Healthy: A View of the World, Man, and God*, ed. and introd. by Nahum N. Glatzer (New York: Noonday Press, 1953). The original German manuscript was first published in 1963 by Joseph Melzer Verlag of Düsseldorf.

39. The original Hebrew text has been reprinted in Gershom Scholem, "Franz Rosenzweig v-sifro 'Kochav Ha-Geulah,'" in *Devarim be-Go* (Tel Aviv: Am Oved, 1975), pp. 407–25.

40. Altmann's article originally appeared in *Between East and West: Essays Dedicated to the Memory of Bela Horovitz*, ed. A. Altmann (London: East and West Library, 1958), pp. 194–214; also reprinted in A. Altmann,

*Studies in Religious Philosophy and Mysticism* (Ithaca: Cornell University Press, 1969). Altmann's classical essay is reprinted in this symposium because it considers matters—Rosenzweig's conception of history and the metahistorical role he attributed to the Synagogue and the Church—otherwise treated but cursorily in the volume. His essay thus adds an important dimension to the volume's deliberations. We wish to thank Professor Altmann, who was unable to accept our invitation to attend the symposium to address this topic, for his kind permission to reprint his essay.

41. Rosenzweig, *Star of Redemption*, p. 151.

42. Ibid., p. 169.

## Chapter 1. Franz Rosenzweig and His Book *The Star of Redemption* (notes added by editor) *(pp. 20–41)*

1. "Patmos" ("Zweite Fassung"), in *Hölderlin: His Poems*, ed. and trans. Michael Hamburger (London: Harvell Press, 1952), pp. 222–25.

2. For a critical evaluation of Rosenzweig's thesis, see C. Jamme and H. Schneider, eds., *Mythologie der Vernunft: Hegels "ältestes Systemprogramm des deutschen Idealismus"* (Frankfurt: Suhrkamp, 1984).

3. Franz Rosenzweig, *Kleinere Schriften*, (Berlin: Schocken Verlag, 1937), pp. 56–78. English translation in Franz Rosenzweig, *On Jewish Learning*, ed. Nahum N. Glatzer (New York: Schocken, 1965), pp. 27–54.

4. Franz Rosenzweig, "Einleitung," in *Hermann Cohens Jüdische Schriften* (Berlin, 1924). Also in Rosenzweig, *Kleinere Schriften*, pp. 244–350.

5. Nehemiah Anton Nobel (1871–1922), a much respected Orthodox rabbi and scholar in Frankfurt.

6. Babylonian Talmud, Megillah 31a.

7. Rosenzweig, *Kleinere Schriften*, pp. 373–99. Excerpts are included in Nahum N. Glatzer, ed., *Franz Rosenzweig: His Life and Thought* (New York: Schocken, 1961), pp. 190–208.

8. In Leo Shestov, *Le pouvoir des clefs*, trans. from the Russian by Boris de Schloezer (Paris, 1928), pp. 307–96.

9. An image from the kabbalistic doctrine of Isaac Luria (1534–72). The repair (*tikkun*) of this supernal event, he taught, is effected through the pious and mystical deeds of man and leads to redemption.

10. In German philosophical parlance *Erfahrung* refers to knowledge mediated through the five senses.

11. Scholem here refers to the physicist Werner Karl Heisenberg (1901–76), who published in 1927 his thesis on "the uncertainty principle."

12. Salomo Ludwig Steinheim (1780–1866) published this four-volume work between 1835 and 1865. Moritz Lazarus (1824–1903) pub-

lished the first volume in 1898, the second posthumously in 1911. A translation of the first volume was published by the Jewish Publication Society in 1900.

13. The reference is to *The Sayings of the Fathers* 2:2, which Samson Raphael Hirsch (1808–88) read thus: "The study of Torah is excellent with *derekh eretz*, that is, worldly occupation, or secular education." (*Derekh eretz* is usually understood as "good manners" or "decorum.") "Torah with *derekh eretz*" became the general slogan of the neo-Orthodox movement founded by Hirsch in Germany.

14. Published posthumously in 1919.

15. Franz Rosenzweig, "Das neue Denken," in *Kleinere Schriften*, p. 389.

16. Cf. Avraham Abulafia, *Iggeret seva netivot ha-torah*, in Adolph Jellinek, *Philosophie und Kabbala*, Erstes Heft (Leipzig 1854), pp. 14–15. (Note supplied by Moshe Idel.)

17. Cf. Ibn Latif, *Rav pae'alim*, in Adolph Jellinek, *Kokhavei Yitshak*, vol. 25 (1860), p. 10, para. 39. (Note supplied by Moshe Idel.)

18. Rosenzweig, "Das neue Denken," p. 385f.

19. The reference is to a hymnic poem by Judah Halevi, "Lord Where Shall I Find Thee."

20. Franz Rosenzweig, *The Star of Redemption*, trans. W. Hallo (New York: Holt, Rinehart and Winston, 1970), p. 238.

21. See introduction to ibid., part 3, pp. 265–97.

22. Gen. 6:16.

23. The Hebrew word *teviah* means both ark and word; for the kabbalists, each word of Scripture, understood in all its hidden meaning, is the Ark of the Torah.

## Chapter 2. Experience in Rosenzweig's New Thinking
*(pp. 42–68)*

1. The following thoughts began as an answer to the reflections that Heinz-Jürgen Görtz develops in his essay "Die Wahrheit der Erfahrung in Franz Rosenzweigs 'Neuem Denken'" (The truth of experience in Franz Rosenzweig's "new thinking"), *Philosophisches Jahrbuch* 88(1981): 389–406. The relationship of my reflections to those of Görtz is that I keep more strictly to the framework of philosophical thinking. Thus for me Rosenzweig's "confirmation theory of truth" is more problematic than for Görtz. I emphasize more strongly than he does the differences between the classical theories of experience and Rosenzweig's theory of experience, and this through a critical comparison of the ultimate principles and evaluations of experience in the two cases. This difference finds its final expression in Rosenzweig's effort to renew the possibility of experiencing, in thought, the miraculous and miracles.

2. Franz Rosenzweig, "Das neue Denken: Einige nachträgliche Bemerkungen zum 'Stern der Erlösung,'" in *Kleinere Schriften* (Berlin: Schocken Verlag, 1937), p. 374. This essay is partially translated as "The New Thinking," in *Franz Rosenzweig: His Life and Thought,* ed. Nahum Glatzer [New York: Schocken, 1961]; this sentence, however, does not appear there. For the remaining quotations from this essay I shall refer to both the German and the English editions; the English version, however, may be somewhat modified for the purposes of this article.

3. In Franz Rosenzweig, *Gesammelte Schriften,* pt. 1: *Briefe und Tagebücher* (The Hague, 1979), 1:484. On the affinity between the concepts of system in Rosenzweig and the later works of Schelling, and on Rosenzweig's opposition to the concept of system in Hegelian idealism, see J. Tewes, *Zum Existenzbegriff Franz Rosenzweigs* (Franz Rosenzweig's concept of existence) (Meisenheim am Glan: A. Hain 1970), p. 9.

4. Ibid., p. 485.

5. Rosenzweig, *Kleinere Schriften,* p. 379; Glatzer, *Life and Thought,* p. 192.

6. Rosenzweig, *Kleinere Schriften,* p. 382; Glatzer, *Life and Thought,* p. 195. Unmistakable here is the criticism directed at Hegel's presentation of sense certainty in *Phänomenologie des Geistes;* see *Phenomenology of Mind,* trans. J. B. Baillie (London, 1931), p. 154.

7. Rosenzweig, *Kleinere Schriften,* p. 395; Glatzer, *Life and Thought,* p. 205. In the letter to Rudolf Ehrenberg (see n. 3) Rosenzweig positively designates the logical-grammatical *and* form as a modern counterform to the speculative categories of Hegelian thought, which he had formerly mistakenly projected into it.

8. Rosenzweig *Kleinere Schriften,* p. 395; Glatzer, *Life and Thought,* pp. 205–6.

9. Thus wrote Eva Ehrenberg in her "discussion" of the *Star of Redemption* in her memoirs, *Sehnsucht: Mein geliebtes Kind* (Munich: Ner-Tamid Verlag, 1963), p. 36. Karl Löwith, in his critical comparison of the thinking of Heidegger and Rosenzweig, has described the transitional epoch in which both stand as "the last epoch so far of German philosophy in which it was productive and had a definite face which was not only the head of monologizing individualists." At the same time he sharply criticizes the seriousness "with which extreme answers are given here to radical questions"—a "seriousness which captivates, but is no longer philosophical and free." See Löwith, "M. Heidegger and F. Rosenzweig: Ein Nachtrag zu 'Sein und Zeit'" (M. Heidegger and F. Rosenzweig: A postscript to "Being and Time"), first published in *Zeitschrift für Philosophische Forschung* 12(2): 161, 186; also see ch. 3, n. 7, below.

10. Rosenzweig, *Kleinere Schriften,* p. 395; Glatzer, *Life and Thought,* p. 206.

11. Rosenzweig, *Kleinere Schriften*, p. 396; Glatzer, *Life and Thought*, p. 206. That here the boundaries of philosophy are overstepped in the direction of theology becomes clear with Rosenzweig's sentence: "Beyond this, only God can verify the truth, and for him only is there only one truth" (p. 207).

12. Franz Rosenzweig, *The Star of Redemption*, trans. William W. Hallo (New York, 1970), pp. 96–97.

13. Rosenzweig, *Kleinere Schriften*, p. 384; Glatzer, *Life and Thought*, p. 196.

14. Particularly instructive is the contrast between the old and the new thinking that Rosenzweig draws with the help of the linguistic expressions *eigentlich* (actually) and *und* (and), particularly in light of Heidegger's thinking and the theme, common to both, of man's being-toward-death, which Heidegger expounds with reference to the existential difference of *Eigentlichkeit* (authenticity) and *Uneigentlichkeit* (inauthenticity); see *Being and Time*, trans. John Macquarrie and Edward Robinson (New York, 1962), paras. 52ff., p. 303. On the relation of Rosenzweig's and Heidegger's thinking see Löwith, "Heidegger and Rosenzweig."

15. Rosenzweig, *Kleinere Schriften*, p. 384; Glatzer, *Life and Thought*, p. 196. Rosenzweig emphasizes the noninterchangeability of the times of reality in the sense that "every single happening . . . has its present, its past, and its future, without which it cannot be known, or can be known only in distorted fashion" (pp. 385, 197–98). To be sure, this ontological thinking about the temporality of what has being is distinguished from related theories of cosmological or anthropological tendency by its methodological multidimensionality. See also nn. 17, 19.

16. Rosenzweig, *Star of Redemption*, p. 8.

17. Victor von Weizsäcker, *Pathosophie, Erster Teil, Einleitung* (Göttingen, 1967), p. 5. Rosenzweig himself expressly places the new theoretical beginnings of von Weizsäcker and Rudolf and Hans Ehrenberg among the "principal presentations of the new science," which he places side by side with *The Star of Redemption;* see Rosenzweig, *Kleinere Schriften*, p. 388.

18. Victor von Weizsäcker, *Anonyma* (Bern, 1964), pp. 10–11. On the concept of pathic existence, see W. Jacob, *Kranksein und Krankheit* (Sickness and disease) (Heidelberg, 1978), pp. 150ff.

19. I use this formula to call attention to the affinity of Weizsäcker's thinking with the great project of a cosmological system of A. N. Whitehead's *Process and Reality*. The latter makes "growing together" (*concrescens*), as the "philosophy of the concrete," the fundamental principle of a theory of living things. On the affinity between Victor von Weizsäcker and Alfred North Whitehead, cf. Jacob, *Kranksein und Krankheit*, pp. 44ff.

20. Cf. Rosenzweig, *Star of Redemption*, p. 106, where Rosenzweig re-

marks that philosophy's "new point of departure is the subjective, the extremely personal self, more than that: the incomparable self, immersed in itself. To this and to its point of view it must hold fast and withal attain the objectivity of science. The most extreme subjectivity, one would like to say deaf and blind egotism, on the one hand, on the other the lucid clarity of infinite objectivity—where is the bridge between them to be found?" The problem arising through Rosenzweig's reference to the theological concept of revelation, which is supposed to assure the scientific status of philosophy, cannot be explored here.

21. See Hegel, *Phenomenology of Mind*, p. 172; also idem, *Science of Logic*, trans. W. H. Johnston and L. G. Struthers (London, 1929), 2:120–27.

22. Hegel, *Science of Logic*, 1:60.

23. Rosenzweig, *Star of Redemption*, p. 121.

24. On the idea of the Hegelian phenomenology of mind as "the science of the experience of consciousness," cf. Werner Marx, *Hegel's Phenomenology of Spirit; Its Point and Purpose: A Commentary on the Preface and Introduction*, trans. Peter Heath (New York: Harper and Row, 1975); also O. Pöggeler, "Die Komposition der Phänomenologie des Geistes," in *Materialien zu Hegels Phänomenologie des Geistes*, ed. H. F. Fulda and D. Henrich (Frankfurt: Suhrkamp, 1973), pp. 329ff.

25. Rosenzweig, *Star of Redemption*, pp. 125–26 (translation modified for the purposes of this article).

26. This criticism applies also, and especially, to the neo-Kantian basic concept of generation; on this cf. Tewes, *Existenzbegriff*, p. 8.

27. Weizsäcker, *Anonyma*, p. 33. On the linking of the here-emphasized basic values of experience in context of life experience and action, cf. R. Wiehl, "Reflexionsprozesse und Handlungen" (Reflective processes and actions), in *Neue Hefte für Philosophie* 9(1976): 31ff.

28. It is above all M. Heidegger who has raised the question of the meaning of human existence in this form—the question of the possible wholeness of this existence—in *Being and Time*, paras. 46ff., p. 279. This specific form of the question leads us back to a connection with the Aristotelian concept of *physis* and an interpretation of this concept. Cf. above all Werner Marx, *Heidegger and the Tradition*, trans. Theodore Kisiel and Murray Green (Evanston: Northwestern University Press, 1971).

29. Among the writings of Schelling's late philosophy, to which Rosenzweig's new thinking is close, we may mention particularly the "Darstellung des Philosophischen Empirismus" (Presentation of philosophical empiricism), in *Einleitung in die Philosophie: Vorgetragen in München, zuletzt im Jahre 1836* (Introduction to philosophy: Lectures given in Munich, for the last time in 1836), in *Werke* (Munich, 1959), 5:271ff. The particular influence of Schelling's late philosophy on Rosenzweig is emphasized by Else

Freund, *Franz Rosenzweig's Philosophy of Existence: An Analysis of the Star of Redemption*, trans. Stephen L. Weinstein and Robert Israel (The Hague, 1979). Worth considering here is Heinz-Jürgen Görtz's reservation, in "Wahrheit der Erfahrung"; also Tewes's remark that Rosenzweig was influenced not only in general, but particularly in his thinking about experience, by Hermann Cohen; Tewes, *Existenzbegriff F. Rosenzweigs*, pp. 10ff.

30. Heidegger, *Being and Time*, para. 37, p. 217.

31. Rosenzweig, *Star of Redemption*, p. 93.

32. Ibid., pp. 94–95.

33. Ibid., p. 67.

## Chapter 3. Rosenzweig's Notion of Metaethics
*(pp. 69–88)*

1. The first number refers to Franz Rosenzweig, *Stern der Erlösung*, 2d ed. (Berlin: J. Kaufmann Verlag, 1930). The second number refers to idem, *The Star of Redemption*, trans. from the 2d ed. of 1930 by William W. Hallo (London: Routledge and Kegan Paul, 1971).

2. The term *metalogic* also appears, e.g., in Schopenhauer.

3. The concept of metaethics has become widely used in contemporary analytical philosophy. It, of course, connotes an analysis of the meanings of the notions or norms employed in the normative presentation of morality. In that sense metaethics is a discourse, above, as it were, the normative presentation of ethical problems. It is an analysis of moral judgments and not an elaboration of a moral code. It is obvious that Rosenzweig uses the term *metaethics* in a different connotation since his employment of the term is not meant to be an analysis of moral notions, but an attempt to go beyond the moral norms in order to analyze the ontological position of man. In this context we may also consider the term *metamathematics* as employed by Hilbert, as well as the term *metalanguage*, in which we analyze or explicate the meanings of the expressions used in our basic language. Such a view eventually presents a hierarchy or a ladder—meta-metalanguage being concerned in turn with the expressions of metalanguage. Rosenzweig does not apply the term *meta* in this hierarchical sense: it does not connote that which is above the level (of ethics) but that which is outside or before it.

4. See Hermann Cohen, "Religion und Sittlichkeit," in *Jüdische Schriften* (Berlin: Schwebcke and Sohn, 1924), 3:143.

5. See Hermann Cohen, *Die Religion der Vernunft aus den Quellen des Judentums* (Leipzig: Gustav Fock, 1919), pp. 23, 215ff.; idem, *Religion of Reason out of the Sources of Judaism*, trans. with an introduction by Simon Kaplan, introductory essay by Leo Strauss (New York: Frederick Ungar Publishing, 1972), pp. 20, 178ff.

6. Cf. the statement by Heidegger: "Keeping silent authentically is possible only in genuine discoursing. To be able to keep silent, *Dasein* must

have something to say—that is, it must have at its disposal an authentic and rich disclosedness of itself." *Being and Time*, trans. John Macquarrie and Edward Robison (Oxford: Basil Blackwell, 1967), p. 208. It must be observed that Heidegger refers here to disclosedness (*Erschlossenheit*) and not to the primary self-enclosure. In addition Heidegger stresses a kind of overreflection of the self capable of mastering itself. Silence is a manifestation of that "overattitude" controlling the basic *Erschlossenheit*. On the phenomenon of silence see Nathan Rotenstreich, "Reflective Silence and Its Sublation," *Clio* 7(3): 423ff.

7. For comparison between Rosenzweig and Heidegger, cf. Karl Löwith, "M. Heidegger and F. Rosenzweig: A Postscript to Being and Time," in *Nature, History and Existentialism*, ed. with a critical introduction by Arnold Levison (Evanston, Ill.: Northwestern University Press, 1966), pp. 51ff.

## Chapter 4. Responsibility Rescued
## (pp. 89–106)

1. Eugen Rosenstock-Huessy, ed., *Judaism Despite Christianity: The Letters on Christianity and Judaism between Eugen Rosenstock-Huessy and Franz Rosenzweig* (New York: Schocken Books, 1971), p. 147.

2. Cited in Nahum N. Glatzer, ed., *Franz Rosenzweig: His Life and Thought* (New York: Schocken Books, 1961), p. 97.

3. Franz Rosenzweig, *Der Mensch und sein Werk: Gesammelte Schriften*, pt. 1: *Briefe und Tagebücher*, ed. Raphael Rosenzweig and Edith Rosenzweig-Scheinmann in cooperation with Bernhard Casper (The Hague: Martinus Nijhoff, 1979), 2:606.

4. Cf. Franz Rosenzweig, "Das neue Denken," in *Kleinere Schriften* (Berlin: Schocken Verlag, 1937), p. 397.

5. Cf. Franz Rosenzweig to Friedrich Meinecke, 30 August 1920, in *Der Mensch und sein Werk*, 2:678–82.

6. Ibid., 1:442.

7. Cf. Franz Rosenzweig, "Urzelle des Stern der Erlösung," in *Kleinere Schriften*, p. 358.

8. Cf. Franz Rosenzweig, *Der Stern der Erlösung*, in *Der Mensch und sein Werk: Gesammelte Schriften*, pt. 2: *Mit einer Einführung von Reinhold Mayer* (The Hague: Martinus Nijhoff, 1976), pp. 158; also cf. 5f.; idem, *The Star of Redemption*, trans. William W. Hallo (New York: Holt, Rinehart and Winston, 1971), pp. 143, 5f.

9. Rosenzweig, *Der Mensch und sein Werk*, 1:353.

10. Rosenzweig, *Star of Redemption*, p. 143; cf. p. 214.

11. Ibid., p. 143.

12. Rosenzweig, "Urzelle," p. 359.

13. Rosenzweig, *Star of Redemption*, pp. 145f., 188f., 242f. "O man,

with your palm branch" is a citation from Schiller's poem "Die Künstler," which he wrote during "the year of the French Revolution."

14. Ibid., pp. 360, 357.
15. Rosenzweig, "Das neue Denken," p. 395.
16. Rosenzweig, "Urzelle," p. 362; cf. idem, *Star of Redemption*, p. 68.
17. Cf. Rosenzweig, *Star of Redemption*, p. 195f.
18. Cf. E. Lévinas, "Rupture de la totalité," in *Totalité et infini*, 4th ed. (The Hague: Martinus Nijhoff, 1974), pp. 5f., 177.
19. Rosenzweig, "Das neue Denken," p. 386.
20. Cf. "Trotzdem aber diese drei Gestalten nie wirklich waren, sind sie die Voraussetzung unserer Wirklichkeit." In Rosenzweig, "Das neue Denken," p. 381. Also cf. "In the place of a language prior to language, we see before us real language." In idem, *Star of Redemption*, p. 109.
21. Rosenzweig, *Star of Redemption*, p. 121; cf. ibid., p. 132.
22. Cf. ibid., pp. 127, 151f.
23. Cf. Aristotle, *Metaphysics*, 1032b2.
24. Rosenzweig, *Star of Redemption*, p. 155.
25. Ibid., p. 82.          26. Ibid., p. 198.
27. Ibid., p. 175; cf. idem, "Urzelle," p. 364. Also see Lévinas's discussion of the "me voici" in the chapter entitled "La gloire de l'infini," in his *Autrement qu'être ou au-delà de l'essence* (The Hague: Martinus Nijhoff, 1974), p. 179f.
28. Cf. Rosenzweig, *Star of Redemption*, p. 166.
29. Cf. ibid., pp. 162–64.
30. Ibid., p. 174. On the relation between speech and revelation, see ibid., p. 148.

31. Ibid., p. 176.          32. Ibid.
33. Ibid., p. 187; cf. ibid., p. 142f. 34. Ibid.
35. Ibid., p. 198.          36. Ibid., p. 204.
37. Ibid.
38. Rosenzweig, "Das neue Denken," p. 387.
39. Rosenzweig, *Star of Redemption*, pp. 214–15. Disappointment (*Enttäuschung*)—rendered by the translator of *Star of Redemption* as "disillusionment"—is a crucial concept in Rosenzweig's thinking. Though it is not identical to the Popperian concept of falsification, it is possibly analogous to it.
40. Ibid., p. 218; cf. ibid., p. 227f. 41. Ibid., pp. 214, 259.
42. Cf. ibid., pp. 209, 211.
43. Rosenzweig, "Das neue Denken," p. 398.
44. Rosenzweig, *Star of Redemption*, p. 236. In another context Rosenzweig speaks of "being at home" in the world (*Einheimischsein*) (ibid., p. 134). One could, however, transform this verb into a transitive one.
45. Cf. ibid., p. 215. Also cf. "ich werde immer nach *neuen* Enttäusch-

ungen *suchen.*" Rosenzweig to Hans Ehrenberg, 6 July 1919, in *Der Mensch und sein Werk*, pt. 1, 2:638.

46. Lévinas, *Autrement qu'être ou au-delà de l'essence*, p. 187.

47. Friedrich Schelling, *Sämtliche Werke*, pt. 1, ed. K. F., A. Schelling (Stuttgart/Ausburg: J. G. Gotla'scher Verlag, 1861), 10:228.

48. Rosenzweig, *Star of Redemption*, p. 160f.; cf. idem, "Das neue Denken," p. 395.

49. As Rosenzweig points out at the conclusion of *Star of Redemption*, the goal of the entire book may be seen in the teaching of *Micah* 6:8, "He has told thee, O man, what is good, and what does the Lord thy God require of thee but to do justice and to love mercy and to walk humbly with thy God."

50. Rosenzweig, "Das neue Denken," p. 397.

51. "Die Kategorie hat keinen anderen Gebrauch zum Erkenntnisse der Dinge, als ihre Anwendung aug Gegenstände der Erfahrung." In Kant, *Kritik der reinen Vernunft*, 2d ed. (1887), p. 146.

52. Rosenzweig, "Das neue Denken," p. 382.

53. Cf. Rosenzweig, *Star of Redemption*, pp. 265, 236.

54. Ibid., p. 95f; cf. ibid., p. 139.   55. Ibid., p. 190.

56. Rosenzweig, "Das neue Denken," p. 396. On Rosenzweig's principle of "verification" (*Bewährung*) also see *Star of Redemption*, p. 170.

57. Namely, in Rosenzweig's essay directed against Buber, "Atheistische Theologie," in *Kleinere Schriften*, p. 278f.

58. Cf. "Wissen oder Unwissen gilt da nichts vor der gemachten Erfahrung." From Rosenzweig to Buber, 5 June 1925, in *Der Mensch und sein Werk*, pt. 1, 2:1040.

59. Rosenzweig, *Star of Redemption*, p. 151f.; cf. ibid., p. 163.

60. Cf. also E. Lévinas, *Totalité et infini*, pp. 29f., 121.

61. Rosenzweig, *Star of Redemption*, pp. 96–97.

62. Cf. "Gott *ist* nicht alles, sondern '*von* ihm und *zu* ihm' ist alles. Also gelehrt ausgedruckt: Er steht zu allem in Beziehung." From Rosenzweig to Gertrud Oppenheim, 30 May 1917, in *Der Mensch und sein Werk*, pt. 1, 1:414.

## Chapter 5. Between Enlightenment and Romanticism (*pp. 107–23*)

1. Franz Rosenzweig, *Hegel und der Staat* (Munich: R. Oldenbourg, 1920); idem, *Stern der Erlösung* (Frankfurt: J. Kaufmann Verlag, 1921).

2. Franz Rosenzweig, "Das älteste Systemprogramm des deutschen Idealismus," in *Zweistromland: Kleinere Schriften zur Religion und Philosophie* (Berlin: Philo Verlag, 1926), pp. 123–75.

3. Cf. Christoph Jamme and Helmut Schneider, eds., *Mythologie der*

*Vermunft: Hegels "ältestes Systemprogramm des deutschen Idealismus"* (Frankfurt: Suhrkamp, 1984).

4. This, of course, is an allusion to Hermann Cohen's posthumous work, *Religion of Reason out of the Sources of Judaism* (1919). Cf. Franz Rosenzweig, "Einleitung in die Akademie-ausgabe der jüdischen Schriften Hermann Cohens," in *Kleinere Schriften* (Berlin: Schocken Verlag, 1937), pp. 299–350.

5. Cf. "Dies Buch, das ich heute nicht mehr geschrieben hätte, konnte ich genau so wenig umarbeiten. Es blieb nur übrig, es so herauszugeben wie es einmal war, in Ursprung also und Absicht ein Zeugnis des Geistes der Vorkriegsjahre, nicht des 'Geists' von 1919." Preface to Rosenzweig, *Hegel und der Staat*, p. xiii. Rosenzweig did, however, include one minor change in the published text. To the original motto that he inscribed on the manuscript in 1909, he added a second: "Hölderlin, *An die Deutschen*. 1800. 1909: 'Aber kömmt, wie der Strahl aus dem Gewölke kommt/Aus Gedanken Vielleicht geistig und reif die Tat? Folgt der Schrift, wie des Haines/ Dunkelm Blatte, die goldene Frucht?' 1919: 'Wohl ist enge begrenzt unsere Lebenszeit, Unserer Jahre Zahl sehen und zählen wir, Doch die Jahre der Völker, Sah ein sterbliches Auge sie?'" For letter to Meinecke, see Franz Rosenzweig, *Der Mensch und sien Werk: Gesammelte Schriften*, pt. 1: *Briefe und Tagebücher* (The Hague: Martinus Nijhoff, 1979), 1:924.

6. See Paul Honigsheim, "Zur Hegelrenaissance in Vorkriegs-Heidelberg: Erkenntnissoziologische Beobachtungen," *Hegel-Studien* 2 (1963): 291–301.

7. Rosenzweig, *Der Mensch und sein Werk*, pt. 1, 2:717.

8. Ibid., pp. 684f., cf. 936f.      9. Ibid., p. 741; cf. p. 768.

10. Ibid., p. 704.      11. Ibid., pp. 824ff., 978, 1039.

12. Ibid., 1:100.

13. Cited in Nahum N. Glatzer, ed., *Franz Rosenzweig: His Life and Thought*, rev. ed. (New York: Schocken Books, 1961), p. 16.

14. Rosenzweig, *Der Mensch und sein Werk*, pt. 1, 1:881.

15. Glatzer, *Life and Thought*, p. 20f.

16. Cf. Weizsäcker report in Rosenzweig, *Der Mensch und sein Werk*, pt. 1, 1:296f.

17. Glatzer, *Life and Thought*, p. 95f.

18. Rosenzweig, *Der Mensch und sein Werk*, pt. 1, 1:342.

19. Glatzer, *Life and Thought*, p. 24.

20. Ibid., p. 35.      21. Ibid., p. 33.

22. Cf. "Vom 'Heil' führt zum 'Schalom' ein näherer Weg als etwa von der ἰδέα (Idea) oder ihrem Abkömmling, dem 'Moralischen.'" In Rosenzweig, *Der Mensch und sein Werk*, pt. 1, 2:700.

23. Ibid., p. 358.

24. See Martin Noth, *Das Geschichtsverständnis der alttestament-lischen Apokalyptik* (Cologne/Opladen: Westdeutscher Verlag, 1954); also see Hans Freyer, *Weltgeschichte Europas* (Wiesbaden: Dietrich Verlag, 1948).

25. Rosenzweig, *Der Mensch und sein Werk*, pt. 1, 2:692f.

26. Ibid., p. 1182.    27. Ibid., 1:146.    28. Ibid., pp. 484ff.

29. Ibid., 2:1154, 1:563.    30. Ibid., 2:291ff.    31. Ibid.

32. From the very beginning Rosenzweig's view differed from Dilthey's relativism. See Wilhelm Dilthey, "Rechnungsabschluss der Gegenwart," in *Gesammelte Schriften* (Stuttgart: Vandenhoeck und Ruprecht, 1966), 14: 589ff. Also, Rosenzweig's thought can not be identified with dialectical theology. Since Gerhard von Rad's *Theologie des Alten Testament* (1960), Christian theology has once again tried to consider history in its totality.

33. Cf. Friedrich Meinecke, *Machiavellism: The Doctrine of Raison d'Etat and Its Place in Modern History*, trans. Douglas Scott (New Haven: Yale University Press, 1957).

34. Rosenzweig, *Der Mensch und sein Werk*, pt. 1, 1:283.

35. Ibid., p. 586. See Otto Pöggeler, "Hegel's Interpretation of Judaism," *Human Context* 6 (1974): 523ff.; idem, "Philosophy in the Wake of Hölderlin," *Man and World* 7 (1974): 158ff.; and idem, "Die neue Mythologie," in *Romantik in Deutschland*, ed. Richard Brinkmann (Stuttgart: Vandenhoeck und Ruprecht, 1978), pp. 341ff.

36. It is only a legend that Hegel's years at Frankfurt were a time of misfortune; rather his crisis belongs to his years at Bern. In his book on the young Hegel, Lukács polemizes against Rosenzweig and Dilthey for distorting the biography of Hegel, but it is Lukács who stresses this legend, drawing from it the totally misleading opinion that Hegel—unhappy in modern society—fled to religion. See my remarks in *Mythologie der Vernunft*, pp. 126–43.

37. Rosenzweig, *Der Mensch und sein Werk*, pt. 1, 2:990.

38. See Meinecke's letter in the second edition of Siegfried A. Kaehler, *Wilhelm von Humboldt und der Staat: Beiträge zur Geschichte deutscher Lebensgestaltung um 1800* (Göttingen: Vandenhoeck and Ruprecht, 1963). For a criticism of Kaehler see Clemens Menze, *Die Bildungsreform Wilhelm von Humboldts* (Hannover: Henn-Verlag, 1975), p. 134.

39. See Hans Ehrenberg, *Die Parteiung der Philosophie: Studien wider Hegel und die Kantianer* (Leipzig: F. Meiner, 1911); and idem, *Hegel* (Munich: Drei Masken Verlag, 1925).

40. Rosenzweig, *Der Mensch und sein Werk*, pt. 1, 1:192f.

41. Cf. "The idealism contained in *The Star of Redemption* as a foundation and presupposition remains the idealism of Hegel," Else-Rahel Rosenzweig, *Franz Rosenzweig's Philosophy of Existence*, trans. Stephen L. Weinstein and Robert Israel (The Hague: Martinus Nijhoff, 1979), p. 6.

Freund also deals with Schelling's late philosophy as informing the development of Rosenzweig's thought. She neglects, however, to point to the central role played by Schelling's *Ages of the World* in shaping Rosenzweig's thought.

42. Rosenzweig, *Der Mensch und sein Werk*, pt. 1, 1 : 363f., 2 : 629, 790.

43. See Emmanuel Lévinas, *Totalité et infini: Essai sur l'extériorité* (The Hague: Martinus Nijhoff, 1961).

## Chapter 6. Franz Rosenzweig on History
*(pp. 124–37)*

1. Cf. Franz Rosenzweig, *Briefe*, ed. Edith Rosenzweig (Berlin, 1935), pp. 40, 41, 43–44.

2. Cf. Carlo Antoni, *From History to Sociology*, trans. Hayden V. White (Detroit: Wayne State University, 1959), pp. 129ff. Rosenzweig refers to the method of *Ideengeschichte* in *Briefe*, pp. 55, 318.

3. Cf. *Briefe*, pp. 43–44, 60–61.

4. In an obituary note on Rosenzweig in *Historische Zeitschrift* (Munich-Berlin, 1930), 142 : 219–20, Meinecke described his former pupil as "der Verfasser des bedeutenden und sehr wirksam gewordenen Werkes 'Hegel und der Staat.'" "Rosenzweig," he continued, "begann als Historiker mit stärkstem philosophischem Einschlag. . . . Der Weltkrieg machte ihn irre an dem zuerst verfolgten Weg, die Höhen der deutschen protestantischen Kultur zu erforschen; darum flüchtete er in die Welt seines Bluts. Aber durch jenes Buch über Hegel hat er der deutschen Geistesgeschichte ein Werk von bleibendem Wert hinterlassen."

Meinecke made another reference to Rosenzweig in a chapter devoted to his pupils in *Strassburg, Freiburg, Berlin, 1901–1919: Erinnerungen von Friedrich Meinecke* (Stuttgart, 1949), p. 97: "Ich nenne weiter ein in der Wissenschaft bekannt gewordenes jüdisches Mitglied dieses Kreises, Franz Rosenzweig, der durch das Hegelkapitel in meinem Weltbürgertum angeregt, das subtile Buch über Hegel und den Staat, geschrieben hat und nach dem Kriege, erschüttert über diesen, wie er fürchtete, endgültigen Zusammenbruch deutscher Ideale, in einem vergeistigten Judentum seine angestammte Bestimmung wieder zu finden glaubte."

5. See n. 4.

6. Cf. *Briefe*, p. 318, and Franz Rosenzweig, *Kleinere Schriften* (Berlin, 1937), pp. 505–7.

7. Cf. *Briefe*, p. 41.          8. Cf. ibid., p. 49.

9. Cf. *Kleinere Schriften*, p. 358: "weil die Unruhe in meinem Denkuhrwerk "1800" heisst ("Hegel" and "Goethe" . . .). Und also von diesem meinem intellektuellen Mittelpunkt aus muss ich alles sehen." See also *Briefe*, p. 706: "Für uns handelt es sich jetzt um 1789 (1781, 1794, 1806)."

10. Cf. Hans Ehrenberg, *Disputation, Drei Bücher vom deutschen Ide-*

*alismus. Fichte. Der Disputation Erstes Buch* (Munich, 1923), pp. 136ff.
The book is dedicated "Dem Freunde Franz Rosenzweig und seinem Werke
"Der Stern der Erlösung."

11. Cf. Schelling, *Philosophie der Offenbarung, Sämtliche Werke,* vol.
4, pt. 2 (1858), p. 332.

12. Ibid., pp. 326–27.

13. Ibid., p. 328: "Johannes ist der Apostel der zukünftigen, erst wahr-
haft allgemeinen Kirche jenes zweiten, neuen Jerusalems, . . . jener nichts
mehr ausschliessenden Stadt Gottes . . . , in die Heiden und Juden gleich
eingehen, . . . die ohne beschränkenden Zwang, ohne äussere Auktorität,
welcher Art sie sey, durch sich selbst besteht, weil jeder freiwillig herbei-
kommt, jeder durch eigne Überzeugung, indem sein Geist in ihr eine Hei-
mat gefunden, zu ihr gehört."

14. On Joachim of Fiore see Ernst Benz, *Ecclesia Spiritualis* (Stuttgart,
1934), and Karl Löwith, *Meaning in History* (Chicago, 1949), pp. 145ff.
and (bibliography) p. 243. A good introduction with selected texts is given
in Alfons Rosenberg's *Joachim von Fiore: Das Reich des Heiligen Geistes*
(Munich-Planegg, 1955).

According to F. Baer, *Sion* (Jerusalem, 1939), 5:1–44, the Franciscan
Spirituals in the thirteenth century, who were followers of Joachim, influenced the author of the *Raya Mehemna,* a kabbalistic interpretation of the
commandments and prohibitions of the Torah. Joachim's doctrine of the
correspondence of the three stages of the Church and of the three persons in
the Christian Trinity may seem to have had some influence on the book
*Temunah* (about 1250) which emanated from the circle around Naḥmani-
des. It describes the various (7) aeons of the world (*Shemitot*) as representing the (7) lower aspects (*Sefirot*) of Divinity. Cf. G. Scholem, *Major Trends
in Jewish Mysticism,* rev. ed. (New York, 1946), pp. 178–80, where direct
influence is, however, considered unlikely. In his *Reshit ha-Kabbalah* (Jeru-
salem-Tel Aviv, 1948), pp. 176ff., Scholem admits that Christian sources
such as the writings of the Franciscan Spirituals may have been known to
the Jewish mystics of Catalonia. He describes in some detail the doctrine of
the book *Temunah* and the kabbalistic speculations that it engendered and
that prepared the ground for the antinomian movement of Sabbatianism in
the sixteenth century.

15. Cf. *Briefe,* p. 706; *Kleinere Schriften,* p. 266.

16. Cf. *Briefe,* pp. 81–82.        17. Cf. ibid., p. 91. See also p. 265.

18. Cf. ibid., pp. 706–7.

19. Cf. ibid., pp. 707–8. See also p. 282.

20. Cf. ibid., p. 686.

21. Cf. Franz Rosenzweig, *Der Stern der Erlösung* (Heidelberg, 1954),
3:25–34. For Schelling's concept of the "growth of the Kingdom" (Mark
4:26ff.) see *Philosophie,* vol. 4, pt. 2, p. 295.

22. Cf. *Briefe,* p. 59.

23. Cf. Max Weber, *Gesammelte Aufsätze zur Religionssoziologie,* vol. 3: *Das antike Judentum* (Tübingen, 1921), where postexilic Judaism is described as the religion of a "Pariah nation." The term is not meant in a derogatory sense but is intended to designate the character of postexilic Judaism as living in a self-imposed social seclusion. In his review of Weber's work, Julius Guttmann interprets the sociological aspects of Jewish exclusiveness in terms that come very close to Rosenzweig's and may have been influenced by him. Cf. *Monatsschrift für Geschichte und Wissenschaft des Judentums,* ed. I. Heinemann, vol. 69, n.f. 33 (1925), pp. 222–23: "Die messianische Hoffnung des Judentums macht die jetzige Welt zu einem Provisorium, dem die gottgewollte Ordnung erst folgen soll. In den Zeiten ihrer unmittelbaren Aktualität führte diese Hoffnung zu völliger Gleichgültigkeit gegen die gegenwärtige Welt. Eine eigentümliche Haltung musste sich ergeben, als nach der Rückkehr aus dem Exil die Hoffnung auf das unmittelbare Eintreten der messianischen Zeit enttäuscht wurde und das Judentum sich in der gegenwärtigen Welt einzurichten hatte. Es musste sich mit ihr abfinden und fühlte sich doch letzlich nicht zu ihr gehörig. Es lebte gleichsam in einem dauernden Provisorium, musste sich den Ordnungen der gegebenen Welt einfügen, die es doch innerlich nicht bejahen konnte. Seine Aufgabe in dieser Übergangszeit bestand darin, in seinem Kreise das göttliche Gebot zu halten, nicht aber diese Welt als solche umzubilden."

24. Cf. *Briefe,* p. 405.

25. See the present writer's article in *Journal of Religion* 24 (4): 258–70, and Nahum N. Glatzer's in *Judaism* 1 (1): 69–79.

26. Cf. *Briefe,* pp. 302, 316–17, 331–32.

27. Cf. ibid., pp. 311–12.

28. Cf. *Der Stern der Erlösung* 3:91.

29. Ibid., pp. 93–94.

30. Ibid., pp. 86, 91, 104–5, 127. Rosenzweig's view of Judaism as standing at the goal of history may be regarded as a Jewish answer to Hegel's and Schelling's interpretations of Judaism. For Hegel the Jewish religion represents the stage of "negativity" against nature ("the angry God") which is inferior to both Hellas and Christianity. See H. J. Schoeps's article, "Die ausserchristlichen Religionen bei Hegel," *Zeitschrift für Religion und Geistesgeschichte* 8 (1): 27–32. Schelling, who was much more sympathetic to Judaism, nevertheless describes it similarly: "Das Judentum war eigentlich nie etwas Positives, es kann nur entweder als gehemmtes Heidentum, oder als potentielles, noch verborgenes Christentum bestimmt werden." Cf. *Philosophie,* vol. 4, pt. 2, p. 148. Whereas the idealist Jewish philosophers (S. Formstecher, S. Hirsch) tried to refute Hegel and Schelling by employing their dialectical method in reverse direction, Rosenzweig takes Judaism completely out of the historical process. In a sense, he may have been influenced by Schelling who, from a Christian point of view, re-

gards Judaism as being outside history: "Indem sie den Übergang zum Christentum versahen und versäumten, schlossen sie sich von dem grossen Gang der Geschichte aus. Sie *mussten* aufhören ein Volk zu seyn, unter die Völker zerstreut und zerstiebt werden. Sie waren nur *etwas* als die Träger der Zukunft . . . es ist im eigentlichen Sinn *ausgeschlossen* von der Geschichte." (Ibid., p. 150).

31. Cf. *Der Stern der Erlösung,* 3:87–88; *Briefe,* pp. 335–36.
32. Cf. *Briefe,* pp. 706–8.   33. Cf. ibid., pp. 74–75.
34. Cf. *Der Stern der Erlösung,* 3:197–98.
35. Cf. *Briefe,* pp. 202, 75, 690.
36. Cf. G. Scholem, *Reshit ha-Kabbalah,* pp. 187–93.
37. Cf. *Der Stern der Erlösung,* 2:114–15, 163–65.
38. Cf. J. L. Fichte, *Die Anweisung zum seligen Leben,* pt. 2: *Sämtliche Werke* (Berlin, 1845), 3:481: "Dieses—bei Gott Seyn nun . . . wird ferner charakterisiert als Logos oder Wort. Wie konnte deutlicher ausgesprochen werden, dass es die sich selbst klare und verständliche Offenbarung und Manifestation, sein geistiger Ausdruck sey,—dass . . . das unmittelbare Daseyn Gottes notwendig Bewusstseyn, theils seiner selbst, theils Gottes sey." Fichte rejects the concept of creation. Cf. pp. 479–80, and tends to equate the *eschaton* with the *Reich der Vernunft* within us. See H. Ehrenberg's analysis and critique in his *Fichte,* pp. 144–46. Fichte's denial of creation was opposed by Schelling, *Philosophie,* vol. 4, pt. 2, pp. 101–3. On the young Hegel's metaphysics of love see Jakob Taubes, *Abendländische Eschatologie* (Bern, 1947), pp. 149ff. Schleiermacher's mysticism belongs to the same climate of thought.

39. Cf. *Der Stern der Erlösung,* 2:154–56, 3:18–20.
40. Cf. *Briefe,* p. 314.
41. Cf. ibid., p. 222. On the *Beseelung* and *Durchseelung* of the world through love see *Der Stern der Erlösung,* 2:195–97.
42. Cf. *Der Stern der Erlösung,* 2:173–77, 196–99.
43. Cf. *Briefe,* p. 60. On the significance of the concept of individuality in German thought see Friedrich Meinecke, *Schaffender Spiegel,* (Stuttgart, 1948), pp. 221ff.
44. Cf. *Briefe,* pp. 212–13. The paradox that "the world can become good only through the good" is quoted here and in *Der Stern der Erlösung,* 2:182.
45. The ideology of progress is refuted, both in its "Islamic" and modern form, in *Der Stern der Erlösung,* 2:177–81.
46. Cf. *Briefe,* p. 55.
47. Cf. *Der Stern der Erlösung,* 2:99.
48. Cf. ibid., p. 176.
49. Cf. Rosenzweig's "Introduction," in *Hermann Cohen's Jüdische Schriften,* ed. Bruno Strauss (Berlin, 1924), 1:lxi–lxii.

50. Cf. *Der Stern der Erlösung*, 2:212–13.

51. Cf. Hermann Cohen, *Ethik des reinen Willens*, 4th ed. (Berlin, 1921), pp. 412–16.

52. Cf. *Briefe*, p. 157.

53. Cf. Karl Löwith, "M. Heidegger and F. Rosenzweig or Temporality and Eternity," *Philosophy and Phenomenological Research* 3 (1942–43): 53ff., where Rosenzweig's position is contrasted with Heidegger's "Sein zum Tode."

54. Cf. *Der Stern der Erlösung*, 2:212–13, 3:172.

55. Cf. ibid., 2:179.          56. Cf. ibid., p. 176.

57. Cf. ibid., pp. 176–77.     58. Ibid.

59. Cf. ibid., 3:87.           60. Cf. ibid., 2:179.

61. Cf. ibid., p. 180.         62. Cf. ibid., pp. 98–99.

63. Cf. ibid., 2:198–99, 3:16–17.

64. Cf. *Kleinere Schriften*, p. 385.

65. Cf. *Der Stern der Erlösung*, 3:16, 119.

66. Cf. ibid., 2:181–82.

67. Paul Tillich, *The Kingdom of God and History* (London, 1938).

68. Cf. *Briefe*, p. 710.

69. Cf. *Kleinere Schriften*, p. 358; *Briefe*, pp. 166, 221. In *Briefe*, p. 710, and *Kleinere Schriften*, p. 358, Rosenzweig credits Eugen Rosenstock with the authorship of this concept. Rosenzweig's letter outlining the idea is found in *Briefe*, pp. 676ff.

70. Cf. *Briefe*, pp. 211, 429ff.    71. Cf. ibid., p. 717.

72. Cf. ibid., pp. 145, 710.          73. Cf. ibid., p. 710.

74. Cf. ibid., p. 227.

75. See n. 4. Meinecke himself reacted to the events of 1918 with a feeling of great despondency. In the words of Carlo Antoni (*Historismus*, p. 147), "Under the tremendous pressure his soul succumbed and abjured historical idealism." It seems that he projected his own despair on Rosenzweig.

76. Cf. *Briefe*, p. 53.        77. Cf. ibid., p. 59.

78. Cf. ibid., p. 298.         79. Cf. ibid., p. 299.

80. Cf. ibid., pp. 55, 409, 476.    81. Cf. ibid., pp. 298–89.

82. Cf. Schelling, *Philosophie*, vol. 2, pt. 4, pp. 3, 4, 121.

83. Cf. *Briefe*, pp. 208, 711, 718.

84. Cf. *Kleinere Schriften*, p. 383.

85. Cf. Schelling, *Philosophie*, vol. 2, pt. 4, p. 322: "Die Geschichte ist die unwiderstehlichste Auktorität. Ich möchte nicht eben das bekannte Schillersche Wort "die Weltgeschichte ist das Weltgericht," mit dem sich jetzt manche viel wissen, besonders nicht in gleichem Sinne wiederholen, wohl aber: die Urteile der Geschichte sind Gottes Urteile." On Hegel's use of Schiller's sentence see Löwith, *Meaning in History*, p. 58.

86. Cf. Ernst Benz, *Schelling, Werden und Wirken seines Denkens*, (Zurich, 1955), pp. 29–55.

87. Cf. Friedrich Schelling, "Stuttgarten Privatvorlesungen" (1810), in *Sämmtliche Werke*, vol. 7, pt. 1 (1860), p. 484. See also Paul Tillich, *Mystik und Schuldbewusstsein in Schellings philosophischer Entwicklung* (Gütersloh, 1912), p. 121.

88. Cf. I. Kant, *Die Religion innerhalb der Grenzen der blossen Vernunft*, in *Werke*, ed. Ernst Cassirer (Berlin, 1923), 6:282; Schelling, *Philosophie*, vol. 2, pt. 4, p. 333; Benz, *Schelling*, pp. 41, 45, 47.

89. Cf. *Der Stern der Erlösung*, 3:16, 119.

90. Cf. ibid., pp. 159–60, 182–83, 195–96.

## Chapter 7. Franz Rosenzweig and the Crisis of Historicism (*pp. 138–61*)

1. See Alexander Altmann, "Franz Rosenzweig on History," ch. 6 in this volume, n. 30.

2. Rosenzweig to Rudolf Ehrenberg, 31 October 1913, in Franz Rosenzweig, *Briefe*, ed. Edith Rosenzweig (Berlin: Schocken, 1935), p. 75.

3. Rosenzweig developed these ideas in the aforementioned letter to Ehrenberg and in his now famous epistolary exchange with Eugen Rosenstock-Huessy. See *Judaism Despite Christianity: The "Letters on Christianity and Judaism" between Eugen Rosenstock-Huessy and Franz Rosenzweig*, ed. E. Rosenstock-Huessy (New York: Schocken Books, 1971).

4. Altmann, "Franz Rosenzweig on History," p. 129. Lionel Kochan suggests that Rosenzweig "seems to be responding to Hegel's essay 'Der Geist des Judentums und sein Schicksal,' which argued that when Abraham heeded the divine command to 'Get thee out of thy country' (Gen. 12:1ff.), he became, in Hegel's words, 'a stranger on earth, a stranger to soil and man alike.'" L. Kochan, *The Jew and His History* (London: Macmillan Press, 1977), p. 107.

5. Altmann, "Franz Rosenzweig on History," p. 129.

6. Diary entry from 22 May 1906, in Franz Rosenzweig, *Der Mensch und sein Werk: Gesammelte Schriften*, vol. 1, *Briefe und Tagebücher, 1900–1918*, ed. Rachel Rosenzweig and Edith Rosenzweig-Scheimann in cooperation with Bernhard Casper (The Hague: Martinus Nijhoff, 1979), p. 44. Rosenzweig's diaries from his student years (1906–13) as a basis for reconstructing his initial encounter with the problem of historicism are discussed extensively in Paul Mendes-Flohr and Jehuda Reinharz, "From Relativism to Religious Faith: The Testimony of Franz Rosenzweig's Unpublished Diaries," *The Leo Baeck Institute Year Book* 22 (1977): 161–74.

7. Diary entry from 29 February 1907; not included in the diary excerpts in the recently published volume of Rosenzweig's *Briefe und Tagebücher* (see n. 6). I have relied on the copy of the diary deposited in the Franz Rosenzweig Archive, Boston (now in the Archives of the Leo Baeck Institute, New York).

8. See Georg G. Iggers, *The German Conception of History: The National Tradition of Historical Thought from Herder to the Present* (Middletown, Conn.: Wesleyan University Press, 1968), p. 152.

9. Rickert, "Geschichtsphilosophie," in *Festschrift für Kuno Fischer* (Heidelberg: Carl Winter Verlag, 1904–5), pp. 101f. Cited in Iggers, *German Conception of History*, p. 158.

10. Diary entry, 24 May 1908, in Rosenzweig, *Briefe und Tagebücher*, 1:81.

11. Subtitled *Studien zur Genesis des deutschen Nationalstaates*, the volume was first published in 1908.

12. Rosenzweig to his mother (Adele Rosenzweig), 30 October 1908, in *Briefe*, p. 40; Rosenzweig to his mother, 13 November 1908, ibid., p. 41.

13. See Franz Rosenzweig, *Hegel und der Staat* (Munich and Berlin: R. Oldenbourg, 1920), p. xiii. In his memoirs Meinecke refers to this fact and warmly praises his former student: "Franz Rosenzweig der durch das Hegelkapitel in meinem Weltbürgertum angeregt, [hat] das subtile Buch über Hegel und der Staat geschrieben." Friedrich Meinecke, *Strassburg, Freiburg, Berlin, 1901–1919. Erinnerungen* (Stuttgart: K. F. Koehler, 1949), p. 97.

14. See Iggers, *German Conception of History*, pp. 195–228. On the presuppositions of "ethical historicism," see the brief but subtle discussion in David H. Fischer, *Historians' Fallacies* (New York: Harper and Row, 1970), pp. 155–57.

15. Cf. Friedrich Meinecke, *Cosmopolitanism and the Nation State*, trans. Robert B. Kimber (Princeton: Princeton University Press, 1970), chap. 1, esp. pp. 21ff.

16. See H. Stuart Hughes, *Society and Consciousness: The Reorientation of European Social Thought, 1890–1930* (New York: Alfred Knopf, 1958), pp. 236–48. Also see Richard W. Sterling, *Ethics in a World of Power: The Political Ideas of Friedrich Meinecke* (Princeton: Princeton University Press, 1958), pp. 267–99.

17. Rosenzweig to Hans Ehrenberg, 4 August 1909, in *Briefe*, p. 44.

18. Rosenzweig to Hans Ehrenberg, undated, probably end of October or beginning of November 1908, ibid., p. 40.

19. A. Altmann, "About the Correspondence," prefatory essay in Rosenstock, *Judaism Despite Christianity*, p. 28. Cf. Rosenzweig to Franz Frank, undated, in *Briefe*, p. 50. On the Baden-Baden circle see Rosenzweig's letters to Hans Ehrenberg (21 December 1909), Walter Sohm (undated), and Franz Frank (undated), in *Briefe*, pp. 47f., 48ff., 50–52. Also see Victor von Weizsäcker's reminiscences of the abortive circle, cited in Rosenzweig, *Briefe und Tagebücher*, 1:96f.

20. Altmann, "About the Correspondence," p. 28.

21. From the opening sentences of a memorandum entitled "Badener

Gesellschaft," found among Rosenzweig's unpublished papers. Cited in *Briefe*, p. 47, n. 1.

22. Rosenzweig to Hans Ehrenberg, 12 December 1909, in *Briefe*, p. 48.

23. Rosenzweig to Franz Frank, undated, in *Briefe*, p. 51.

24. Ibid., p. 55.

25. Cf. "Und, wie immer der Sprung vom Nichts ins Etwas, eine grosse Sache, grösser als alle künftigen Schritte vomk Etwas zu Mehr.—Überhaupt ist dies das Resultat dieses Winters, d.h. das diesen Winter fertiggewordene, dem Werden nach wohl ältere, Resultat für mich in wissenschaftlicher Beziehung: dass ich nun Tendenz zur extensiven historischen Universalität habe; früher wie du weisst nur die zur intensiven. Das Vehikiel dahin war mir die Theologie. [Max] Lenz statt Meinecke diesen Winter war insofern für mich gradezu providentiell; denn in Meinecke steckt kein universalhistorischer Trieb, während er bei Lenz das Beste ist. Was sich mir freilich als Universalgeschichte auftut, ist eigentlich nur der Stoff; das Material zum Hinundherspringen; nicht Hegels 'Gang' noch Rankes 'Mar.'" (That is, neither the process of universal history à la Hegel, nor a factual story à la Ran*ke*.) Rosenzweig to Hans Ehrenberg, 14 February 1911, in *Briefe*, p. 59.

26. See Eugen Rosenstock, "Einleitung," and Franz Rosenzweig und Eugen Rosenstock, "Judentum und Christentum," (correspondence discussed in n. 3), in Rosenzweig, *Briefe*, appendix 1, p. 639.

27. Rosenzweig to Rudolf Ehrenberg, 31 October 1913, in *Briefe*, p. 71f. Translated in Altmann, "About the Correspondence," p. 32f.

28. Harold Stahmer, "Introduction," in Rosenstock, *Judaism Despite Christianity*, p. 2. Cf. "But the ghostly edifice of scholarship for its own sake—about which I have the bad conscience of a heretic—falls down for me if one merely crows three times like a young cock." Rosenstock to Rosenzweig, circa December 1916, in ibid., p. 162.

29. Stahmer, "Introduction," p. 24.

30. E. Rosenstock-Huessy, "Prologue/Epilogue to the Letters: Fifty Years Later," in *Judaism Despite Christianity*, p. 74.

31. Rosenzweig to Hans Ehrenberg, 6 December 1913, in *Briefe*, p. 82.

32. Franz Rosenzweig, "Atheistische Theologie," in Rosenzweig, *Kleinere Schriften* (Berlin: Schocken Verlag, 1937), p. 281.

33. Cf. n. 3.

34. Paraphrase by Altmann, "About the Correspondence," p. 43f. Cf. Rosenstock to Rosenzweig, 28 October 1918, in Rosenstock, *Judaism Despite Christianity*, pp. 118–23.

35. Rosenzweig to Gertrud Oppenheim, 30 May 1917, in *Briefe*, p. 211.

36. Rosenzweig, "Atheistische Theologie," pp. 280, 279, 283f., 279, 289.

37. Ibid., p. 290.
38. Rosenzweig, *Briefe*, p. 123.
39. Fredrich Schelling, "Philosophie der Offenbarung," in *Sämtliche Werke*, vol. 4, pt. 2 (1858), p. 332; cited in Altmann, "Franz Rosenzweig on History," p. 000.
40. Ibid. See Karl Löwith, *Meaning in History* (Chicago: University of Chicago Press, 1949), pp. 145ff.
41. Harold Stahmer, *"Speak That I May See Thee": The Religious Significance of Language* (New York: Macmillan, 1968), pp. 121–24.
42. E. Rosenstock-Huessy, *Ja und Nein: Autobiographische Fragmente* (Heidelberg: Lambert Schneider, 1968), p. 154f.
43. Rosenzweig, *Briefe und Tagebücher*, 1:183.
44. Franz Rosenzweig, "Realpolitik" and "Nordwest und Sudost," *Archiv für exakte Wirtschaftsforschung* 8 (4): 537–42, 546–53. "Realpolitik" reprinted in Rosenzweig, *Kleinere Schriften*, pp. 409–14. I wish to thank Rafael Rosenzweig for providing me with a rare offprint of "Nordwest and Sudost."
45. Rosenzweig, "Realpolitik," p. 413.
46. Ibid.
47. This part of the monograph is sixty-one typewritten (folio) pages—apparently transcribed by Edith Rosenzweig from her husband's handscript. I wish to thank Steven S. Schwarzchild for bringing my attention to this essay and for providing me with a photostat of the copy of the essay he received from Harold Stahmer, who found it among the papers of the late Eugen Rosenstock-Huessy, whose literary estate he administers. I also wish to thank Rafael Rosenzweig for authenticating the essay and granting me permission to cite it. Rosenzweig's first outline of the essay dates from 1910–11; at the time he saw the essay as complementing his work on Hegel. See Rosenzweig's letter to Gertrud Oppenheim of 1 May 1917, in *Briefe*, p. 198. We also learn from his correspondence that he originally considered giving the essay the subtitle "Zur Geschichte der geschichtlichen Welt." Rosenzweig to his parents, 20 January 1917, ibid., p. 152.
48. See Rosenzweig to E. Rosenstock, 11 March 1917, in *Briefe*, p. 172.
49. Ibid., p. 172f. Cf. "Sie haben natürlich recht. 'Ökumene' ist unangenehm gelehrt und 'schön'[. . .]" (p. 172).
50. Ibid., p. 173.
51. See Rosenzweig to Rosenstock, 25 December 1917, in *Briefe*, p. 272. I wish to thank Rafael Rosenzweig for providing me with a copy of this manuscript—thirty-one typewritten folio pages, also apparently transcribed by Edith Rosenzweig from her husband's script.
52. Rosenzweig to Hans Ehrenberg, 26 December 1917, in *Briefe*, p. 273 (Rosenzweig's emphases).
53. Cf. "Das eigentliche Kriegsergebnis steht schon am Tag des Krieg-

ausbruchs fest und wird im Krieg nur *bestätigt,* nicht geschaffen. So ist also dieser Krieg *nicht,* wie Meinecke behauptet, politische unproduktiv und also zwecklos . . . gewesen. Meineckes Grundfehler ist, dass er malgré tout doch immer in *Staaten* denkt und nicht in Staatenverbänden." Rosenzweig to his parents, 1 October 1917, in *Briefe,* p. 245 (Rosenzweig's emphasis).

54. See Rosenzweig, "Realpolitik," p. 414; also see Rosenzweig to Hans Hess, 30 September 1917, in *Briefe,* p. 239, and Rosenzweig to Margrit Rosenstock, 14 December 1917, ibid., p. 266.

55. Rosenzweig to parents, 20 July 1917, ibid., p. 218.

56. See Rosenzweig, *Briefe und Tagebücher,* 1 : 423, n. 1.

57. Rosenzweig to Hans Ehrenberg, 4 May 1918, in *Briefe,* pp. 307–9.

58. Rosenzweig to Hans Ehrenberg, 21 April 1918, *ibid.,* p. 302.

59. I wish to thank Rafael Rosenzweig to providing me with a copy of the preface, which consists of two typewritten folio pages. Regarding Rosenzweig's change of heart, cf. "Dass und was ich in Ökumene über Afrika geschrieben habe, weiss ich nicht mehr. . . . Und trotz allem, ich kann mich nicht vor dem Frieden fürchten; ich habe eben jetzt, wo er im Osten aufgeht zum ersten Mal wieder zu denken gewagt und bin für einen Augenblick aus meinem Schutzpanzer herausgekrochen—es wird *doch* gehen. Nun gerade, weil die Welt 'vertiert, entsehnt, entseelt, glaubenlos' . . . geworden sein wird, grade darum werden es die *Menschen nicht* sein." Rosenzweig to Rosenstock, 15 December 1917, *ibid.,* p. 269 (Rosenzweig's emphasis). Also see Rosenzweig's letter to Hans Ehrenberg of 26 December 1917, where he indicated that he "deliberately" pushed the study of history aside in favor of the study of Jewish texts. Ibid., p. 274f. In an undated letter, probably from autumn 1919, Rosenzweig refers to his "Globus" essay as "passé as my Hegel book." *Briefe und Tagebücher,* 1 : 651.

60. The image of the sea as a source of hope seems to have fascinated Rosenzweig since his youth. In a memoir Gertrud Oppenheim reports that in July 1903 she accompanied her cousin Franz and his family to Switzerland. In a museum in Basel they saw Boecklin's painting *Odysseus at the Sea:* the wayward Greek standing in a blue jacket looking longingly at the sea. The sixteen-and-one-half-year-old Franz chose this painting—with a citation from Goethe's *Iphigenie in Tauris,* "das Land der Griechen mit der Seele suchend"—for his ex libris. I wish to thank David Strassler of Jerusalem for showing me a copy of this memoir (consisting of ten typewritten pages), which he received from Gertrud Oppenheim upon a visit to Johannesburg, South Africa, where she spent her last years.

61. See nn. 2, 3.

62. This, of course, is Rosenzweig's term; see *The Star of Redemption,* trans. W. Hallo (New York: Holt, Rinehart and Winston, 1971), p. 328.

63. Rosenzweig, *Hegel und der Staat,* p. xii.

64. Ibid. The volume was prepared before the war, and only reluctantly

did he agree to publish it in 1919. Cf. "Dies Buch, das ich heute nicht mehr geschrieben hätte, konnte ich genau so wenig umarbeiten. Es blieb nur übrig, es so herauszugeben wie es einmal war, in Ursprung also und Absicht ein Zeugnis des Geistes der Vorkriegsjahre, nicht des 'Geists' von 1919" (p. xiii).

65. Attributed to Rosenzweig by Siegfried A. Kaehler in a letter to Meinecke, 22 January 1919. Friedrich Meinecke, *Ausgewählter Briefwechsel* (Stuttgart: K. F. Koehler, 1962), p. 329.

66. Rosenzweig to Meinecke, 30 August 1920, in N. N. Glatzer, ed., *Franz Rosenzweig: His Life and Thought*, 2d rev. ed. (New York: Schocken Books, 1961), p. 62. Not included in the 1935 edition of Rosenzweig's *Briefe*, but now found in the recently published *Briefe und Tagebücher*, 2:678–82.

67. Glatzer, *Life and Thought*, p. 93.

68. Ibid.

69. Rosenzweig to Rosenstock, 15 December 1917, in *Briefe*, p. 268.

70. Eugen Rosenstock-Huessy, *Out of Revolution: Autobiography of Western Man* (Norwich, Vt.: Argo Books, 1969), p. 5.

71. Ibid., p. 7.                    72. Ibid., p. 10.

73. In Rosenstock, *Judaism Despite Christianity*, p. 168.

74. Ibid.

75. Rosenzweig to his parents, 17 December 1917, in *Briefe und Tagebücher*, 1:501f.

76. Diary entry from 30 March 1922, *ibid.*, 2:769. Cf. "In order [to enter the Kingdom] the world thus requires an effect from without *in addition* to its own inner growth, the growth of which is precarious because never certain of enduring." Rosenzweig, *Star of Redemption*, p. 225. Prior to writing *The Star* (to be more exact, prior to writing the composition of the preface to "Ökumene"), Rosenzweig emphasized the role of revelation (qua orientation) as the force rendering genuine history possible. Cf. "Only for Jews and Christians exists that firm orientation of the world in space and time; the actual world and actual history exist; North, South, Past, Present exist, and are not 'of God' . . . but they came of God, ought to become, and only therefore are." Rosenzweig to Rosenstock, circa December 1917, cited in Rosenstock, *Judaism Despite Christianity*, p. 166.

77. Rosenzweig summarized his critique of "the historical *Weltanschauung*" in *Star of Redemption*, pp. 97–104. Of all the varied aspects of the modern sensibility, according to Rosenzweig, critical historical consciousness has had the most devastating effect on theology. It has undermined "the *auctoritas* of tradition" and its witness to historical revelation and God's truth. Bereft of the firm ground of tradition, contemporary theology then "calls upon philosophy to build a bridge from creation to revelation. . . . [Theology] looks longingly to philosophy as the authentic *auctoritas*." *Star of Redemption*, pp. 106–8.

78. Thus, despite his "existential" concern with the temporal finitude of man, Rosenzweig would not have accepted the absolute historicity taught by Heidegger. See the illuminating discussion in Karl Löwith, "M. Heidegger and F. Rosenzweig or Temporality and Eternity" *Philosophy and Phenomenological Research* 3 (1): 53–77. Also see Kochan, *Jew and His History*, pp. 99–114; and Rivkah Horwitz, "The Conception of Jewish History in the Thought of Franz Rosenzweig," *Proceedings of the American Academy of Jewish Research* 37 (1969): 1–23 (in Hebrew).

79. Rosenzweig, *Star of Redemption*, pp. 328, 224, 226.

80. Altmann, "Franz Rosenzweig on History," p. 000.

81. Rosenzweig, *Star of Redemption*, p. 339.

82. Cited in Kochan, *Jew and His History*, p. 106.

83. Rosenzweig, *Star of Redemption*, p. 208. Cf. "Loved by God, man is closed off to all the world and closes himself off. . . . His soul opens for God, but because it opens only for God, it is invisible to all the world and shut off from it. The mystic rotates his magic [Gyges'] ring on his finger in arrogant confidence, and at once he is alone with 'his' God, and incommunicable to the world. . . . He wants wholly and solely to be God's favorite, and nothing else. To be this . . . he must deny the world, and since it will not be denied, he must in reality repudiate it. . . . He must treat it [the world] as if it were not created" (pp. 207ff.).

84. Ibid., p. 260.

85. Franz Rosenzweig, "Das neue Denken," in *Kleinere Schriften*, p. 392.

86. Rosenzweig, *Star of Redemption*, p. 412.

87. Ibid., p. 379.                    88. Ibid., p. 419.

89. Rosenzweig to Gertrud Oppenheim, 31 May 1917, in *Briefe*, p. 212.

90. Rosenzweig, *Star of Redemption*, p. 224. Rosenzweig's conception of the ontological "Must" of perfection that is "not yet in existence" invites comparison to Ernst Bloch's ontology of the future as "not yet" (*noch nicht*).

91. Rosenzweig held that the idea of progress obtained its logical fullness in Hermann Cohen's concept of infinite or asymptotic perfection. With allusion to Cohen, he pointed out the delusional hope sponsored by this concept: The idea of progress "discloses its real nature soon enough through the concept of endlessness. Even if there is talk of 'eternal' progress—in truth it is but 'interminable' progress that is meant. . . . Were the Kingdom only to grow, with mute, insensate, compulsive propulsion, ever progressing, progressively further into the endlessness of time, with no end ahead of it outside of endlessness, then indeed the act [of love] would be lame. Then the ultimate would be endlessly far away, and therefore the proximate, and the neighbor, also inaccessible." *Star of Redemption*, p. 227f. Rosenzweig's critique of the idea of inevitable, historically immanent progress conflates with his rejection of historicism. See his discussion, "Islam and the Idea of Progress," ibid., p. 225.

92. Ibid., p. 227.

93. See Rosenzweig to Hans Ehrenberg, 19 April 1922, in *Briefe*, p. 580. Cf. "[W]ithout this 'wish to bring about the Messiah before his time' and the temptation to 'coerce the kingdom of God into being,' without these, it [the future] is only a past distended endlessly and projected forward." Rosenzweig, *Star of Redemption*, p. 227. In a letter to Rudolf Hallo, dated 4 February 1923, Rosenzweig observed that the dialectic of redemption and history requires that "the supra-human powers, of which Judaism is one," be recurrently secularized. "Die Ewigkeit der Mächte bewährt sich in ihrer Fähigkeit, sich immer neu zu säkularisieren." *Briefe*, p. 476.

## Chapter 8. Franz Rosenzweig and the Kabbalah
*(pp. 162–71)*

1. Franz Rosenzweig, *Kleinere Schriften* (Berlin: Schocken, 1937), p. 289.

2. Ibid., p. 284.                    3. Ibid., p. 289.

4. *Pesikta de Rav Kahana* 12:6; *Midrash Tehilim* 123:2; *Yalkut Shimoni*, Jesaia para. 705, *Sifra* Deut. 346. Rivka Horwitz has kindly drawn my attention to the usage of the same Midrash in Buber's "Jewish Religiosity" (1916), which might have influenced Rosenzweig; see Martin Buber, *On Judaism*, ed. N. N. Glatzer (New York: Schocken, 1973), pp. 84–85. Buber, indeed, used the Midrash together with kabbalistic concepts, and this may have given Rosenzweig the impression that the statement belongs to the kabbalistic literature.

5. Rosenzweig does not mention which of the early mystics were the source of the new or atheistic theology. In Martin Buber's doctorate, written in 1904, we find the following passage discussed by Rosenzweig: "the doctrine of Valentine Weigel that 'God became God' only after He created the world contains his opinion that the self-knowledge of God takes place in man." Cited in Rosenzweig, *Kleinere Schriften*, p. 518. A similar doctrine, in a more developed way, we find in the writings of the Arab mystic Ibn Arabi; see H. Corbin, *Creative Imagination in the Sufism of Ibn Arabi* (Princeton: Princeton University Press, 1965), p. 197.

6. Franz Rosenzweig, *The Star of Redemption*, (New York: Holt, Rinehart and Winston), p. 171.

7. Rosenzweig, *Kleinere Schriften*, pp. 285–86, 288.

8. Ibid., p. 286.                    9. Ibid., p. 288.

10. This piece, written several years before Rosenzweig visited Eastern Europe during the war, shows that it was *not* the personal encounter with Eastern European Jewry that influenced his opinion on the commandments, but his knowledge of Lurianic Kabbalah. On the influence on Rosenzweig of Eastern European Jewry as well as Hermann Cohen in this mat-

ter, See J. Heinemann, *Ta'ame Hamitzvot Besifrut Yisrael* (Jerusalem: Histadruth Ha-Zionit, 1956), 2:198–99.

11. What Rosenzweig says in connection with the mystics' view of *The Duties of the Heart*—"Only of late it was proven that . . ."—shows that as early as 1914 he had already read a scholarly article discussing this subject. Early mystics read *The Duties of the Heart;* the "Raavad" was the initiator of the two translations of the book, as mentioned by Judah ibn Tibbon in the introduction to his translation of the work. For other influences of Bachya's book on the kabbalists in Provence, see G. Scholem, *Les origines de la kabbale* (Paris: Aubier Montaigne, 1966), pp. 236, 238, 319.

12. Rosenzweig, *Star of Redemption*, p. 410.

13. Ibid., pp. 410–11.    14. Ibid., p. 411.

15. Ibid., p. 409.

16. On the Sabbatean-kabbalistic background of the Star of David, which is the Star of Redemption, see G. Scholem, "The Star of David: History of Symbol," in *The Messianic Idea in Judaism* (New York: Schocken, 1972), pp. 257–81.

17. Rosenzweig, *Star of Redemption*, p. 409. Buber, too, ascribes the re-union of God with the Shekhina as a result of human action, emphasizing the redemptive overtones of this action; see Buber, *On Judaism*, p. 28. However, Rosenzweig's discussion includes explicit details missing in Buber's essay.

The surrender of God to man, or his "selling Himself" to man, is a basic idea that appears over and over in Rosenzweig's work and seems to be rooted in the kabbalistic idea about the Shekhina. See for example, *Kleinere Schriften*, pp. 78, 209, 211, 213, 214.

18. Ibid., p. 66.    19. Ibid., p. 360.

20. Rosenzweig himself rejected the idea of emanation as a theological solution; see *Star of Redemption*, pp. 136ff.

21. An allusion to the term *dunkler Grund* (the dark ground or somber basis), which appears in the "germ cell" of *The Star of Redemption*. Cf. Franz Rosenzweig, "Urzelle des Stern der Erlösung," in *Kleinere Schriften*, pp. 357–72.

22. Rosenzweig, *Star of Redemption*, p. 26.

23. One cannot accept as certain the opinion expressed by Julius Guttmann, in *Philosophies of Judaism*, trans. D. W. Silverman (New York: Holt, Rinehart and Winston, 1964), p. 384, that the duality of the idea of God in Rosenzweig's theology is "undoubtedly" derived from Schelling. It seems to me that Rosenzweig's opinion on the essence of God, "which is hidden precisely by being revealed," may have been influenced by a mystic idea, found inter alia in the theology of Rabbi Moshe Cordovero that "revelation is the cause of the hidden": see Yosef ben Shlomo, *Torat Ha-elohut Shel Rabbi Moshe Cordovero* (Jerusalem: Mosad Bialik, 1965), pp. 95–98. A similar

idea is, however, also found in Schelling, who, as scholars have shown, was almost certainly influenced by the Kabbalah; see X. Tilliette, *Schelling: Une philosophie en devenir* (Paris: J. Vrin, 1970), 2:244, n. 69.

24. Commentary of Rabbi Bachya ben Asher on Genesis 1:1, ed. C. D. Chavel (Jerusalem: Ha-Rav Kook, 1966), p. 21; commentary on *Sefer Yetsirah* by Rabbi Moshe Botarel (Jerusalem: Levin-Epstein, 1965), p. 19. Commentary on the *Ten Sefiroth* by Rabbi Yaakov ben Yaakov Hacohen, published by G. Scholem in *Institute for Jewish Studies* 2 (1927): 227, etc. On the Ismaiyliya background of this dictum, see G. Vajda, *Juda ben Nissim ibn Malka, philosophe juif marocain* (Paris: La rose edituré, 1954), p. 65.

25. Rosenzweig, *Star of Redemption*, pp. 29, 27.

26. In his lecture "Franz Rosenzweig and His book *The Star of Redemption*," included in this volume, Scholem uses the term *inner logic* in connection with language to denote mystic approach; the source for this idea may be traced to the *Iggeret Sheva Netivoth Hatorah* by Rabbi Abraham Abulafia, published by A. Jellinek in Leipzig in 1854, which Rosenzweig could conceivably have read. Scholem cites the kabbalist Rabbi Yitzchak ibn Latif's doctrine on thought bound to time, an idea that finds its source in the book *Rav Pe'alim*, a treatise extant in two editions by Jellinek (1860) and Schoenblum (1885). On the significance of *inner logic* see M. Idel, "On the History of the Interdiction against the Study of Kabbalah before the Age of Forty," *Association of Jewish Studies Review* 5 (1980): xvii, n. 7 (in Hebrew).

27. Rosenzweig, *Star of Redemption*, p. 408.

28. On the connection between the theological process and the Chair or the Chariot, see X. Tilliette, *Schelling*, 2:225, n. 73 where the author comments on the possible connection between Schelling and Jewish ideas.

29. Rosenzweig, *Star of Redemption*, p. 409.

30. Pico della Mirandola, *Opera Omnia* (Basel, 1557), p. 113. On the Jewish background of Pico's thesis, see M. Idel, "The Magical and Neoplatonic Interpretations of the Kabbalah in the Renaissance," *Jerusalem Studies in Jewish Thought* 1 (4): 77 (in Hebrew).

31. Rosenzweig, *Kleinere Schriften*, p. 528. A similar idea also appears in two other places in Rosenzweig's article: see ibid., p. 540, and his lectures; see R. Horwitz, "Franz Rosenzweig, Unpublished Writings," *Journal of Jewish Studies* 20 (1969): 73–75; see also Rosenzweig, *Star of Redemption*, p. 230.

32. *Yosher Levav* 1, 3:15; see G. Scholem, *Major Trends in Jewish Mysticism* (New York: Schocken, 1965), p. 399, n. 9; and Horwitz, "Unpublished Writings," p. 74. G. Scholem also mentions the early version of this idea, which appears in *Rav Pe'alim* by Rabbi Yitzchak ibn Latif; see n. 26.

33. Rosenzweig, *Kleinere Schriften*, p. 531.

34. Rosenzweig, following Hermann Cohen, rejects this approach; see ibid.

35. It appears that he considered the book *Shiur Koma,* "an internal Jewish act of personification," dating from early Kabbalah. This opinion is very different from Graetz's view; he saw the book as a work written during the period of the *Geonim,* under the influence of Islamic anthropomorphism. It fits, however, with the opinion of Moses Gaster on *Shiur Koma;* see M. Gaster, "Das Shiur Komah," *Monatschrift für Geschichte und Wissenschaft des Judentums* 37 (1893): 179–85, 213–30.

36. A similar, but less positive description is found with Graetz: "The Kabbalah is a daughter of embarrassment: its system was the way of escape from the dilemma between the simple anthropomorphic interpretation of the Bible and the shallowness of Maimonist philosophy." H. Graetz, *History of the Jews* (Philadelphia: Jewish Publication Society, 1956), 3 : 549.

37. Rosenzweig, *Kleinere Schriften,* p. 532.

38. Schelling, under the influence of the Bible and of Boehme, used many anthropomorphic expressions. See Tilliette, *Schelling,* 1 : 549.

## Chapter 9. The Concept of Language in the Thought of Franz Rosenzweig
*(pp. 172–84)*

1. For a masterful discussion of Nietzsche's and Sartre's, as well as other modern writers', views of the crisis of language, see George Steiner, *Language and Silence* (New York: Atheneum, 1967).

2. Franz Rosenzweig, *Briefe und Tagebücher,* ed. Rachel Rosenzweig (The Hague: Martinus Nijhoff, 1979), 1 : 471.

3. Rosenzweig to Eugen Rosenstock, 27 November 1971, in *Briefe und Tagebücher,* 1 : 483f.

4. A long letter from Rosenzweig to Rudolf Ehrenberg, 18 November 1917, in *Kleinere Schriften* (Berlin: Schocken, 1937), pp. 357–72.

5. Franz Rosenzweig, *The Star of Redemption,* trans. William W. Hallo (Boston: Holt, Rinehart and Winston, 1964). The numerals in the text refer to pages in the Hallo edition.

6. Rosenzweig to Gertrud Oppenheim, 14 March 1922, in *Briefe und Tagebücher,* 2 : 758; with reference to Margarete Susman, "Der Stern der Erlösung," in *Der Jude* (Berlin: Jüdischer Verlag, 1921–22), 6 : 259ff.

7. Rosenzweig paraphrases Shabbat 133b: "Be thou like Him: just as He is gracious and compassionate, so be thou gracious and compassionate."

8. Franz Rosenzweig, "Das neue Denken," in *Der Morgen,* vol. 1, 1925; later in *Kleinere Schriften;* in English, "The New Thinking," in *Franz Rosenzweig: His Life and Thought,* ed. N. N. Glatzer (New York: Schocken, 1953), pp. 190–208.

9. Rosenzweig, "The New Thinking," p. 199.
10. Ibid., p. 201.

Chapter 10. Franz Rosenzweig in Perspective
*(pp. 185–201)*

1. Franz Rosenzweig, *Der Mensch und sein Werk: Gesammelte Schriften,* pt. 1: *Briefe und Tagebücher,* vol. 2: *1918–1929* (The Hague: Martinus Nijhoff, 1979), p. 760.

2. Ibid., p. 822.               3. Ibid., p. 771.
4. Ibid.                        5. Ibid., p. 747.
6. Ibid., p. 768.              7. Ibid., p. 760.
8. Ibid., p. 767.
9. Franz Rosenzweig, *The Star of Redemption,* trans. W. Hallo (New York: Holt, Rinehart and Winston, 1971), pp. 220–22.
10. Rosenzweig, *Briefe und Tagebücher,* 2:770.
11. Ibid., pp. 770–71.          12. Ibid., pp. 1003, 1114.
13. Rosenzweig, *Star of Redemption,* pp. 294–96.
14. Rosenzweig, *Briefe und Tagebücher,* 2:774.
15. Rosenzweig, *Star of Redemption,* pp. 210–11.
16. Rosenzweig, *Briefe und Tagebücher,* 2:774.
17. Ibid.                       18. Ibid., p. 769.
19. Ibid., p. 801.
20. Rosenzweig, *Star of Redemption,* p. 47.
21. Ibid., p. 219.
22. Cf. Rosenzweig, *Briefe und Tagebücher,* 2:783, n. 747.
23. Cf. ibid., p. 775, n. 738.
24. Cf. ibid., pp. 776–77, n. 738.
25. Cf. ibid., p. 783, n. 747.
26. Cf. ibid., p. 785, n. 750.
27. Ibid.
28. Cf. ibid., p. 791, nn. 764, 772.

Chapter 11. Recollections of a Disciple
*(pp. 202–13)*

1. Franz Rosenzweig, *The Star of Redemption,* trans. William A. Hallo (New York: Holt, Rinehart and Winston, 1970), pp. 3, 424.
2. Immanuel Kant, *A Critique of Pure Reason,* trans. Norman Kemp Smith (New York: St. Martin's Press, 1929), p. 653.
3. Ibid., Valentine ed. (Leipzig: Meiner Verlag, 1919), p. 685.
4. Franz Rosenzweig, "'Urzelle' des Stern der Erlösung," in *Kleinere Schriften,* ed. Edith Rosenzweig (Berlin: Schocken Verlag, 1937), pp. 357–72.

5. Ibid., p. 369.

6. Franz Rosenzweig, "Das Neue Denken," in *Kleinere Schriften*, pp. 373–99.

7. Rosenzweig, *Star of Redemption*, pp. 3–89.

8. Else-Rahel Freund, *Franz Rosenzweig's Philosophy of Existence: An Analysis of "The Star of Redemption,"* trans. Stephen L. Weinstein and Robert Israel, ed. Paul Mendes-Flohr (The Hague: Martinus Nijhoff, 1979).

9. E. Simon, "Franz Rosenzweig und das Jüdische Bildungsproblem," *Korrenspondenzblatt des Vereins zur Gründung einer Akademie für die Wissenschaft des Judentums* (1913); reprinted in E. Simon, *Brücken: Aufsätze* (Heidelberg: Verlag Lambert Schneider, 1965).

10. Rosenzweig to Hans Ehrenberg, 18 March 1921, in Franz Rosenzweig, *Briefe*, ed. Edith Rosenzweig with the cooperation of E. Simon (Berlin: Schocken Verlag, 1935), p. 399.

11. Franz Rosenzweig, "The Builders: Concerning the Law," in Rosenzweig, *On Jewish Learning*, ed. N. N. Glatzer (New York: Schocken, 1965), pp. 72–94.

12. Ibid., pp. 76–79.

13. *Judaism Despite Christianity: The "Letters on Christianity and Judaism" between Eugen Rosenstock-Huessy and Franz Rosenzweig*, ed. E. Rosenstock-Huessy (New York: Schocken, 1971).

14. Rosenzweig, *Briefe*, p. 507f.

15. This is a statement by Richard Koch, who movingly recorded his memories of Rosenzweig in Eugen Mayer, ed., *Franz Rosenzweig: Eine Gedenkschrift* (Frankfurt: Vorstand der Israelitischen Gemeinde Frankfurt a.M., 1930), pp. 24–30.

16. Nahum N. Glatzer, *Franz Rosenzweig: His Life and Thought* (New York: Schocken, 1953). This volume has, since its original publication, been reprinted many times.

17. Franz Rosenzweig, "It Is Time: Concerning the Study of the Judaism," in Rosenzweig, *On Jewish Learning*, pp. 27–54.

# Contributors

ALEXANDER ALTMANN *(1906–1987) was Professor Emeritus, Brandeis University.*

BERNHARD CASPER *is Professor, University of Freiburg.*

NAHUM N. GLATZER *is Professor Emeritus, Brandeis University.*

MOSHE IDEL *is Associate Professor, Hebrew University of Jerusalem.*

PAUL MENDES-FLOHR *is Associate Professor, Hebrew University of Jerusalem.*

STÉPHANE MOSÈS *is Professor, Hebrew University of Jerusalem.*

OTTO PÖGGELER *is Professor, University of Bochum.*

NATHAN ROTENSTREICH *is Professor Emeritus, Hebrew University of Jerusalem, and Vice-President of the Israel Academy of Sciences and Humanities.*

GERSHOM SCHOLEM *(1897–1982) was Professor, Hebrew University of Jerusalem.*

ERNST AKIVA SIMON *is Professor Emeritus, Hebrew University of Jerusalem.*

REINER WIEHL *is Professor, University of Heidelberg.*

# Index of Names

# Subject Index

Education, Jewish, 11, 22–23, 212;
Freies Jüdisches Lehrhaus, 12, 14,
22–23, 204
Emancipation, 28, 122, 125, 127, 128,
171
Empiricism, 45, 55, 56, 101, 204
Enlightenment, 5; God in, 105; Hegel
between Romanticism and, 16, 110,
122; and Johannine Christianity, 17,
147; and Romanticism, 109–10,
116, 123
Eschatology: and eternity, 159; and history, 129–30, 134, 137; and Johannine Christianity, 125–26, 128, 146;
in Lurianic Kabbalah, 165; and
Zionism, 194–95
Essence: of finite being, 79; of God, 72,
84–85, 166–68, 170, ,243 n.23; vs.
reality, 10, 32–33, 36
Eternity, 38, 39, 132–33, 134, 137,
159–61
Ethics, 2, 15, 31, 80; and absolute in
classical metaphysics, 104; in H. Cohen, 30, 81–83, 133; in idealism, 91
Exile: of God, 131, 166; of Jewish
people, 117, 120, 123, 130, 159; and
revelation, 166
Existence, 7, 26, 32, 223 n.28; and
death, 40; "in the distinctive" ("Sein
im Besonderen") 75; pathic existence
(Weizsäcker), 49–50; in Rosenzweig's thought, 87–88; in Schelling,
8–9; and truth, 39
Existentialism, 8, 11, 87–88
Experience, 10, 16, 27, 35, 36, 42–68
passim, 104, 187; and cognition,
44–45, 52, 54–56, 60; in Hegel,
57–59, 61, 63–64; and miracle,
64–67; particularity and multiplicity
of, 48–50, 54–58, 63, 64; and perception, 53, 54, 57, 61; vs. reason
31–33; of responsibility, 101–4;
connecting system and subjectivity,
43–45; traditional concepts of,
52–54

Factuality, 51, 96, 105; of existence (in
Schelling), 8, 102; of experience, 44,
101–3
Faith, 2, 5, 6, 11, 27; combining elements of God, World, Man, 34, 36,
37; and philosophical system, 37,
119, 205; and rational thought in

idealism, 32, 34, 66; and rational
thought in Rosenzweig, 10, 12, 56,
60, 144
Finitude, 76–79, 83–84, 86, 87. See
also Death
Freedom, 2, 3, 9, 66, 88; of individual,
16, 76–77, 83, 91, 95
Freies Jüdisches Lehrhaus (the free Jewish house of learning), 12, 14, 23,
118, 186, 196, 204

God: his essence, 32, 72, 84–85,
166–68, 170; freedom of, 76, 77; his
role in history, 4, 16–17, 132, 137,
143; in idealism, 9, 24, 32, 137; as
isolated element, 33, 36; in mysticism, 163–68; in negative theology,
71, 84; relationship with man, 7,
15–16, 18, 37, 61, 96–101, 106,
131, 133, 144, 163, 169, 174,
176–77, 180, 191–93; transcendence of, 74, 84, 163–64, 188; and
World and Man, 31–33, 36, 37, 39,
51–52, 57, 60, 61, 66, 71–73, 75,
82, 85, 86, 92–95, 105, 106, 165,
174, 191, 204

Hegelianism, 109, 114, 118. See also
Hegel, Rosenzweig's relation to
Hermeneutic Ambiguity, 63, 66
Historicism, 17, 90, 114, 132, 157; crisis of, 139, 140, 144–45; Meinecke's
ethical h., 141; Rosenzweig's rejection of, 156, 159
History, 125, 140, 151, 152; eternity
in, 134; in Hegel, 4, 16, 118, 132,
136–37, 143; and idea, 119, 122;
and meta-history, 17, 154–55; and
redemption, 129, 130, 134, 158–59;
and religion, 117, 132, 142; and revelation, 128, 131, 134–35, 144–45;
Rosenzweig's rejection of providence
in, 136–37. See also Judaism, its
metahistorical significance
Hochschule für die Wissenschaft des
Judentums, 11, 22, 23

I, the. See Self, the
Idealism: passim, esp.: "generation"
(Erzeugung) in, 91, 95; history in,
136–37; the individual in, 25–26,
73, 91, 119; and Johannine Church,
126; and language, 176; one-dimen-

sionality of, 51–52, 119, 206; and
revelation, 131; system of, 10;
"truth" in, 45. See also Hegel; Kant;
Whole, the
Individual, the. See Self, the
Irreducibility, 72–73, 75, 93
Islam, 36, 42, 175
Isolation (Separateness): of God,
World, Man, in Islam, 36; of God,
World, Man, in pure thought,
32–34; of God, World, Man, in the
"new thinking," 93, 101; overcoming
of, 94, 95, 96. See also Self-Enclosure

Jewish Law (Commandments), 169; in
Rosenzweig's argument with M.
Buber, 7, 112, 206–8; and metahistorical significance of Judaism,
130, 159–60; and unification of
God, 164–65
Judaism (Synagogue), 36, 42, 187;
Rosenzweig's affirmation of, 1, 2, 6,
11, 12, 16, 110–12, 115, 129, 157,
209; and Christianity, 17, 36,
38–39, 116–17, 128, 129–31,
138–39, 156, 160, 180, 194, 197,
232n.30; and history, 128–31,
138–39, 164; and humanity, 13; its
metahistorical significance, 17,
128–31, 138–39, 156, 159, 160,
164, 189, 193–94, 197, 232n.30;
Orthodoxy, 28, 29, 206–7; Reform,
28, 29. See also Jewish Law;
Mysticism

Kabbalah: and anthropomorphism,
169–71; attitudes against in nineteenth century, 29; influence on
Rosenzweig, 6, 17, 35, 162–71;
Lurianic Kabbalah, 165–67, 171
Kingdom of God, 37, 98, 103, 106,
128–34, 137, 159, 161. See also
Eschatology
Knowledge, 15, 39, 45; and existence
(Schelling), 8, 9; principles of, in
classical theories of experience, 52,
54; and experience, in Victor von
Weizsäcker, 50; messianic theory of,
42, 46, 48, 66, 104; and negation,
32–33, 75; in Hegel, 57–59, 64;
and reality, 85, 199; and language,
172–73. See also Cognition

Language, 18, 172–84 passim; of creation, 175; and liturgical community,
178–81, 183; and knowledge,
172–73; of logic, 175; of mathematics, 34–35, 175; in mysticism, 168;
philosophy of, 37; of revelation, 175,
205; and silence, 86, 175; and system, 43–44; and transformation of
elements, 96, 98. See also Dialogue;
Speech; Speech-Thinking; Word,
Primal
Liturgy, 38–39, 190, 193, 194, 197
Love, 26, ,93; of God, 7, 15–16,
96–101, 106, 131, 133, 163, 174,
176, 177, 178, 180, 192; of neighbor, 16, 98–103, 131–32, 174, 178,
179, 180; and redemption, 178; in
revelation, 137, 176–78

Man: vs. the "All," 26, 70, 91; self-
awareness of, 78–80, 85–86; self-
enclosure of, 76, 78, 80, 82–83, 85,
87; in Rosenzweig's system, 61–62,
85, 86, 88, 119; and creation,
94–95, 192; in existentialism,
87–88; as isolated element, 33–34;
and speech, 17–18, 60, 98, 117,
176–77, 183; responsibility of, 15,
16, 90, 91, 95–104, 105, 106. See
also God, relationship with man;
God, and World and Man; Love, of
God; Love, of neighbor; Self, the
Mathematics, 33, 35, 93, 175
Messianic Theory of Knowledge. See
under Knowledge
Messianism. See Eschatology
"Meta-," 69–70, 72, 74
Metaethical, the, 15, 69–70, 73, 74,
80–82, 84, 87, 90, 95, 96, 224n.3
Metalogic, 69, 71, 72, 80, 82
Metaphysics, 69, 71, 72, 80, 82, 104
Miracle, 7, 15, 27, 36, 37, 84, 87; as a
boundary of philosophy, 64–68; and
confirmation theory of truth, 46, 48;
and nature, 65
Multidimensionality, 54, 55, 57, 59, 61
Multiplicity: of experience, 57, 62; of
factuality, 44–45; of phenomena,
53; of philosophical standpoints, 55;
of truths, 46; and unity, 54–55
Mysticism, 131; attitudes toward, 29;
and creation, 168; God in, 166–68;